To Elizabeth Mack

with esteem and good

wishes

[illegible signature]

Jönköping 8/21/10

Economics of Knowledge

Economics of Knowledge

Theory, Models and Measurements

Åke E. Andersson

Professor, Department of Economics, Jönköping International Business School, Jönköping, Sweden

Martin J. Beckmann

Professor, Department of Economics, Brown University, USA and Professor of Applied Mathematics, Munich Technical University, Munich, Germany

Edward Elgar

Cheltenham, UK • Northampton, MA, USA

Published by
Edward Elgar Publishing Limited
The Lypiatts
15 Lansdown Road
Cheltenham
Glos GL50 2JA
UK

Edward Elgar Publishing, Inc.
William Pratt House
9 Dewey Court
Northampton
Massachusetts 01060
USA

A catalogue record for this book
is available from the British Library

Library of Congress Control Number: 2009925917

ISBN 978 1 84720 675 6

Printed and bound by MPG Books Group Ltd, UK

Contents

Figures

Tables

Boxes

Preface

Motto: First come I, my name is Jowett.
There is nothing but I know it.
What I don't know isn't knowledge.
I'm the master of this college.
(Henry Charles Beeching, 1880)

Knowledge is no stranger to economic discourse. In contemporary economic thinking, knowledge surfaces in discussions of the sources of growth, comparative advantages and the nature of high-tech industries. But since Machlup (1962b) a broader view of knowledge in economics has been absent. Sociology has stolen a march on economics by looking into the institutions of science and the social structures behind research activities: it also started bibliometrics, the exploitation of citation indexes.

In the spirit of interdisciplinary exploration our study of the economics of knowledge began at the Institute for Futures Studies in 1995. Since these golden days we have not only studied scientific collaboration at a distance but experimented with it (Andersson at the KTH (Royal Institute of Technology) in Stockholm and the Jönköping International Business School in Jönköping, Beckmann at Brown University in Providence, RI and at the Technical University of Munich). Now a book by two authors can never be of one piece. While one of us (A) has analysed some topics in depth (Chapters 1, 6–8), the other (B) has cast a wide net to capture as many economic aspects of knowledge as could be found and placed them in some order (Chapters 2–5). While not aiming at perfection we hope that a reasonable integration of the two approaches has been achieved.

While Machlup, who opened up this field (1962b), was mainly seeking to identify and measure the 'knowledge industries', our intention has been more analytical. To steer our way through a multitude of theoretical problems just barely mentioned in the general introduction, we have constructed and explored diverse economic models. The division of labour has been for Andersson to focus on firm and household demand for knowledge, macroeconomics and policy issues while Beckmann has plunged into the microeconomics of knowledge. A full integration of these approaches could not be achieved and would have been premature in view of the state of the area. In fact we have been selective and perhaps idiosyncratic in our choice of problems, which is not improper in a new field.

We gladly acknowledge the contributions of Olle Persson in Chapter 4. Professor Tönu Puu has also given us drawings of the logistic and a Frischian Production Function.

We have benefited from lively discussions with our friends and colleagues Tönu Puu, whose interest in the economics of culture has touched at various points on our subject, Kiyoshi Kobayashi, Wei-Bin Zhang, Charlie Karlsson and Börje Johansson.

We are grateful to David Emanuel Andersson for important and skilful improvements of content and language and to Kristofer Månsson for checking formulas. The invaluable typing work of Ms Gunvor Albihn on our almost undecipherable manuscripts at various stages of incompleteness cannot be sufficiently praised and appreciated. Ms Sandy Fleig has supported us at various stages of the project.

Of the greatest importance for the completion of this project has been the complicated and excellent editorial contribution by Dr Ulla Forslund Johansson. Mr. David Fairclough of Edward Elgar has been extremely helpful in the completion of the manuscript.

We wish to thank the following who have kindly given permission for the use of copyright material.

1. Akadémiai Kiadó, Springer Science and Business Media BV for article 'The thirteen most cited journals in economics', *Scientometrics*, **42** (2), 267–71.
2. Blackwell Publishing for article 'Diversification versus concentration: a note on the allocation of effort among risky research projects', *Pacific Economic Review*, **5** (3), 291–98.
3. Springer Verlag for article 'Scientific collaboration as spatial interaction', in M.J. Beckmann, B. Johansson, F. Snickars and R. Thord (eds) (1998), *Knowledge and Networks in a Dynamic Economy*, Heidelberg: Springer Verlag, 287–91.
4. Physica Verlag for article 'Bidding for research funds', in U. Leopold-Wildburger, G. Feichtinger and K.P. Kirchner (eds) (1999), *Modelling and Decisions in Economics: Essays in Honor of Franz Ferschl*, Heidelberg: Physica Verlag, 229–38.
5. Akadémiai Kiadó, Springer Science and Business Media BV for article 'Locating the network of interacting authors in scientific specialties', *Scientometrics*, **33** (3), 351–66.

We are also grateful for permission to quote empirical material from the studies of R. Asplund and P.T. Pereira (eds), *Returns to Human Capital in*

Europe, The Research Institute of the Finnish Economy, and to the World Bank for permissions to quote empirical material in working papers on returns to investments in education.

The authors also gratefully acknowledge financial support from The First Savings Bank Foundation

The work has also been supported by CESIS (Centre of Excellence for Science and Innovation Studies).

October, 2008

Åke E. Andersson Martin Beckmann

1 The Study of Knowledge in Economics

Knowledge was rarely analysed by economists before the 1980s. If it was mentioned at all, it was in some disguised form such as human capital, technology or innovations. The recent interest in the role of knowledge in the growth of economies is closely related to the consequences of the secular expansion of education in the industrial economies, the rapid growth of producer services and other knowledge-based industries and the increasing focus of manufacturing industries on industrial research and development (R&D).

The average duration of the formal education of the labour force in industrializing countries was less than three years around 1900. In 2004, the Scandinavian countries, Germany and the United States had a labour force of which more than 80 per cent had at least 12 years of formal education. Current trends indicate that the average level of formal education in the OECD region as a whole will exceed 13 years before the year 2020.

In the early stages of industrialization, scientific and technological research is of minor importance. Newly industrialized countries such as Greece, Turkey or Mexico allocate about half a per cent of their GDP to research and development investments. The relative share of GDP used for research and development was even lower when countries such as the United States, Britain or Germany started industrializing in the 19th century.

By 2005 the picture had changed completely, as Table 1.1 illustrates. In the OECD region, 2.25 per cent of total combined GDP was allocated to R&D expenditures. In Sweden, Finland and Japan the share allocated to R&D investments exceeded 3 per cent. There is however substantial variability among developed economies. Spain, Italy and Portugal only allocated around 1 per cent of GDP to research and development.

The relative role of industrial research and development is remarkable. Scientific research – as measured by higher education research and development (HERD) – is less than one-fifth of total research and development expenditures (GERD) in the OECD region. This is in stark contrast to the early 20th century, when the small universities of Europe and the United States held most of the scant resources for research, while industrial entrepreneurs scavenged for those parts of scientific research output that could form a new base for industrial manufacturing. Technological development could then be seen as exogenous to economic processes (cf. Schumpeter, 1934). The situation is completely different in modern economies. Research and education is developing interdependently with material investments and the harnessing of economies of scale and scope. Scientific, technological and economic expansions have all become inextricable components of an endogenous growth process.

Table 1.1 Research and development (R&D) in OECD economies, 2005

	R&D GDP %	R&D workers, %	HERD* GDP %
Sweden	3.89	1.25	0.8
Finland	3.48	1.65	0.7
Japan	3.33	1.10	0.4
South Korea	2.99	0.79	0.3
Switzerland	2.93	0.61	0.7
United States	2.62	0.97	0.4
Germany	2.46	0.70	0.4
Denmark	2.45	1.02	0.6
Austria	2.42	0.68	0.6
OECD	2.25	0.73	0.4
France	2.13	0.80	0.4
Canada	1.98	0.77	0.7
Belgium	1.82	0.76	0.4
United Kingdom	1.78	0.55	0.5
Australia	1.76	0.84	0.5
Luxembourg	1.56	0.68	0.0
Norway	1.52	0.92	0.5
Czech Republic	1.42	0.48	0.2
Ireland	1.26	0.59	0.6
Spain	1.12	0.57	0.3
Italy	1.10	0.30	0.4
Hungary	0.94	0.41	0.3
Portugal	0.80	0.41	0.3
Greece	0.49	0.37	0.2

Note: * HERD is R&D in higher education.

Source: OECD Science and Technology Indicators (2007b).

THE CONCEPTS OF KNOWLEDGE

Knowledge is extensively discussed in other sciences. The longest tradition is in philosophy with more recent contributions in cognitive science and computer science. The analysis of knowledge or *epistemology* has a long tradition in philosophy going back to Plato and Aristotle. Of some importance for our analysis are theories first proposed by the philosopher Bertrand Russell and the philosopher and economist Frank Ramsey, which have recently been combined and reformulated by Nils-Eric Sahlin (1990). Russell states in *The Problems of Philosophy*:

> What we firmly believe, if it is true, is called knowledge, provided it is either intuitive or inferred (logically or psychologically) from intuitive knowledge from which it follows logically. What we firmly believe, if it is not true, is called error. What we firmly believe, if it is neither knowledge nor error, and also what we believe hesitatingly, because it is, or is derived from, something which has not the highest degree of self-evidence, may be called probable opinion (Russell, 1912, p. 81).

Building upon Russell, Ramsey concludes – in the formulation by Sahlin (ibid., p. 93) – that '[k]nowledge is not true justified belief but rather a belief is knowledge if it is obtained by a reliable process and if it always leads to success'. What is then the success or value of knowledge?

In order to discuss this issue, Ramsey introduced utility and probability into the analysis of knowledge acquisition. In his paper 'Weight or the value of knowledge', Ramsey ([n.a.], 1990) shows how to assess the value of new knowledge to a scientist. Suppose that f_1 is a scientifically warranted but currently unknown proposition and f_2 represents not knowing the proposition. Ramsey then claims that the importance of being able to generate the new knowledge requires an evaluation of the probability of acquiring the new knowledge; an assessment of the subjective value or utility of the finding; and an allocation of potential resources (e.g. time) to creative research, in order to compare the situation where the new knowledge is found with the situation where it is not found. Ramsey proposes the use of expected utility as the criterion to be used in the optimization.

Assume that the expected utility for the scientist of new knowledge (e.g. a new proved proposition) equals:

$$u = Pf(x) + (1 - P)g(x) \tag{1.1}$$

where

P = probability of research success
$f(x)$ = research activity in case of successful search for new knowledge
$g(x)$ = research activity in case of unsuccessful search for new knowledge
x = share of time allocated to further research.

Moreover, the probability P can be assumed to depend on resources, I, allocated to the research process. Thus:

$$u = P(I)f(x) - [1 - P(I)]g(x) \tag{1.2}$$

which is maximized at the best combination of I and x.

In his article, Ramsey assumed that the probability P would be predetermined. He later questioned this assumption, as pointed out by Sahlin (1990). With the assumption that P is predetermined, Ramsey proved the proposition that u″ is larger than zero. Assuming an endogenous probability $P(I)$ yields the following maximization problem:

$$\text{Max } u = P(I)f(x) - [1 - P(I)]g(x) \tag{1.3}$$

subject to the resource constraint: $T(x, I) = 0$. The associated Lagrangian is assumed to be concave and differentiable. Maximization implies:

$$P(I)f'(x) + [1 - P(I)]g'(x) - \lambda T'(x) = 0 \tag{1.4}$$

$$P'(I)[f(x) - g(x)] - \lambda T'(I) = 0$$

$$T(x, I) = 0.$$

Since $f(x)$ should be greater than $g(x)$ and $\lambda T'(I)$ is greater than zero, it follows that $P'(I)$ should also be greater than zero at the optimum. Greater potential scientific benefit from the new knowledge (as measured by f) implies that more resources (I) should be allocated to increasing the probability of research success.

The creative potential of a proposition, model or theory is central to Ramsey and to his follower Braithwaite:

> It is only in theories which are not intended to have any function except that of systematizing empirical generalizations already known that the theoretical terms can harmlessly be defined. A theory which is hoped may be expanded in the future to explain more generalizations than it was originally designed to explain must allow more freedom to its theoretical terms than would be given them were they to

be logical constructions out of observable entities. A scientific theory which, like all good scientific theories, is capable of growth must be more than an alternative way of describing the generalizations upon which it is based, which is all it would be if its theoretical terms were limited by being explicitly defined. (Braithwaite, 1968, p. 76)

CONCEPTS IN THE ANALYSIS OF KNOWLEDGE

Information

Information and knowledge have been discussed and analysed by a number of economists. An example is Arrow (1971), who discusses at some length the role of information in the economic system. Arrow's analysis builds on the conceptualization by Shannon and Weaver (1949) – a communications engineer and a statistician. They were concerned with the problem of optimizing the capacity of telephone lines. In their optimization there was a trade-off between investment cost and quality of reception. Increasing the quality of reception implies increasing cost. Their problem was then to judge the quality of reception for the telephone user. The elementary concept of their analysis is called *bit*, defined as the smallest information carrying unit. A bit is represented by 0 or 1, indicating false or true. Two states X and Y carry information $I(X,Y)$ according to:

$$I(X,Y) = H(X) + H(Y) - H(X,Y) \tag{1.5}$$

where

$$H(X,Y) = \sum_{x,y} P(x,y) \log_2 P(x,y).$$

Later on, the Shannon–Weaver approach to the information problem has been refined by information theorists such as Kullback and Leibler (1951), and in economics by Snickars and Weibull (1977). Information is often slightly redefined in the sense that the elementary concept is instead *nits*, being measured in terms of natural logarithms rather than on the log-2 scale.

The information of a message can thus be defined and measured as the deviation between the actual and the expected message, as represented by the following equation:

$$I = \sum p_i \ln(p_i/q_i) \tag{1.6}$$

where

I = information
p_i = actual message I
q_i = expected message I.

The approach is clearly probabilistic and information is equivalent to *surprise* in the sense that only a large deviation between the actual and the expected message has large information content. I is approximately equal to the common χ^2 measure. All kinds of data and other descriptive information can easily be transmitted via an encoding and decoding procedure with the use of digital representations. From this point of view, information as represented above is also quite useful in economic and econometric analysis.

Unfortunately, the concept of information has been misused recently. A common mistake is to equate information and knowledge, as for example, Bill Gates (1995) does when describing the 'information society'.

Information and knowledge are not synonymous terms. Instead, information should be regarded as a necessary input in the knowledge formation process, while knowledge is the ability to transform old information into new information.

Data

At a slightly more complex level we have data – representing a string of information bits. In economics, data are useless unless they are defined by a variable of interest with its attendant unit of measurement as well as a spatio-temporal delimitation. A datum such as the number 81 648 000 000 is meaningless without a combination of variable definition and measure such as the gross national product in Swedish kronor and a spatio-temporal delimitation such as Sweden in 1962. Data are thus information strings, consisting of definitions of descriptors, spatio-temporal delimitations and the associated numerical data. Well-organized data with proper definitions can be represented as unique and reversible information.

Patterns

A pattern is an n-dimensional structure. A pattern can be represented algebraically, geometrically or topologically. The configuration of streets in a city, the location of factories on a map and the geometric structure of a human face are all examples of patterns. A rapidly expanding scientific field is oriented towards pattern formation, cognition and recognition. Much of the analysis within this field deals with the problem of the non-uniqueness of pattern formation and cognition (Haken, 1998). Figure 1.2 is an example of a simple two-dimensional pattern that is non-unique in the perception system of humans. The perception of this figure contains both *hysteresis*, in the sense that perception depends on the starting knowledge of the perceiver, and *instability*, which refers to sudden leaps between the perceived figures.

The non-uniqueness of a pattern leads to problems of irreversibility between the levels of information, data and patterns. This implies problems with the decoding and encoding of patterns by information or data. Tõnu Puu (1997a) shows how a geographic pattern can exhibit structural instability as a result of specific infinitesimal changes to the parameters that determine the optimal location pattern.

Concepts and Mechanisms

A proper conceptualization or reconceptualization is central to the formation of scientific knowledge. Concepts are at the core of theories and models. The Keynesian revolution is an example of how new concepts are formed and related to one another in a new theory. The assumption of fixed factor and output prices enabled Keynes to radically change the macroeconomic conclusions from those of earlier economists such as Leon Walras and Alfred Marshall. In Keynes's theory, the only variable macroeconomic entities are total income, investment, the rate of interest and employment, which is the implication of his new macroeconomic conceptualization. In the earlier neo-classical theory, the assumption of price flexibility guarantees that the economy attains general equilibrium with full employment of all resources. By contrast, in Keynes's theory it is possible for general equilibrium to be compatible with substantial underemployment of labour and capital.

Different concepts can be brought into relation with each other by dynamic or static equations as well as other models which can be tested for reliability. We will have arrived at new knowledge after successfully completing appropriate logical or empirical reliability tests. If embodied in some individual, we say that such an array of models and reliability tests constitutes *scientific skill*.

Scientific creativity, which we define as one or more dynamic changes to the components of knowledge, can occur at all of the afore mentioned stages – with the exception of information. Information consists of the irreducible modules or primitive building blocks that are combined and recombined in the pursuit of new knowledge.

COMMUNICATION OF KNOWLEDGE

It is easy to transfer information between different points in space by electronic and other communication media. The spatial friction associated with information transfer is negligible. By contrast, the transfer of knowledge tends to be much more affected by such friction. The analysis of the spatial frictions associated with knowledge transfer constitutes one of the main objectives of this book.

Figure 1.1 illustrates the relationships between different types of information and knowledge that are relevant to economic analysis.

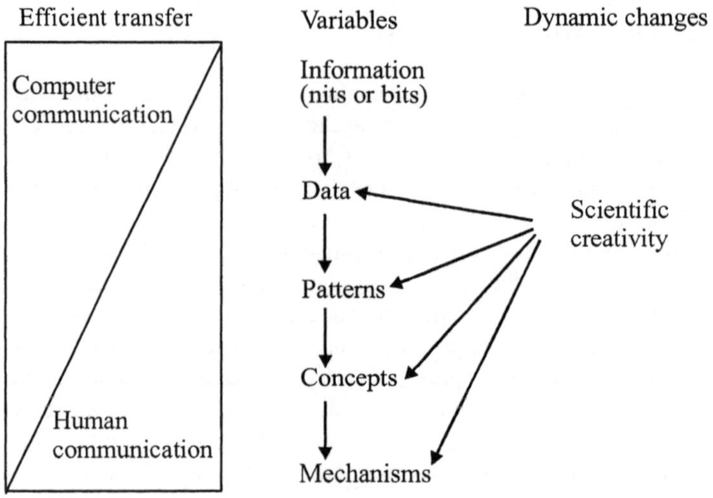

Figure 1.1 Communication and concepts of information and scientific knowledge

Established knowledge which has been reformulated into standard pedagogical forms can be transmitted by books, lecture notes, the internet and other media. New concepts, causal mechanisms, theories and models that have only recently developed as parts of a creative process are much more dependent on person-to-person interaction in a 'process of persuasion'. The efficiency of persuasion and negotiation declines with increasing distance between the parties that are involved in the interaction. The importance of negotiations and persuasion in scientific creativity is probably a reason for the stability of scientific institutions such as universities, workshops and conferences.

CREATIVITY VERSUS PRODUCTIVITY

Productivity is conventionally defined to be the amount of a given good (i.e. a good with fixed characteristics) that can be produced with a given set of inputs. Labour productivity is thus defined to be the output per unit of labour input. Creativity is a much less well-defined concept. We find the following definition serviceable:

> Creativity is a flow of ideas from an individual or group of individuals, which is perceived by relevant specialists to be new and at least potentially useful for other creators, consumers or producers.

Most of us have received an education that is adapted to the demands for preconceived notions of specialized labour in industry or public administration. Most of the attendant occupations have been defined according to a basic understanding of the principle of division of labour, and its productivity-enhancing properties. The traditional interpretation of the division of labour is that each worker should specialize in performing specific highly specialized tasks, without much room for improvization or changing work routines.

Industrial society was based on the division of labour and the hierarchical organization of firms. Research and development in such a society became a sort of tinkering, which was oriented towards improving the techniques for producing a given set of goods. Creativity was looked upon as a social exception which only involved a small group of scientists, artists and inventors.

The first stage of re-evaluating the economic and political importance of creative work occurred during the Second World War, when political decision-makers realized that mathematicians, chemists and physicists were indispensable in military and other strategic projects. A large-scale example was the Manhattan Project, within which scientists were organized into secret research groups with the aim of transforming the knowledge of theoretical physics into the atom bomb (Fermi, [1954] 1994). On the basis of this experiment in organized creativity, the American 'think tank' became a way of improving the coordination between creative scientific research and the development and innovation of new products – for both military and civilian uses – in the post-war American economy. The Cowles Commission and the Rand Corporation are examples of such think tanks.

A thoroughgoing integration of creative research and technological development would, however, not be realized before the end of industrialism. By the early 1970s, manufacturing employment had already begun its long decline in North America and Western Europe. It was becoming increasingly obvious that highly industrialized societies could no longer expect increasing employment of labour from the production of standardized material goods.

In the 1970s, many economic analysts expected the traditional service industries to become the new guarantors of full employment. Few analysts expected that creativity in science, technology and design would become the most important factor for explaining the growth of real income, employment and general welfare in the emerging post-industrial society.

New developments in the structure of some regions, for example the San Francisco Bay Area with Silicon Valley, the Boston Region with Route 128 and Cambridge, England, reflected a new type of interaction between creative scientists – both from universities and from industry. These were the first visible manifestations of the increasing importance of creativity in the economic system. Since the 1960s, the role of creativity as a factor of economic development has been channelled in somewhat surprising directions.

First, there has been a rapid increase in resources that are allocated to scientific research. The number of published journal papers in natural science, engineering and medicine increased at a pace of about 7 per cent per year from 1975 to 1990 (Andersson and Persson, 1993).

Second, industrial research and development (R&D) has become a strategic part of the growth policies of firms and governments in the OECD region since the late 1960s. This development has no doubt encouraged the numerous attempts to analyse the interdependencies between R&D and economic growth (see for example Uzawa, 1965; Shell, 1966; Andersson and Mantsinen, 1980; Romer, 1990).

MECHANISMS OF CREATIVITY

Creativity is a process based on inherited and socially acquired capacities. As a process it is dynamic, because creativity always means the emergence of something genuinely new. Discoveries of causal mechanisms and inventions based on these discoveries are outcomes of creative processes. Discovery implies a capacity to find patterns in a seemingly chaotic world. Real creativity springs from the ability to comprehend and explain the mechanisms generating such patterns. The detection of a hidden pattern and its transformation into something meaningful is often something that occurs suddenly within the brain. The mathematician I.N. Stewart and the psychologist P.L. Peregoy (1983) employ a series of experiments to show how the brain can discover initially hidden structures. Their experiments support the claim that the perception–cognition system of the brain is best represented as non-linear dynamic equations.

Using the following images (see Figure 1.2) they were able to show that the perception of a man is suddenly transformed into a clear perception of a woman after three to six steps from left to right and the perception of a woman is suddenly transformed into a man, when starting from the right and moving three to five steps to the left.

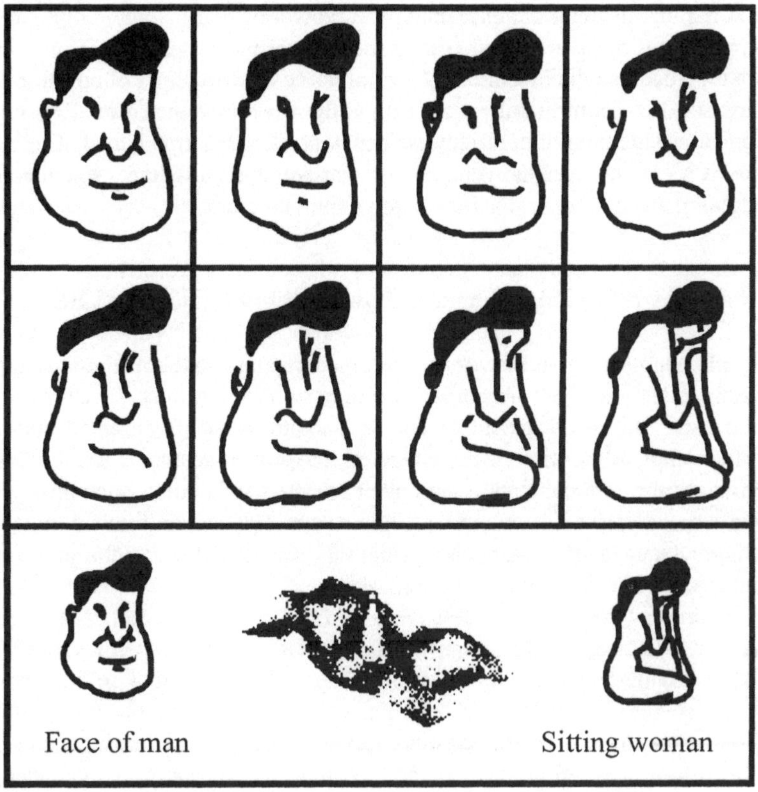

Source: Kruse and Stadler (1993).

Figure 1.2 The structural instability of perception

This result implies that the brain has a tendency to be anchored in the original perception and that it needs a critical level of information before it can give up the initial interpretation in favour of a new one. The brain thus reinforces and stabilizes the already known. The conservative nature of the brain tends to limit creativity. Expressed differently, creativity requires a certain degree of instability of the brain. Such instability is evidently present in most of us.

Inventions and discoveries are different labels for created ideas. An invention mostly originates with a scientist who perceives a surface structure before suddenly realizing that beneath this superficial structure there is a more important deep structure. The newly discovered deep structure can subsequently be used for the formation of a new principle or theory which becomes instrumental in generating inventions.

We should in this context note that there are two types of creativity. The first type denotes the invention of a completely new principle of construction, composition or conceptualization, providing a new structuring of some set of problems. This type of creativity is fundamental or *infrastructural*. The other type of creativity uses the principle of 'variations on a theme', which means the exploitation of a pre-existing creative infrastructure.

CREATIVE CAPACITY – ACQUIRED OR INHERITED?

Are all people born creative? There are indicators that creativity is not a genetic deviation from the normal but rather a general human capacity. One indicator is the development of the capacity to speak. Even small children create completely new spoken sentences. These new sentences are linguistic constructs for communicating with other children and adults. Sometimes they even seem surprised at their own linguistic discoveries and inventions. The individual's capacity for linguistic creativity seems to develop through social interaction from early childhood until old age.

Simonton (1984) uses extensive empirical material to show that early exposure to scientifically or artistically creative individuals is of importance for developing the creativity of young people. Formal schooling does not in general compensate for the lack of artistic and other creative inspiration in the homes of children. A reason for this deficiency could be that most educational systems have focused on the diffusion of already well established knowledge, which has been considered appropriate as a preparation for a 'normal career' in manufacturing firms or bureaucracies. The implication is that schools have primarily encouraged the development of discipline and adaptation to one's social environment as well as specialized skills that can be employed in cooperation with others for solving well-specified problems as efficiently as possible.

Pre-university education has therefore rarely been directed towards independent problem formulation or the generation of different ways of solving such problems. Instead, most education emphasizes learning how to solve pre-formulated problems in a way that is pleasing to the teacher. Such learning of well-established techniques has in fact been common at all levels of education, and especially during the first years of primary education.

Gudmund Smith and Ingegerd Carlsson (1990) find that the typical development of creativity during childhood and adolescence exhibits a cyclical pattern. Some parts of the 'creativity cycle' favour absorption of formal education, while other parts of the cycle favour the development of creativity. The typical ages at which creativity develops most rapidly seem to be between five and seven, ten and 12 as well as 17 and 19 years of age. In the education systems of most industrialized nations the two latter creativity peaks are used by schools for especially intensive teaching and examinations, which crowds out both conscious and spontaneous creativity development. Smith and Carlsson have even claimed that an educational programme that gives priority to creativity development may need to be set free from fixed, centrally decided curricula.

THE CREATIVE PERSONALITY

The transformation from an industrial society towards a society which is based on the exploitation of knowledge – with increasing product complexity as a by-product – will require better policies for developing and using human creativity. Finding and supporting people with creative skills has become much more important than during the industrial era.

Smith and Carlsson (ibid.) and their research team have investigated empirical commonalities among creative individuals. The most important results can be summarized as six observations.

First, a typical characteristic of creative people is the ability not only to formulate a problem but also to be persistent in the pursuit of its solution. Sometimes the problem in question is not conceived as especially interesting by anyone else and is often looked upon as somewhat strange or even bizarre by others. Second, the creative personality entails the development of a subjective and quite emotional relationship to the problem during the period of problem-solving. The solution to such an independently formulated problem is often not obviously profitable or even interesting for anyone but the creator. A third trait is an interest in aesthetically satisfying solutions to the generated problem. Fourth, one of the most important personality traits of creative individuals is what Smith and Carlsson calls the *oceanic capacity*. This is the capacity to envisage almost infinite possibilities when a new creative solution turns out to be correct. It further implies an instant and yet sustainable reward that is of greater importance than external rewards in the form of money or fame. Fifth, creative persons tend to be victims of angst, which according to Smith and Carlsson is *the* most natural companion to creative activities. The final observation is that it does not seem to be the case that a goal-oriented and affluent home is the best breeding ground for the development of creativity among children. Remarkably often creative persons seem to have come from disadvantaged homes.

In his book *How to Solve It*, the mathematician George Polya (1945) claims that the most important approach to creative problem formulation and problem-solving is the use of heuristics (i.e. suitable analogies): 'Analogy pervades all our thinking, our everyday speech and our trivial conclusions as well as our ways of expression and the highest scientific achievements' (Polya, ibid., p. 37). While this is obvious in both pure and applied mathematics, Polya's argument is that it is true of all creative activities.

Production requires a predictable and structurally stable process in order to be efficient. Creativity is almost diametrically opposed to such stability. The creator has to accept fundamental uncertainty and its companion – structural instability. This implies that creativity can only be pursued by individuals who accept a career with an embedded uncertainty regarding income and wealth.

In the scientific world, the income stream of creative people is normally secured through a combination of subsidies and payment for other work than creative scientific research. In universities much of the salaried time is used for conventional teaching, administration and other non-creative activities. The financial rewards for creativity are primarily determined by the decisions-makers who allocate public or private funds. The allocations tend to be based on earlier research performance and an estimate of the likelihood of success as evaluated by some more or less credible peer group.

In decisions concerning industrial R&D it is common to calculate the financial rewards according to methods that resemble those that are used for the evaluation of the returns to material investments. This implies that decision-makers estimate the expected net present value and risk. Because of the public nature of knowledge, the risk is very large and different procedures address the problem of how to protect privately funded inventions. The most common procedure of protecting new material products is *patenting*. Patents are usually sought in all countries that the patentee deems as non-negligible markets for firms that are likely to imitate the new knowledge in the absence of patent protection. Patent rights are regulated by international treaties and give the property right to the proceeds from the new product for a time period of no more than 20 years. However, most patent holders can only benefit from their patents for approximately 10 to 15 years, because of normal production delays after a patent has been granted.

CREATIVE SCIENTIFIC ORGANIZATIONS

Universities are organizations that are designed to produce a number of products, such as graduates at different levels and in different academic fields, textbooks, laboratory tests, expert reports, scientific papers and books.

The factors of production include information, stored in libraries and computers, human capital embodied in professors and administrators and physical capital such as computers and lecture halls. This implies that universities are firms that engage in *joint production*. The total revenue of such firms is the sum of the revenues from each of its valued outputs. The cost is a function of the cost of producing each of its outputs, which may include positive and negative interaction effects among the various production processes within the firm. An example is the following net revenue (or profit) function, first proposed by Stackelberg (1932):

$$\text{Net revenue} = \sum p_i(x) \cdot x_i - C(x_1, \ldots, x_n) \tag{1.7}$$

where

$p_i(x)$	=	the price of produced service i
x_i	=	the quantity produced of service i
$C(x)$	=	cost of production as determined by the vector of services.

Necessary optimality conditions are:

$$p_i + \sum_j \frac{\partial p_j}{\partial x_i} x_i = \frac{\partial C}{\partial x_i} \qquad (i = 1, \ldots, n) \tag{1.8}$$

where x_i indicates a specific service and p_j is the price of service j. The sum of marginal price effects weighted by the quantities plus the price of the service itself is optimized when it is equal to the marginal cost of producing the service. As the quantities are weighted marginal price effects, there are economies of both scale and scope in the production of university services.

It is also possible that the cost functions reveal joint production benefits. A research team with different specialists could give rise to labour-cost-reducing synergies that arise from cooperative problem-solving. In that case there will be another gradient component that should be added on the right-hand side of the optimality condition.

When determining the amount to be produced of a certain service (e.g. elementary statistics lectures), it is not enough to consider the marginal effect on the price of that service itself. The decision-maker has to take the marginal price effect on all other affected services into account. The marginal effect on prices of the other services could be positive (e.g. on prices of courses in economics, biology, medicine and business administration if some knowledge of statistics would be helpful in passing the tests of those disciplines). It could even be the case that the sum of the positive marginal effects on the prices of other services is great enough to justify offering the service free of charge.

Joint production is especially important in the structuring of universities to undertake scientific research, applied research and development and teaching activities. Interaction effects are not independent of field – medicine and technology are examples of fields with especially strong interaction effects.

It should be obvious that the willingness to pay among industrial firms for scientific research is minimal. However, the willingness to pay for applied research and technological development projects may be substantially increased if a university has a top-ranking position as a centre of creative scientific research in terms of publication and citation records and prize-winning achievements. Similarly, some teaching by famous creative scientists can increase the marketing value to students of a university, even if most of their courses are taught by less creative professors.

CREATIVITY RANK, SIZE AND ORGANIZATION OF UNIVERSITIES

There have recently been numerous attempts to rank universities according to their creativity, as reflected by scientific publication and citation data. Table 1.2 presents the world's 20 most creative universities according to one such attempt.

The relative importance of the United States is obvious from this table. Only three out of the 20 top-ranked universities are located outside of the United States. Psacharopoulos (2005) sees this as an indication of Europe's diminishing weight in the world of scientific creativity. However, location is not the only important explanatory variable in this context. As we have seen above, size does matter. Extending the data set to the 50 top-ranked universities offers clear indications that the optimal size of a university falls in the range between 10 000 and 25 000 students (with the exception of universities that specialize in medicine or technology). Table 1.3 shows the relation between size and rank.

Size matters to the extent that a very large population of students does not contribute to creativity. Indeed, some of the world's best universities have surprisingly small student populations. Examples include Princeton University with 7 200, the University of Chicago with 13 400 and Stanford University with 14 900 students.

Table 1.2 Scientific creativity ranking of universities

World Rank	University	Country
1	Harvard University	United States
2	University of Cambridge	United Kingdom
3	Stanford University	United States
4	University of California at Berkeley	United States
5	Massachusetts Institute of Technology (MIT)	United States
6	California Institute of Technology (Caltech)	United States
7	Columbia University	United States
8	Princeton University	United States
9	University of Chicago	United States
10	University of Oxford	United Kingdom
11	Yale University	United States
12	Cornell University	United States
13	University of California at San Diego	United States
14	University of California at Los Angeles	United States
15	University of Pennsylvania	United States
16	University of Wisconsin at Madison	United States
17	University of Washington at Seattle	United States
18	University of California at San Francisco	United States
19	Johns Hopkins University	United States
20	Tokyo University	Japan

Source: Shanghai Institute of Technology (2005).

Table 1.3 University rank by number of students

Rank	Student population ≤ 25 000 %	Student population > 25 000 %
1–10	90	10
11–30	55	45
31–50	30	70

Source: Shanghai Institute of Technology (2005).

Table 1.4 shows the relation between the share of private funding of tertiary education and the number of top-ranked universities in a number of countries.

Universities ranked among the top 100 are extremely rare in countries with socialized funding of higher education and scientific research. Countries with a private sector contribution of 30 per cent or more account for 73 out of the world's top 100 universities. A reasonable size in combination with private funding seems almost to be a necessary condition for scientific success.

Specialization is another important factor that affects the likelihood of academic success as indicated by world ranking. Six of the top 50 universities are in fact quite small, but they achieve their success by being highly focused in their research (see Table 1.5).

Table 1.4 Private funding of tertiary education in OECD countries and number of top 100 universities

	Private funding of tertiary education (percentage share of total funding)	Number of top 100 universities
United States	66.7	51
Japan	54.5	5
Australia	43.8	2
Canada	38.5	4
United Kingdom	30.0	11
Spain	25.0	0
Ireland	20.0	2
Netherlands	16.7	2
Sweden	11.8	4
Italy	11.1	1
Germany	10.0	7
France	9.1	4
Portugal	9.1	0
Belgium	7.7	0
Austria	0.0	1
Denmark	0.0	1
Finland	0.0	1
Greece	0.0	0
Norway	0.0	1

Source: Psacharopoulos (2005).

The average size of these specialized universities is approximately 6 000 students. The California Institute of Technology – ranked as the world's sixth-best university – has only 2 086 students.

We can sum up our findings by pointing to three factors that jointly seem to provide necessary conditions for sustainable scientific success:

1. Moderate size – between 2 000 and 25 000 students. The average student population of the top ten universities is 17 000.
2. Substantial share of private funding – seven out of the top ten universities are private.
3. Academic specialization.

Table 1.5 The six best specialized universities

University	Specialization
Massachusetts Institute of Technology	Technology; Quantitative business management and economics
California Institute of Technology	Technology
University of California at San Francisco	Medicine
Erdgenössiche Technische Hochschule	Technology
University of Texas – Southwestern Medical Center at Dallas	Medicine
Karolinska Institute	Medicine

CREATIVITY AND INNOVATIONS

The British Department of Trade and Industry defined innovation as 'the successful exploitation of new ideas' while the American Heritage Dictionary defines it as 'the act of introducing something new: something newly invented'. Creativity thus precedes innovation; the innovator need not be creative. However, innovators are dependent on the existence and effectiveness of creators.

Innovation of new technological and organizational ideas is crucial to the development of economic efficiency. The economic role of innovated knowledge is analysed in a microeconomic context in Chapter 7 and from a macroeconomic point of view in Chapter 8. In this chapter, our discussion is limited to remarks on an attempt to measure the relative innovation performance of national economies.

The most thorough analysis of the relative innovativeness of different economies has been conducted by the German Institute for Economic Research (DIW). DIW has developed a ranking of national innovativeness which encompasses measurements of seven innovation-related variables:

1. Education and availability of inventive engineers and creative scientists
2. Research and development activity
3. Regulations and competitive climate
4. Funding of innovators; risk-taking
5. Demand for new products
6. Networking (active intra-industry networking and networking with higher education and research establishments)
7. Implementation in production.

Table 1.6 Countries ranked by innovation index, science index and economic growth

Rank	Country	Innovation index 2007	Science index 1988–90	GDP growth rate per year 1996–2006
1	Sweden	7.0	131	3.1
2	United States	6.9	100	3.2
3	Switzerland	6.8	142	1.8
4	Finland	6.7	87	3.8
5	Denmark	6.0	105	2.1
6	Japan	5.6	39	1.1
7	United Kingdom	5.4	106	2.8
8	Germany	5.2	63	1.5
9	Netherlands	5.0	93	2.5
10	Canada	4.9	117	3.5
11	France	4.6	65	2.3
12	Ireland	4.4	n.a.	7.2
13	Belgium	4.4	65	2.3
14	Austria	4.1	60	2.2
15	South Korea	3.9	n.a.	4.2
16	Spain	1.4	29	3.8
17	Italy	1.0	36	1.4

Note: n.a. = not available.

Sources: DIW (2007); Database: Science Citation Index (1988–1990); OECD National Accounts (2007a).

The measurement of the role of creativity in innovation performance focuses on three indicators; state promotion of R&D, which includes the total volume of government spending on R&D and related tax concessions; the extent to which public sector research and higher education establishments liaise with industrial firms; and the quality of basic research, which is evaluated on the basis of quantitative indicators of journal publications and journal citations.

The magnitudes of the seven variables are weighted so that the contribution of each variable to the overall index should reflect its relative importance for innovativeness. Table 1.6 gives the rank-ordered 2007 innovation index for 17 developed economies. The table also includes a science index which is based on bibliometric data for the period 1988 to 1990, which means that the science index precedes the innovation index by almost two decades.

Table 1.6 shows that there are no perfect positive associations between knowledge accumulation, technological innovation and economic growth – at least not in the short or medium run. Highly creative and innovative economies might for example have low savings and investment rates or substandard conditions for new firm start-ups. The United States is an example of an economy which has had relatively low savings and investment propensities while Sweden is an example of a country which has had low levels of firm start-ups. By contrast, Ireland and South Korea are examples of economies with low rankings on the innovation index but with a recent history of rapid economic growth.

CREATIVITY, INNOVATIONS, GROWTH AND TRADE

The role of scientific and applied creativity in the process of economic growth is analysed at some length in Chapter 8. The implications for international trade and location are not discussed at any length in this study. However, there is a certain theory of trade and location – product cycle theory – that, at least implicitly, depends on dynamics of creativity and innovations. This theory has been examined and discussed in Andersson and Johansson (1984) and Johansson and Andersson (1998).

The starting point of that analysis is illustrated by Figure 1.3.

The process of changing division of labour is inherently dynamic in this theory of location and trade. At each sufficiently short period of time allocation in space is determined by comparative advantages. But these advantages are changing with the progress of technological knowledge by creativity and innovations. The birth of new products and processes is given by the creative/innovative activities in the left uppermost corner of Figure 1.3. These birth processes are primarily located in the knowledge-based regions. If the new products (and their production processes) are dependent upon supply of knowledge and information resources, production will remain in the K-regions. When maturation of the technology occurs, comparative advantages of other regions will induce relocation and changes in the pattern of trade. Production would then move to developed non-K-regions, if a high capital intensity is optimal and where advantages of large-scale production can be realized.

For labour-intensive products a relocation to developing regions will occur. A brake on the relocation process can happen (as illustrated by the lower left corner of Figure 1.3) if a policy of protectionism is politically introduced. The larger the shares of resources going into R&D investments (or the larger the creativity and innovation capacity), the more rapid would be the relocation of production and trade flows.

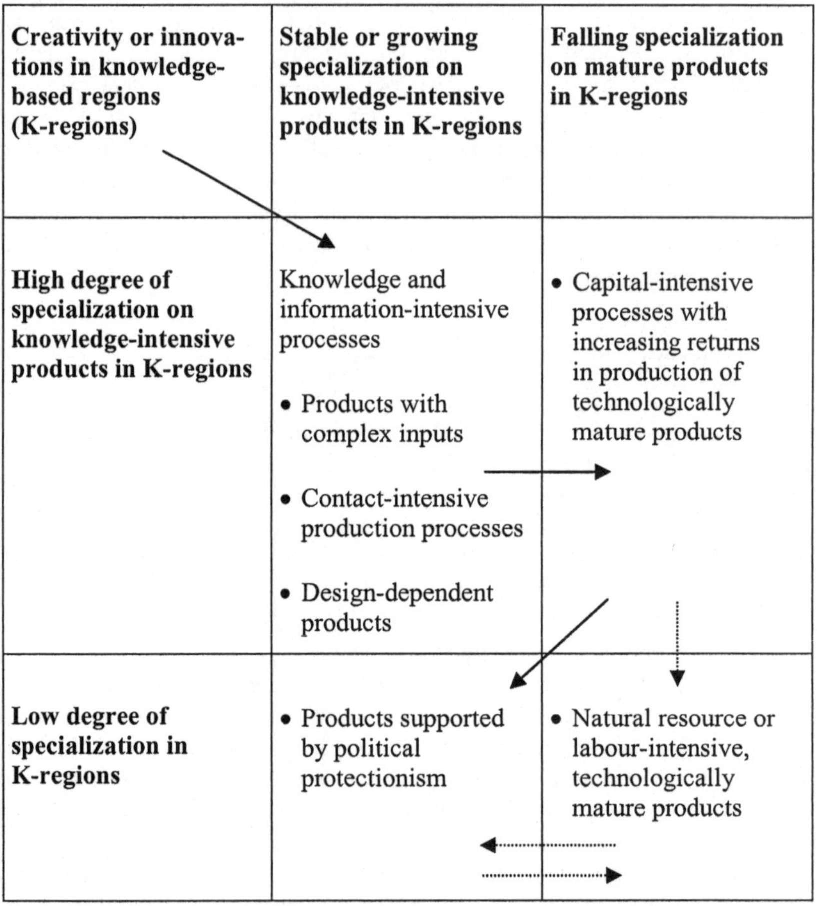
Creativity or innovations in knowledge-based regions (K-regions)
Stable or growing specialization on knowledge-intensive products in K-regions
Falling specialization on mature products in K-regions
High degree of specialization on knowledge-intensive products in K-regions
Knowledge and information-intensive processes
• Products with complex inputs
• Contact-intensive production processes
• Design-dependent products
• Capital-intensive processes with increasing returns in production of technologically mature products
Low degree of specialization in K-regions
• Products supported by political protectionism
• Natural resource or labour-intensive, technologically mature products

Note: Continuous arrow = dominant flow; dashed arrow = non-dominant flow.

Figure 1.3 Spatial dynamics of product cycles

2 Stock of Knowledge

Knowledge is voluminous and diverse, from an object of man's highest aspirations down to mere amusement or tools in production. The question 'what is knowledge?' is fundamental in philosophy. For economic analysis a simple working definition is needed; we propose knowledge as sets of related ideas and associated facts.

From the arcane world of ideas, knowledge is brought into the real world of material objects through embodiment; first in persons, and then in documents – such as notes, working papers, published articles, books, blue-prints or computer files and programs. The embodiment in persons comes through original discovery or learning – learning from teachers or documents.

Knowledge embodied in documents can be counted and measured in some way. With such quantification we can obtain a proxy variable for knowledge, however crude it may be. The accumulation of documents in a field of knowledge gives rise to the notion of a stock of knowledge. Such a stock of knowledge is reminiscent of a physical stock of capital and may be called a stock of mental capital. Like physical capital, a stock of knowledge is heterogeneous and thus difficult to measure. It may increase through the discovery of new knowledge and decrease through the discovery of errors or redundancies. When entire subjects are found to be irrelevant or misleading and therefore dropped, their stock of knowledge disappears entirely.

The transfer of knowledge from embodiment in persons to documents is propelled by institutional mandates for prompt communication of discoveries to the scientific community; an exchange of knowledge for prestige, in other words, the recognition of 'priority'. In the case of applied knowledge the acquisition of property rights to an item of knowledge through patents or copyrights also requires disclosure in documents.

Like material goods, knowledge in documents can be a consumption good or a factor of production.

TYPES OF KNOWLEDGE

Following Machlup (1962b, p. 2), we illustrate knowledge by listing his many types of knowledge:

Box 2.1 Types of knowledge according to Machlup (1962b)

Practical knowledge	Professional knowledge Business knowledge Workman's knowledge Politician's knowledge Household knowledge Other practical knowledge
Intellectual knowledge (satisfying intellectual curiosity; regarded as part of liberal education, humanistic and scientific learning, general culture; acquired as a rule in active concentration with an appreciation of the existence of open problems and cultural values)	Liberal education General culture Scientific learning Historical facts National culture
Pastime knowledge (satisfying the non-intellectual curiosity or a desire for light entertainment including local gossip, news of crime, accidents and scandals, light novels, stories, jokes, games, etc; acquired as a rule in passive relaxation from serious pursuits; apt to dull one's sensitiveness)	Entertainment
Spiritual knowledge (related to one's religious knowledge of God and of the ways of the salvation of the soul)	Ethics Religion
Unwanted knowledge (knowledge apart from one's interests; accidentally acquired, aimlessly retained)	

Some types of knowledge are of a binary (zero/one) nature. The answer to a question is known or not known. Other types of knowledge may be increased (more or less) continuously and may be treated as a continuous variable. In scientific knowledge, a fundamental distinction is that between basic and applied knowledge. Basic research produces basic knowledge which is not directed towards usefulness. This reminds us of what Hardy (1940) said in celebration of pure mathematics: 'mathematics, may it never be of use for anything'.

SIGNIFICANT KNOWLEDGE – AN IRON LAW?

How many articles are significant in the flood of publications in a scientific field? This is an important question even apart from 'how to recognize the significant articles' (de Solla Price, 1961; Kochen, 1969; Holub et al., 1991). As a rough estimate for the field of economics, Borchardt (1978, p. 488), citing Kochen (ibid.) states in translation that 'a law of important articles [is] that the number of important articles in the field of economic theory increases to the extent of the square root of the total number of all published articles'. A related estimate of the number of important scientists among all scientists in a particular field by de Solla Price (1963) is a cubic root.

To test Kochen's 'square root law', Holub et al. (1991) look at modern growth theory in economics since the late 1930s in 46 journals that together account for 2 681 articles. Important articles were defined as having received 30 citations or more. It turned out that these included (with four exceptions) all articles indicated as important in textbooks and surveys.

The slope coefficient in the log-linear relationship was close to 0.5 in the 'foundations of growth theory' and 'optimal growth theory' categories. In other categories, the coefficient was slightly greater, but within the 95 per cent confidence interval. Can a theoretical explanation be given to this square law (or cubic law or any other power law)? Clearly it cannot result from any given frequency distribution of talent among the authors in a field, for that would yield a proportionate rather than square root relationship. In the model below, we interpret 'significant articles', K, as a proxy for ideas or knowledge content, and literature, L, as measured stock of knowledge.

The relationship between knowledge and the literature (all publications) is in fact not a static one but the result of ongoing dynamic processes. We postulate that new knowledge is produced from the existing knowledge K and the literature L and assume a Cobb–Douglas production function:

$$\dot{K} = f(K,L) = aK^{\beta}L^{\alpha} \tag{2.1}$$

$$\dot{K}K^{-\beta} = \frac{1}{1-\beta}\frac{d}{dt}\left(K^{1-\beta}\right) = aL^{\alpha}$$

$$K(t)^{1-\beta} = a(1-\beta)\int_0^t L^{\alpha}(t)\,dt. \tag{2.2}$$

As an empirical observation, the literature in an active field grows exponentially:

$$\dot{L} = gL.$$

Now substitute

$$\frac{dL}{gL} = dt \tag{2.3}$$

in (2.2):

$$K^{1-\beta} = a(1-\beta)\int \frac{L^{\alpha}}{gL}\,dL$$

$$= \frac{a(1-\beta)}{g}\frac{L^{\alpha}}{\alpha}$$

or

$$K = cL^{\frac{\alpha}{1-\beta}} \tag{2.4}$$

which is a power relationship.

Holub's iron law means that $\alpha/(1-\beta) = 1/2$ and a cubic law means that $\alpha/(1-\beta) = 1/3$. In any meaningful relationship $\alpha/(1-\beta) < 1$ implies that $\alpha + \beta < 1$. In other words, the result implies decreasing returns to scale.

CITATION ANALYSIS CONTINUED: THE MOST CITED JOURNALS IN ECONOMICS[1]

Holub et al. (1991) used citation counts for estimating the relationship of significant articles to all articles published in a field. In this section we propose a method of weighting each citation along with the cited documents or authors, and apply it to a ranking of scientific journals. Palacios-Huerta and Volij (2004) examine this method and alternative schemes of 'impact measurement'.

How many readers an economic journal has, is not known and difficult to discover. To measure a journal's impact we can however use citation data compiled from the *Social Science Citation Index* (SSCI) published by the

Institute for Scientific Information (ISI). The impact factor divides the number of citations a journal receives from all other journals in the database by the number of papers published in it, and has been used extensively in bibliometric studies (Bonitz, 1985; Bonitz, 1990; Marshakova-Shaikevich, 1996). This has included evaluation of economic journals (Moore, 1972; Liebowitz and Palmer, 1984; Taylor and Johnes, 1992). Stigler et al. (1995) provides a thorough analysis of the economic journal literature and examines its citation network. The aim of this section is more modest. We want to derive a ranking of economics journals from their citation matrix, distinguishing between impact factor, defined conventionally as the ratio of citations received to papers published in a journal, and the impact value, to be described below. In Stigler et al. (ibid.), this ranking is achieved by means of 'export scores' based on the ratios of 'citations sent to journal A by journal B to citations received by B from A'.

The impact factor treats all citations as equally important, while we also use the values of journals (to be discovered) as weights. Thus a journal's impact value, v_i, is proportional to the weighted citations it receives:

$$v_i = \alpha \sum_j c_{ij} v_j$$

or, equivalently:

$$\lambda = \frac{1}{\alpha}$$

$$\lambda v_i = \sum_j c_{ij} v_j$$

so that the proportional factor λ is the eigenvalue of the citation matrix, c_{ij}. Here c_{ij} is the number of citations articles in journal i received from articles in journal j.

For a positive matrix (c_{ij}), the existence of a positive eigenvalue with the greatest absolute value among all eigenvalues (as well as the associated positive eigenvector) is assured by Perron's theorem (Perron, 1907; Debreu and Herstein, 1953). The greatest eigenvalue corresponds to the smallest possible proportionality factor.

Suppose some journal i dominates another journal k in the sense of receiving more citations in some and not fewer citations in any journal j, then $v_i > v_k$ (see Appendix 2.1). In this sense, *Econometrica* dominates the *Economic Journal* (see Table 2.1).

The citation matrix, showing citations from and to these thirteen journals, is displayed in Table 2.1. Here the data have been retrieved from the online version of SSCI. The citing window is the same as for the impact factors, but the cited window could not be delimited, which means that citations prior to the volume for 1981 are included. In Table 2.2, the impact factors – which are based on a 16-year citation period (1981–96) – are listed together with the eigenvector components.

The high impact factor of *JEL* is apparently due to the fact that its citations are divided by relatively few articles. The impact values show a different picture. In the citation matrix the *JEL* is in fact dominated by several other journals, including *Econometrica*, *JPE* and *AER*. The strong impact value of the *QJE* is perhaps surprising, while those of *AER*, *Econometrica*, *RES* and *JPE* are to be expected. The impact values are more plausible than impact factors since they use more information: the whole citation matrix rather than column sums. They do not depend on the total number of articles in each journal.

We have demonstrated how the impact of economics journals may be estimated as the result of weighted citations, the weights being the values of various journals that are discovered as part of the estimation process. This idea may be extended to finding the impact of various authors in a field with one important difference: self-citations are to be omitted. In journals self-citations simply refer to papers published in the same journal, which are certainly relevant and legitimate.

CLASSIFICATION OF KNOWLEDGE

For knowledge to be cumulative, new knowledge must be placed into the context of existing knowledge. Finding an 'address' for new (or any) knowledge is tantamount to classifying knowledge. Fundamentally the problem of classification is philosophical, and deals with how to best divide the vast areas of knowledge. A practical aspect is the need of libraries to put order into their document (book) holdings.

Classification is subdivision of sets, and for practical usefulness the criteria for subdivision must be clear and easy to apply. Another consideration is that – on average – the classification code should be as short as possible. This requires that at any stage, the subdivision should result in classes of about the same size. Division into equal halves results in a binary code. In any code based on partition, the length of the code measures the specificity of the subject class. It can be argued that specificity also means 'depth', and that the degree of possible classification specificity reveals the depth of a field of knowledge. As illustrations we list a few well-known systems of classification in Appendix 2.2.

Table 2.1 Citation matrix for 13 most cited economics journals

Cited journal (all cited years)	Citing journal (citing time-window 1981–96)												
	JEL	*EM*	*JPE*	*QJE*	*AER*	*RES*	*RJE*	*JET*	*JIE*	*EJ*	*JPE*	*IER*	*ECO*
Journal of Economic Literature	121	27	72	41	144	19	40	35	12	71	53	38	32
Econometrica	153	1072	468	353	864	541	372	950	236	501	426	583	250
Journal of Political Economy	155	126	377	177	467	154	143	184	138	182	192	187	110
Quarterly Journal of Economics	94	132	205	411	456	162	130	165	144	205	227	193	120
American Economic Review	170	175	317	290	1027	190	243	187	209	380	363	273	174
Review of Economic Studies	62	252	161	155	290	303	135	289	106	203	214	240	103
Rand Journal of Economics	87	152	226	208	474	194	721	190	68	165	182	188	124
Journal of Economic Theory	38	263	110	70	187	182	132	661	36	92	133	224	62
Journal of International Economics	25	14	58	65	129	47	6	14	522	102	50	147	66
Economic Journal	75	51	76	68	179	54	62	54	73	450	141	85	134
Journal of Public Economics	51	94	114	94	201	92	61	108	51	128	783	89	80
International Economic Review	29	103	84	45	123	73	46	133	94	86	85	268	57
Economica	81	50	75	76	181	62	52	59	93	189	120	64	238

Source: Beckmann and Persson (1998b).

Table 2.2 Impact factors and impact values for economics journals, 1981–96

	Impact factor	Impact value (eigenvector components)
American Economic Review	13.59	0.944
Quarterly Journal of Economics	13.65	0.589
Econometrica	29.01	0.570
Review of Economic Studies	12.41	0.479
Journal of Political Economy	24.42	0.396
Journal of Public Economics	5.98	0.391
Journal of Economic Theory	8.01	0.390
Economic Journal	7.66	0.275
Economica	4.28	0.256
International Economic Review	5.17	0.212
Rand Journal of Economics	11.78	0.210
Journal of International Economics	8.01	0.208
Journal of Economic Literature	32.22	0.149

Source: Beckmann and Persson (1998b).

The Dewey Decimal classification, now rarely used, has suffered from its poor prediction of knowledge expansion in different fields, resulting in some very large decimal terms or signatures in subjects undergoing rapid growth. Division into ten classes at every stage is also more troublesome than simple bisection.

While bisection into equally large parts (measured by subjects rather than stocks of books) has the appeal of simple logic, its application results in lengthy labels, that is numbers composed of the digits 0 and 1, which are rather vulnerable to error.

A subject i, of size s_i, is identified through n_i equi-partitions:

$$2^{-n_i} = s_i.$$

The information content of a binary classification system is:

$$-\sum_i s_i \log_2 s_i = -\sum_i n_i e^{-ni}.$$

The depth of a library's holdings of x_i books in subject i:

$$-\sum_i x_i n_i = -\sum x_i \log_2 s_i$$

may be defined through the subdivisions that generate *i*. A library containing only books on broad (general) subjects is then revealed to have little specificity or 'depth'.

NOTE

1 An earlier version of this section, 'Citation analysis continued: the most cited journals in economics', was published as 'The thirteen most cited journals in economics' (Beckmann and Persson, 1998b).

APPENDIX 2.1: MATHEMATICAL NOTE

$$\lambda v_i = \sum_j c_{ij} v_j$$

$$\lambda v_k = \sum_j c_{kj} v_j$$

$$\lambda(v_i - v_k) = \sum_j (c_{ij} - c_{kj}) v_j > 0$$

since $c_{ij} \geq c_{kj}$ and with strict inequality for some j, and $v_j > 0$ for all j.

APPENDIX 2.2: EXAMPLES OF KNOWLEDGE CLASSIFICATION SYSTEMS

1. Dewey Decimal System

0 General
1 Philosophy
2 Theology
3 Sociology
4 Philology
5 Natural science
6 Useful arts
7 Fine arts
8 Literature
9 History
310 Statistics
320 Political science
330 Economics
340 Law
350 Public administration
360 Social pathology and services
370 Education
380 Commerce and communication
390 Customs and folklore
410 English
420 German
430 French
440 Italian
450 Spanish
460 Latin

470 Classical Greek
490 Other
510 Mathematics
520 Astronomy
530 Physics
540 Chemistry
550 Earth science
560 Paleontology
570 Life sciences
580 Botany
590 Zoology
1971: 18 980 entries

Category 5 had the most rapid growth

2. Cutter

A General works
B Philosophy
C Christianity and Judaism
D Ecclesiastical history
E Biography
F History
G Geography and travel
H Social sciences
J Civics, government, political science
K Legislation
L Sciences and arts together
M Natural history
N Botany
O Zoology
P Anthropology and ethnology
Q Medicine
R Useful arts, technology
S Constructive arts (engineering and building)
T Manufacturers and handicrafts
U Art of war
V Recreation, sports, games
W Art
X Philology
Y English and American literature
Z Book arts

3. Library of Congress

A	General works, polygraphy
AE	General encyclopaedias
AG	Dictionaries
B	Philosophy, psychology, religion
BC	Logic
BD	Speculative philosophy
95-101	Metaphysics
143-236	Epistemology
240-1	Methodology
BF	Psychology
BH	Aesthetics
BJ	Ethics
BL	Religion, mythology, rationalism
BM	Judaism
BP	Islam, Baha'ism, Theosophy
BR	Christianity
C	Auxiliary sciences of history
CC	Archaeology
CJ	Numismatics
CT	Biography
D	History, general and Old World
DA	Great Britain
DB	Austria, Czechoslovakia, Hungary
DC	France
E-F	History, America
E 184-	United States, general
F 1-975	United States, local history
2511	Brazil
G	Geography, anthropology, recreation
GA	Mathematical geography
GB	Physical geography
GC	Oceanography
GN	Anthropology
GV	Recreation
561-1197	Sports
H	Social sciences
HA	Statistics
HB	Economics
HC	Economic history and conditions, natural production
HD	Land, agriculture, industry

4801-8942	Labour
HE	Transport and communication
HF	Commerce
HG	Finance
1501-3542	Banking
HJ	Public finance
HM	Sociology
HN	Social history
HQ	The family, marriage, women
HV	Social pathology, social and public welfare, criminology
HX	Socialism, communism, anarchism
J	Political science, official documents
JC	Political theory, theory of the state
JK	United States
JN	Europe
JS	Local governments
JV	Colonies, emigration, immigration
JX	International law, international relations
K	Law
L	Education
M	Music and books on music
N	Fine arts, visual arts
NA	Architecture
NB	Sculpture
NC	Drawing, design, illustration
ND	Painting
NE	Print media
P	Language and literature
PA	Classical
PB	Modern European
PC	Romance
PD	Germanic
Q	Science
QA	Mathematics
8-10	Mathematical logic
76	Computer science
QB	Astronomy
QC	Physics
QD	Chemistry
QE	Geology
QH	Natural history
301-559	General biology, including life, genetics, evolution

573-671	Cytology
QK	Botany
QL	Zoology
QM	Human anatomy
QP	Physiology
QR	Microbiology
R	Medicine
RA	Public aspects
RB	Pathology
RD	Surgery
S	Agriculture
SB	Plant culture, forestry
SF	Animal culture
T	Technology
TA	Engineering, general, civil engineering, general
TC	Hydraulic engineering
TT	Handicrafts
TX	Home economics
U	Military science
V	Naval science
Z	Bibliography and library sciences

3 Production of Knowledge

In paradise, knowledge came as fruit, whose plucking proved to be expensive. Since then chance discoveries by sheer luck have occurred. But as Pasteur said; 'chance favours the prepared mind'. New knowledge must be produced by patient and intelligent work and it is a product of labour (and other resources) – just as goods and services are.

Knowledge rarely progresses in big leaps or by scientific revolutions (cf. Kuhn, 1970). Instead it tends to occur in a piecemeal fashion, by addressing (smaller or larger) bits of problems. Much of this work is organized as projects. Although it may seem degrading to some scholars, research – the generation or discovery of new knowledge – is treated as an economic activity here. Even without a profit motive, as in basic research, scientific research is a goal-directed activity in which rational decision-makers engage. These decisions include at least the following: what problem(s) to choose, whether to seek financial support; what assistants and other resources to acquire; how to proceed from stage to stage; whether and when to terminate a project; and finally how and where to publish and what to do next.

We must also study research as a production process using inputs such as scientific effort (labour), the existing stock of knowledge, and tools such as computers and laboratory equipment – for the production of new knowledge as an output. To bring research into the field of economic theory, we must discover appropriate production functions (see section 'Production functions' below).

What happens in a certain scientific field is not just the story of individual researchers experiencing successes or failures. It is also a question of the dynamics of scientific specialties. As such, it involves the movements of scientists into and out of a specialty and the mining and possible exhaustion of its subject matter (Chapter 8).

The pursuit of science was not always an economic activity carried out by professionals as an occupation to earn a living. Just a few centuries ago, it was instead an avocation of private scholars – amateurs who sought knowledge purely for its own sake. The scale and pace of today's knowledge industry goes beyond such private pleasures.

This does not mean that today's scholars are in the game purely for the money. As we shall see, prestige-seeking is an important motivating force, with monetary gain being an unavoidable indirect objective.

RESEARCH PROJECTS: PROBLEM SELECTION

As a first problem in the economics of research we consider research project selection. Since basic research, by definition, does not envisage applications or specific uses, its benefits are elusive, and any cost–benefit analysis would be fuzzy. Thus researchers feel comfortable following their own preferences, often guided by their knowledge from past experience. Still, in asking for support from a foundation such as the National Science Foundation (NSF), indicators of 'scientific worth' – and sometimes of 'social value' – are usually called for. By contrast, selection of applied research projects should be guided by profit expectations. This forces the researcher to estimate probabilities of costs and outcomes, while the economic evaluation (that is, estimation of potential revenues) should be the province of management using market research. We will consider one type of risk assessment that is relevant to both basic and applied research.

Scientists as free agents will follow their interests based on their experience, which corresponds to their acquired knowledge. Not only from career considerations, but also for reasons of self-esteem, it can be vital to do problems that promise early success. Selection may then be a matter of strategy. Since research is a risky activity, the following issue may confront a research director or anyone approaching a critical career stage: for optimal results, should one focus all one's efforts on a single project or should one diversify?

DIVERSIFICATION VERSUS CONCENTRATION[1]

Capital budgeting (Kaufman, 1986) is perhaps the best known example of allocating a scarce resource among competing risky projects. A similar problem situation arises with regard to the use of human resources in a research organization. Clearly, the outcome of any research undertaking is risky, sometimes to the point that even probabilities of success are hard to estimate. But decisions must be made. As we show, they should depend on the horizon and will thus be different when aiming for short-run success as against long-run expected results.

Consider a number of research projects whose probability of success as a function of effort x are of the form $\phi(x) = 1 - \exp(-x/a)$. This is modelled on search theory (Stone, 1975). The discovery of a solution is treated as a process of 'random search'. Only with infinite effort ($x \rightarrow \infty$) will a solution be found for sure. Here, a is the expected time to discovery – a measure of a problem's difficulty. Now let there be $i = 1,...,N$ projects of scientific worth (b_i) and search effectiveness (a_j). How should the available research capacity (c) be allocated among the projects? There are two common objectives:

1. To maximize the chance of at least one success
2. To maximize the expected value of results.

The first objective, or 'safety first', takes a short-term view, while the second is more appropriate in the long run. One might expect the more risky situation described by 'safety first' to call for a diversification of effort.

At Least One Success

The probability of all projects failing is:

$$\prod_i e^{-\frac{x_i}{a_i}} = e^{-\sum_i \frac{x_i}{a_i}}$$

so that the probability of at least one success equals:

$$1-e^{-\sum_i \frac{x_i}{a_i}}. \qquad (3.1)$$

To maximize this subject to a 'budget constraint' regarding effort is equivalent to:

$$\max_{x_i>0} \sum_{i=1}^{N} \frac{x_i}{a_i} \qquad (3.1a)$$

$$\text{subject to} \sum_i x_i \leq c. \qquad (3.2)$$

By the Neyman–Pearson lemma, the solution is:

$$x_i = \begin{Bmatrix} c \\ 0 \end{Bmatrix} \text{for } i\text{:} \quad a_i \begin{Bmatrix} = \\ > \end{Bmatrix} \min{}_j a_j \qquad (3.3)$$

that is, 'all or nothing'. Contrary to naïve intuition, all effort should be concentrated on one project, the most promising in view of 'research effectiveness' ($1/a_i$) which becomes the only relevant criterion, since the safety-first principle ignores scientific worth (b_i).

The Long View

In the long view, the Bernoulli principle of maximizing expected utility is appropriate (Luce and Raiffa, 1957). Interpreting 'scientific worth b_i' as utility, this implies:

$$\max \sum_{i=1}^{N} b_i \left[1 - e^{-(x_i/a_i)}\right] \tag{3.4}$$

$$\text{subject to } \sum_i x_i \leq c. \tag{3.2}$$

Maximizing the Lagrange function:

$$\sum_{i=1}^{N} b_i \left[1 - e^{-(x_i/a_i)}\right] + \lambda \left[c - \sum_{i=1}^{N} x_i\right]$$

yields

$$x_i \begin{Bmatrix} = \\ \geq \end{Bmatrix} 0 \Leftrightarrow \frac{b_i e^{-(x_i/a_i)}}{a_i} \begin{Bmatrix} < \\ = \end{Bmatrix} \lambda. \tag{3.5}$$

The solution is:

$$x_i = a_i \left[\log\left(\frac{b_i}{a_i} \Big/ \lambda\right)\right]_+ \tag{3.5a}$$

and

$$x_i = 0 \text{ whenever } \frac{b_i}{a_i} < \lambda. \tag{3.5b}$$

Solution (3.5a), rewritten as:

$$\frac{x_i}{a_i} = \log\left(\frac{b_i}{a_i} \Big/ \lambda\right) \tag{3.5c}$$

clearly states that the effort x_i on project i in relation to the project's difficulty a_i should equal the logarithm of the cost–benefit ratio b_i/a_i divided by the marginal cost–benefit ratio λ – a reasonable result.

The 'efficiency price λ' is here revealed as a 'marginal cost–benefit ratio'

(Andersson, 1997). To calculate λ, assume first that all projects i are activated: $x_i > 0\ \forall i$, which happens when the ratios b_i/a_i are not too disparate. Then:

$$c = \sum_{j=1}^{N} x_j = \sum_{j=1}^{N} a_j \left(\log\frac{b_j}{a_j} - \log\lambda \right)$$

yields

$$\log\lambda = \frac{\sum_{j=1}^{N} a_j \log\frac{b_j}{a_j}}{\sum_{j=1}^{N} a_j} - \frac{c}{\sum_{j=1}^{N} a_j}$$

so that

$$x_i = \frac{a_i}{a}c + a_i\left(\log\frac{b_i}{a_i} - \overline{\log\frac{b}{a}} \right) \tag{3.6}$$

where

$$a = \sum_j a_j \quad \text{and} \quad \overline{\log\frac{b}{a}} = \frac{\sum_j a_j \log\frac{b_j}{a_j}}{\sum_j a_j} \tag{3.7}$$

is a weighted average of the parameters $\log(b_j/a_j)$, which in combination with a_j represents weights to be attached to projects j. When some $x_j = 0$, the sums in (3.6) and (3.7) should be extended over only those j for which $x_j > 0$.

Thus, while for short-term results concentration of effort is better, the long-run strategy should be diversification of effort to equalize returns at the margin.

An example

As an example, consider $N = 2$ with $b_1 = b_2 = 1$, $a_1 = 1$, $a_2 = 0.5$, $c = 1$. Then:

$$\overline{\log\frac{b}{a}} = \frac{1}{2}\ln 2$$

$$\log\lambda = \frac{1}{3}\ln 2 - \frac{2}{3} = -0.436$$

$$x_1 = -\ln\lambda = 0.436$$

$$x_2 = 1 - x_1 = 0.564$$

where the more promising project number two receives the larger but not the entire available effort. In fact, both projects are undertaken in the long run, as long as the a_i and b_i do not differ by more than a factor h, where:

$$h = \frac{a_1 b_2}{a_2 b_1}. \tag{3.8}$$

Are the Results Robust?

The choice of an exponential return function $e^{-\lambda x}$, while rather plausible, is specific. How robust are the conclusions?

Suppose we assume (in conformity with the general theory of production) that returns are initially increasing and later decreasing, as shown in the conventional diagram (Figure 3.1). That is to say:

$$f(x) \text{ is convex for } x \leq m$$

$$f(x) \text{ is concave for } x \geq m$$

Let m be the turning point of project i, and suppose the time horizon limits total input:

$$\sum_i x_i \leq c < \sum_i m_i.$$

In this case we cannot enter the concave regime of diminishing returns with all projects and thus satisfy the second-order conditions under equalization of returns at the margin, which is the conventional solution to an allocation problem. Instead we must maximize in the convex domain. Consider just two projects $i = 1,2$ and let $f_i(x_i)$ be convex. To allocate an available labour force, c, for maximal results means

$$\max_x f_1(x_1) + f_2(x_2)$$

$$\text{subject to } x_1 + x_2 \leq c.$$

A convex function achieves its maximum on the boundary of the admissible set; that is, for either:

$$\left.\begin{matrix} x_1 = c,\ x_2 = 0 \\ x_2 = c,\ x_1 = 0 \end{matrix}\right\} \text{ when } f_1(c) \begin{Bmatrix} \geq \\ \leq \end{Bmatrix} f_2(c).$$

The earlier conclusions about concentration of effort are thus still valid for the allocation of a resource when the returns are of the increasing/decreasing type. The previous distinction between short and long run arises here from the difference between sufficient and insufficient availability of the resource to enter the domain of diminishing returns with all (active) projects.

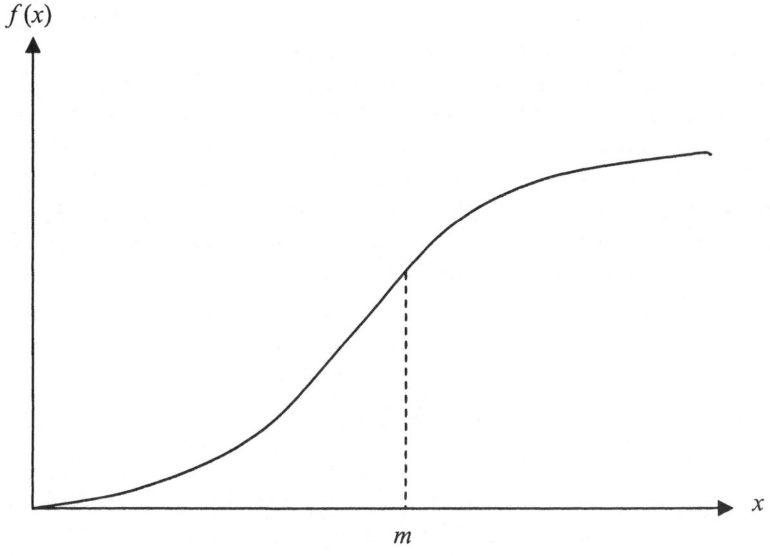

Figure 3.1 Production function for a single input

STAGES

Research projects tend to move through stages, sometimes in predetermined order such as $i = 0,1,\ldots,N$. More generally these stages are nodes in a directed graph or network, through which a path must be found to completion in stage N.

A well-known useful tool in the management of projects, including research projects, is Critical Path Analysis (CPA) or PERT, which lists the steps to be taken in their proper order and estimates the remaining time needed after each step (these techniques need not be described here). A more interesting situation is when choices are open for reaching the next stage, giving rise to intermediate research decisions. To illustrate, let v_i be the expected value of the final outcome of the research project, conditional on one's having reached stage i. Let S_i be the set of stages j that can be aimed for next. The decision process can then be formalized as a dynamic programme:

$$v_N = u \qquad v_i = \max_{j \in S_i} - c_{ij} + P_{ij} v_j \tag{3.9}$$

where u is the final payoff, c_{ij} is the expected cost (or time) of moving from i to j, and P_{ij} is the probability of a successful transition. For instance, when $u = 1$ if reaching N is an answer, then v_j is the intermediate and conditional probability of success, with $c_{ij} = 0$ (i.e. cost or delay is no object).

A special skill of an experienced researcher is to be able to select ways of moving on that avoid dead ends and head more or less straight to the target N. When the next stage is uncertain but depends on the selected strategy k, so that P_{ij}^k is the probability of a successful move to j, then the optimal choice, k, maximizes the expected probability of successfully reaching N. This best strategy is given by Equation (3.10), since costs c_{ij} are here ignored, and corresponds to Richard Bellman's well-known 'principle of optimality' (Bellman, 1957):

$$\begin{aligned} v_N &= 1 \\ v_i &= \max_k \sum_j P_{ij}^k v_j . \end{aligned} \tag{3.10}$$

In commercial applied research, with final outcomes in a set N having values u_n and transitions ij, the value of being in state i is determined by:

$$v_n = u_n \tag{3.11}$$

for terminal states $n \in N$ and:

$$v_i = \max_j P_{ij} \left(v_j - c_{ij} \right). \tag{3.12}$$

The project should then be terminated whenever $v_i < 0$.

Stages: An Example

Table 3.1 and Figure 3.2 show typical steps in economic research.

Table 3.1 Research stages

Stage	Description
0	Give up
1	Vague idea
2	Quick literature search
3	No reference
4	Problem has been discussed
5	Problem is solved
6	Decision to go ahead
7	References collected
8	Grant application written and submitted
9	Grant approved
10	Grant rejected
11	Application rewritten
12	Work started
13	Mathematical model set up
14	Theoretical approach chosen
15	Empirical approach chosen
16	Data search completed
17	No data found
18	Some data obtained
19	Model estimated/tested
20	Results not significant
21	Results significant
22	Model revised
23	Mathematical analysis of model
24	Failed
25	Some results
26	Results written up as paper
27	Paper submitted to journal
28	Rejected
29	Accepted for revision
30	Paper rewritten
31	Accepted
32	Paper published

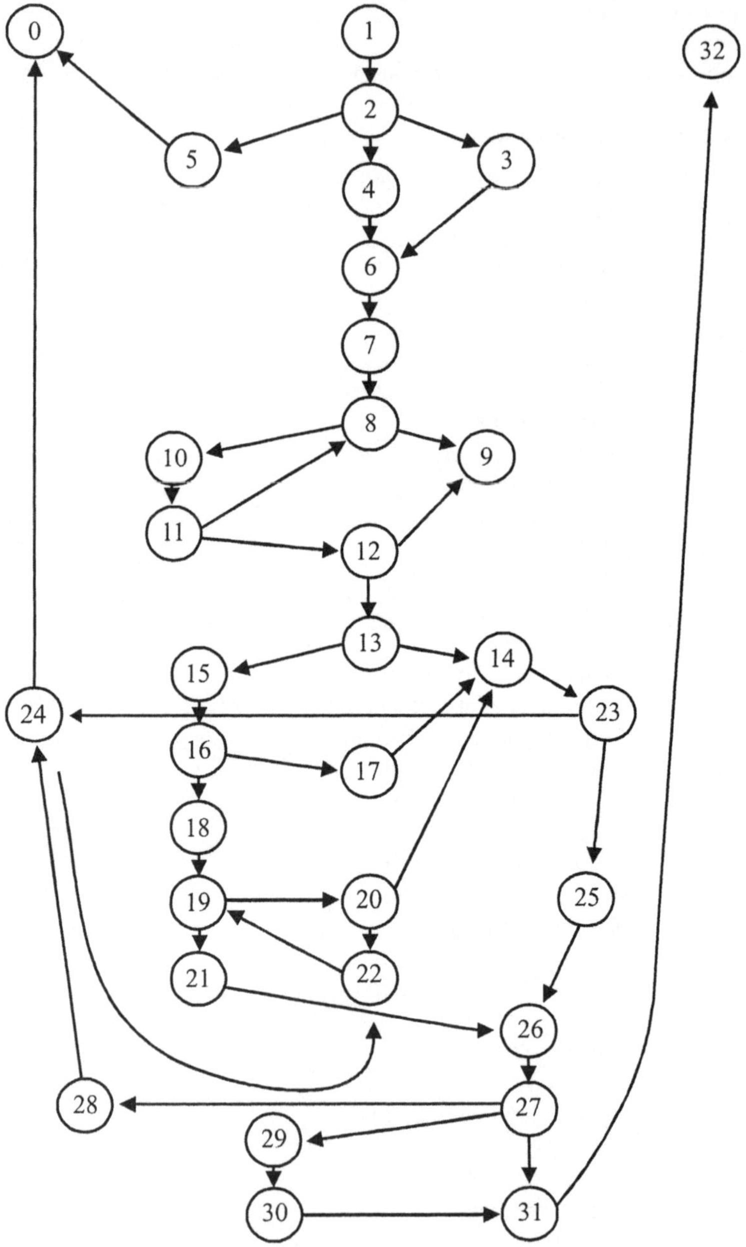

Figure 3.2 Graph of producing a scientific paper

TERMINATION: THE ONE-ARMED BANDIT[2]

Not all research is successful and the probability of failure may at times even be foreseen. Decisions are therefore needed on when to terminate a research project. Although this is painful and will cost prestige it may be better than to incur further opportunity costs:

$$v_i = \max\left(0, \max_{j \in S_i} - c_{ij} + v_j\right) \qquad v_N = u$$

a modification of Equation (3.12).

The first alternative, termination, is optimal when it is due to the expected cost, c_{ij}, and the probabilities, P_{ij}, of progression to further stages in the second alternative: continuation yields negative results.

A famous stopping rule problem is the one-armed bandit in which, for example, a new type of medical treatment is tried out in analogy to a coin or slot machine experiment of locating a slot machine with positive expected payoff: let a tossed coin show head with unknown probability P; whose prior density distribution is assumed to be uniform over the unit interval. The expected value of P, given m trials and k heads so far, is then easily calculated, using Bayes's rule:

$$E(P) = \frac{k+1}{m+2}.$$

A gambler may bet one dollar for each toss of this coin. Assuming utility to be proportional to money (as one would in playing a slot machine) and letting the future be discounted by $\rho < 1$, we raise two questions:

1. Should one start this game?
2. When should one stop?

A Bayesian gambler should never quit while he is ahead. Let $v_n(k,m)$ be the expected winnings when k heads have come up in m trials and n gambles are still contemplated:

$$v_n(k,m) = \qquad (3.13)$$

$$\left[\frac{2k-m}{m+2} + \rho\frac{k+1}{m+2} v_{n-1}(k+1, m+1) + \frac{m-k+1}{m+2}\rho v_{n-1}(k, m+1)\right]_+$$

$$v_0(k,m) = 0.$$

Now:

$$v_1(k,m) = \frac{2k-m}{m+2}$$

is the expected payoff of a single play. Observe that $2k - m$ is the fortune won so far.

Theorem: If $2k > m$, then $v_n(k,m) > 0$ for all n, which implies that the optimal strategy is to continue playing as long as the net gain is positive.

Proof (induction):

$$v_n(k,m) =$$

$$\underset{>0}{\frac{2k-m}{m+2}} + \underset{>0}{\frac{k+1}{m+2}\rho v_{n-1}(k+1,m+1)} + \underset{\geq 0}{\frac{m-k+1}{m+2}\rho v_{n-1}(k,m+1)} > 0.$$

Should the game be started? Yes. Consider:

$$v_1(0,0) = \max\left(\frac{0}{2},0\right) = 0 \quad v_1(0,1) = 0 \quad v_1(1,1) = \frac{1}{3}$$

$$v_2(0,0) = \rho\left[\frac{1}{2}v_1,(1,1) + \frac{1}{2}v_1(0,1)\right] = \frac{\rho}{6} > 0$$

Theorem: $v_n(k,m)$ is non-decreasing in n.

Proof (induction):

$v_1(k,m) \geq 0 = v_0(k,m)$. Suppose $v_n(k,m) \geq v_{n-1}(k,m)$. Consider

$$v_{n+1}(k,m)$$

$$= \left[\frac{2k-m}{m+2} + \rho\frac{k+1}{m+2}v_n(k+1,m+1) + \rho\frac{m-k+1}{m+2}v_n(k,m+1)\right]_+$$

$$\geq \left[\frac{2k-m}{m+2} + \rho\frac{k+1}{m+2}v_{n-1}(k+1,m+1) + \rho\frac{m-k+1}{m+2}v_{n-1}(k,m+1)\right]_+$$

$$= v_n(k,m)$$

Therefore, for $n \geq 2$:

$$v_n(0,0) \geq v_2(0,0) = \frac{\rho}{6} > 0.$$

Thus the game is always worth starting. It can be shown that the game should be stopped after a loss of:

$$\frac{1}{4}\frac{\rho^2}{(1-\rho)^2}$$

or more. In particular, when $\rho \leq 2/3$ one should 'stay with the winner', that is, one should continue only as long as one's accumulated earnings are positive.

From the consideration of research projects we now turn to the more formal aspects of knowledge production.

PRODUCTION FUNCTIONS

Knowledge Production from Labour: Writing

Scholars possess knowledge (they are in fact embodiments of knowledge). If they want to utilize this to their economic advantage, they can do so by teaching or by research or by doing both. If they are individuals of independent means, they may be content to do neither and play the role of pundits or amateur scientists. In the following we use the designation scientist for those individuals of learning (scholars) who are (also) engaged in the creation of new knowledge through research. Scientists are thus researchers.

We shall view research from an economic perspective as production. Production converts inputs into something else, called an output. In scientific research the inputs are scientific effort as labour and existing knowledge as capital. The output is new (i.e. additional) knowledge. There may be other inputs such as the use of laboratory equipment or computers, but these may be treated as complements of labour. In order to get a general understanding of the functional relationships, such complements are ignored. There are various ways or modes by which knowledge is produced, and the production functions vary accordingly.

Writing may be seen as transforming knowledge from its embodiment in (the mind of) a person into a document such as an article, monograph or book. As it adds to the published stock of knowledge it is one form of knowledge production, often the last stage in a research project. Writers may set for themselves a daily quota of a certain number of manuscript pages. This gives rise to an output, Q, which is proportional to the time devoted to writing, t, or more precisely

$$Q = Q(t) = \min\left[qt, K_0\right]$$

where q is the number of pages completed per unit of time, or productivity. Here, K_0 is the intended size of the document (book).

Equating time input with labour input, $t = L$ (see Figure 3.3):

$$Q = Q(L) = \min\left[qL, K_0\right]. \tag{3.14}$$

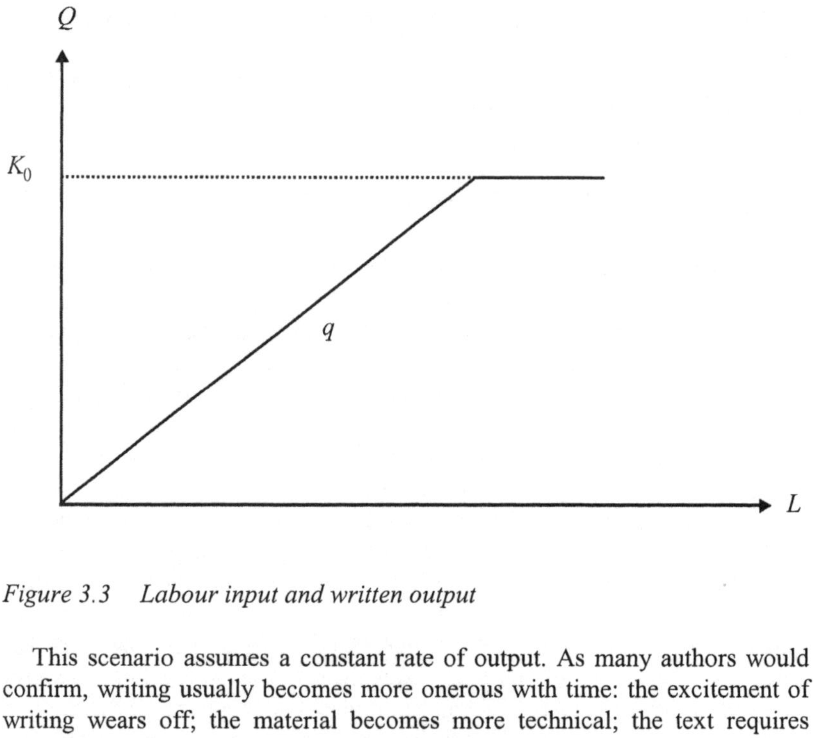

Figure 3.3 Labour input and written output

This scenario assumes a constant rate of output. As many authors would confirm, writing usually becomes more onerous with time: the excitement of writing wears off; the material becomes more technical; the text requires checking and (cross-) referencing. As an example, let:

$$q = \frac{1}{1 + at}$$

then:

$$dQ = \frac{dt}{1 + at}$$

integrating:

$$Q(t) = \frac{1}{a}\ln(1 + at) \tag{3.15}$$

$$Q(L) = b\ln(1 + aL) \qquad b = \frac{1}{a}$$

a production function with decreasing returns (see Figure 3.4).

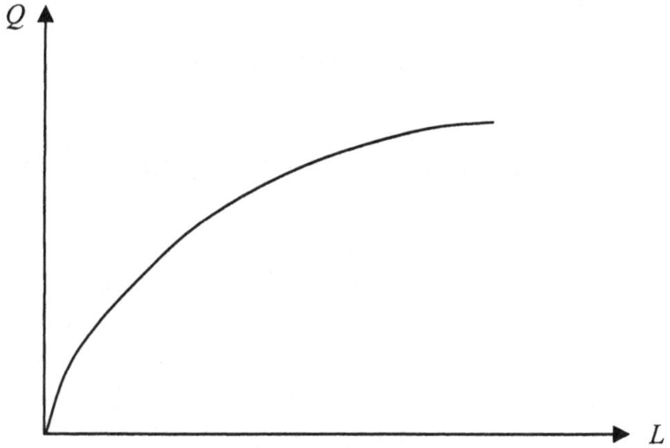

Figure 3.4 Written output

Alternatively, assume that writing must be preceded by a fixed amount R_1 of reading relevant literature. Then the output is:

$$Q = f\left(L - R_1\right) \tag{3.16}$$

where we have measured the relevant literature, R_1, as 'reading time'. The simplest function, *f*, is once again piece-wise linear:

$$\max\left[0, \min q\left(t - R_1\right), K_0\right]. \tag{3.17}$$

When smoothed, this function becomes a classical production function with initially increasing and then decreasing returns – a so-called 'sigmoid curve'.

In Equation (3.17) and Figure 3.5, the speed of writing is at first zero, then constant (= q), then zero again. In a smoother scenario, a writer's speed rises at first to be slowed down later. A simple formula would be:

$$q(t) = at - t^2$$

yielding an output:

$$Q(L) = \frac{a}{2}L^2 - \frac{1}{3}L^3 \tag{3.18}$$

which is also known as a Frisch production function (Frisch, 1962) (Figure 3.6). When the writer's revenue is proportional to the number of pages written, gQ, she should stop when:

$$g = \frac{dQ}{dt} = \frac{dQ}{dL} = aL - L^2$$

At this point the price – that is, the marginal revenue – equals the marginal product.

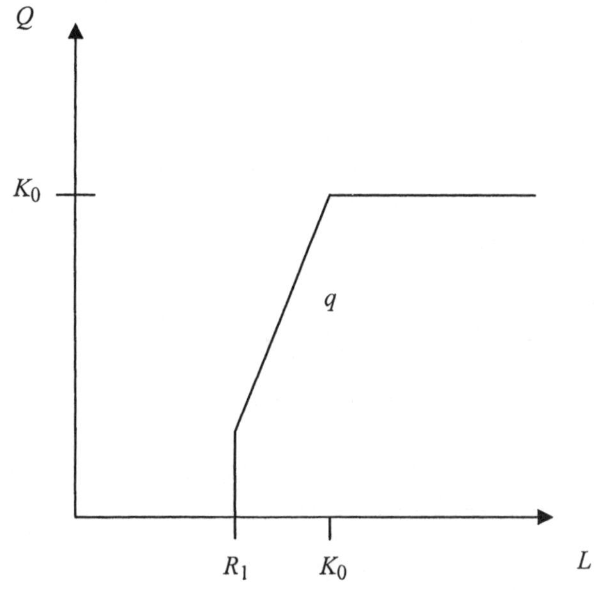

Figure 3.5 Output from reading and writing

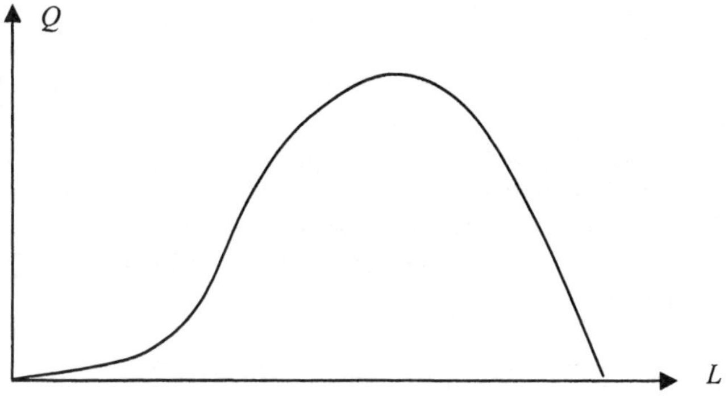

Figure 3.6 Frisch production function (Source: Puu, 2003)

Search

The quest for the solution to a given problem is a type of search. In systematic search at rate q of an area A (of potential solutions), the probability of discovery with an input L is:

$$P(L) = \frac{qL}{A} \qquad (3.19)$$

implying a proportional production function. When searching an unlimited area in which potential answers are equally distributed, a random search may be appropriate. Here, random means that the probability of a result during a small time interval, Δt, is $\lambda \Delta t$, where we at first assume λ to be constant. Search theory, an important subject in early operations research, addresses the questions of whether to start and when to stop.

Let v be the net value of the search, that is the value u of the solution minus the expected search cost. Let the opportunity cost (or money cost) per unit of time to the researcher be c, and let t be the time already spent on search. The decision to continue or stop means:

$$v(t) = \max\left[0, -c\Delta t + \lambda \Delta t \cdot u + (1 - \lambda \Delta t) v(t + \Delta t)\right]. \qquad (3.20)$$

Stopping yields $v = 0$ whereas continuing costs $c\Delta t$ and yields a chance $\lambda \Delta t$ of the prize u or the opportunity to continue with $v(t + \Delta t)$. Stopping is best when:

$$-c + \lambda u = 0 \qquad (3.21)$$

observing that

$$v(t+\Delta t)=0. \tag{3.22}$$

Equation (3.21) means that expected revenue equals marginal cost for the next time interval (Δt). Notice that when λ is a constant, the right-hand side is independent of t, implying that $v(t)$ equals v. The constancy of v means that a search should either never be started or never be stopped. In fact, continuing search means that:

$$v=-c\Delta t+\lambda\Delta t\cdot u+(1-\lambda\Delta t)v$$

$$v=u-\frac{c}{\lambda} \tag{3.23}$$

independent of time.

The value of the search – at any time – equals the certainty of prize (u) minus the cost c over the expected (continuing) time of search; $1/\lambda$. With continuing random search what is the probability of discovering $P(t)$ by time t? Let $Q = 1 - P$ be the probability of no discovery yet:

$$Q\,(0)=1$$

$$Q(t+\Delta t)=Q(t)\cdot[1-\lambda(t)\Delta t]$$

$$\frac{\Delta Q}{Q}=-\lambda\Delta t$$

$$\ln Q=-\int_0^t\lambda(x)\;dx$$

$$P(t)=1-Q(t)=1-e^{-\int_0^t\lambda(x)dx}.$$

With search time $t = L$ (labour), the production function is:

$$P(L)=1-e^{-\int_0^L\lambda(x)dx}$$

and with a constant discovery rate λ it is:

$$P(L)=1-e^{-\lambda L}. \tag{3.24}$$

That a search should either never be started or never be stopped is also true when the chance of discovery $\lambda(t)$ increases with the time t already spent. This happens, for example, in systematic search when the unexplored area shrinks over time, which means that the chance of discovery is an increasing function of time.

When the chance of discovery $\lambda(t)$ decreases because the researchers become tired or the object has a tendency to disappear, then Equation (3.21) dictates the best time to stop. If missed, then at later times the inequality:

$$\lambda(t)u < c$$

signals that the search should cease.

The mathematician Richard Bellman stopped researching any problem that would not yield an answer in one day 'since there are so many other interesting problems to pursue'. Among the mathematicians of his time he was arguably the most productive in terms of significant publications.

Pioneering Research

In a new field with little or no literature, knowledge inputs accumulate with ongoing research efforts. Such research generates initially increasing and then decreasing returns, which is characteristic of single-input production activities in general.

Consider therefore the unfolding stock of knowledge $K = K(t)$ in a single-person research project. The individual researcher does not start at the 'zero level' but rather with some initial $K(0)$, say K_0. As the project develops, K should grow at a rate that is at first constant but eventually decelerates by the approach of a knowledge limit, $K = A$, for that particular problem:

$$\dot{K} = \gamma K(A - K).$$

This can also be read as follows: progress results from the impact of prior knowledge on potential new knowledge, $A - K$. The coefficient γ can be made to equal unity by a suitable choice of time units, while the level A can be made to equal unity by the choice of units for measuring knowledge. Thus:

$$\dot{K} = K(1 - K) \tag{3.25}$$

the well-known equation for logistic growth, so that:

$$K(t) = \frac{1}{1 + ae^{-t}} \tag{3.26}$$

where:

$$a = \frac{1-K_0}{K_0} = \frac{1}{K_0} - 1 \qquad (3.27)$$

which is a decreasing function of the level of prior knowledge K_0.

As before, let t stand for the amount of labour (research effort) expended. The production function:

$$Q(L) = \frac{1}{1+ae^{-L}} \qquad (3.28)$$

exhibits increasing returns followed by decreasing returns after a turning point, at

$$L_1 = \ln a.$$

The range of increasing returns is thus an increasing function of $a = (1/K_0) - 1$, in other words, the smaller the initial level (K_0) of knowledge, the larger the increasing returns. Observe that the maximum attainable knowledge for the project is now scaled at $K = 1$. If the potential knowledge is A, the result is changed to:

$$K(L) = \frac{A}{1+ae^{-t}}.$$

When a reaction speed γ is reintroduced one obtains:

$$K(L) = \frac{A}{1+ae^{-\gamma L}}$$

while a is determined by K_0 – as before – in Equation (3.27) (Figure 3.7).

Two-factor Production Functions

So far time (i.e. labour) has been the only variable factor in knowledge production. When studying knowledge production at different times – or under conditions when available knowledge as input is also variable – it becomes necessary to include the stock of knowledge explicitly as a factor input into knowledge production. Compared to conventional production of goods and services, this means that knowledge plays the role of capital. Just as it is difficult to measure capital inputs, so it is with knowledge inputs. The best one can do is using proxy variables such as the literature on a subject for the existing knowledge of the subject. In choosing a production function we follow the general economic theory of production.

In Equation (3.17), the literature (the stock of knowledge) appears as an obstacle to writing, since output is assumed to be merely quantitative, with no consideration of quality. However, the stock of knowledge should in fact be considered a factor of production, with labour (L) and knowledge (K) being treated as factors of production which are to some extent substitutable (but also complementary). In the microeconomic theory of production, the CES function (Arrow et al., 1961) has proved to be a convenient and flexible choice.

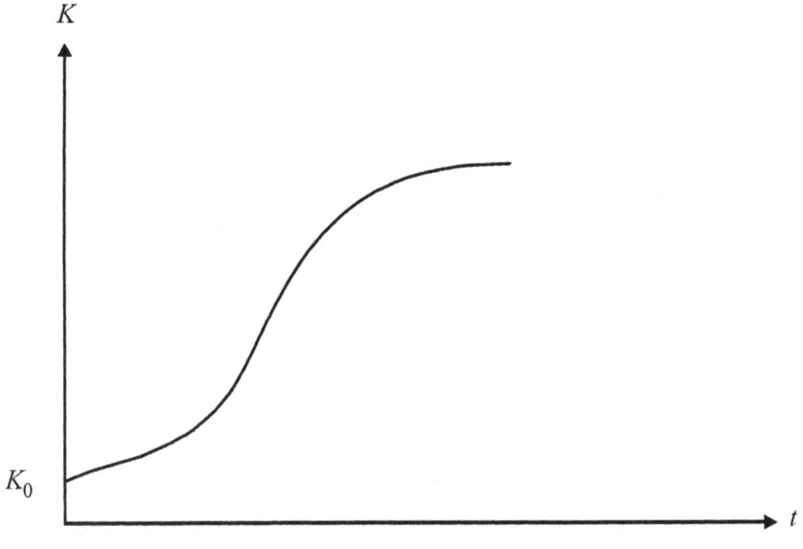

Figure 3.7 Logistic production of knowledge in pioneering research (Source: Puu, 2003)

Deviating from its original formulation, we use the more convenient notation:

$$f(x,y) = \left(\alpha x^{\rho} + \beta y^{\rho}\right)^{\frac{1}{\rho}} \tag{3.29}$$

$$\alpha, \beta > 0 \quad \rho \le 1.$$

Beckmann and Künzi (1984, pp. 56–65) provide an exhaustive discussion of its various properties. The function is concave when:

$$0 < \rho \le 1. \tag{3.30}$$

When $\rho > 0$, a single input, $x > 0$ or $y > 0$, will also yield a positive output, $\alpha^{(1/\rho)}x$ or $\beta^{(1/\rho)}y$ respectively. When $\rho < 0$, then both inputs are indispensable. In the context of knowledge economics, $\rho > 0$ is the normal case, which means that it is possible for new knowledge to be produced by labour without explicit introduction of a second input from a given stock of knowledge *K*, and one author can be productive without a co-author. As extreme cases, we should note:

$$\rho = -\infty \qquad f(x,y) = \text{Min}(x,y),$$

the Leontief fixed coefficient production function:

$$\text{when } \rho = 0 \quad f(x,y) = x^{\alpha} y^{\beta}, \tag{3.31}$$

the Cobb–Douglas production function first mentioned by Wicksell (1898), characterized by constant factor elasticities (α, β).

The CES function is linear and homogenous, implying constant returns to scale, except in the Cobb–Douglas case when:

$$\alpha + \beta \begin{Bmatrix} < \\ = \\ > \end{Bmatrix} 1, \quad \text{implies} \begin{Bmatrix} \text{decreasing} \\ \text{constant} \\ \text{increasing} \end{Bmatrix} \text{ returns to scale.}$$

We may use and estimate production functions for knowledge production that involve inputs in other combinations, such as labour and research funds. Production functions may also be applied to teaching, with inputs from both teachers and students.

Mathematically, (3.29) represents a 'generalized mean' (Hardy et al., [1934] 1967). It is characterized by an inequality:

$$\left(\alpha x^{\rho} + \beta y^{\rho}\right)^{\frac{1}{\rho}} \le \left(\alpha^{\frac{1}{1-\rho}} + \beta^{\frac{1}{1-\rho}}\right)(x+y). \tag{3.32}$$

It is sometimes convenient to focus on the specification $\rho = 1/2$, which is simple and captures the essential relations:

$$\left(\alpha\sqrt{x} + \beta\sqrt{y}\right)^2 = \alpha^2 x + 2\alpha\beta\sqrt{xy} + \beta^2 y. \tag{3.33}$$

Generalizations to all $0 < \rho \leq 1$ are usually straightforward, so that this specification is robust.

Consider, for $y = 1$:

$$\left(\alpha x^{\rho} + \beta\right)^{\frac{1}{\rho}} = \beta^{\frac{1}{\rho}}\left(1 + \frac{\alpha}{\beta}x^{\rho}\right)^{\frac{1}{\rho}}$$

and let $\rho = (1/2) + \varepsilon$. It can be shown that:

$$\left(1 + \frac{\alpha}{\beta}x^{\frac{1}{2}+\varepsilon}\right)^{\frac{1}{\frac{1}{2}+\varepsilon}}$$

$$= 1 + 2\frac{\alpha}{\beta}\sqrt{x} + \left(\frac{\alpha}{\beta}\right)^{2} x + M\varepsilon$$

differing from $\left[1 + (\alpha/\beta)\sqrt{x}\right]^{2}$ only by terms proportional to ε, thereby proving robustness.

Consider (3.32) with $\rho = 1/2$:

$$\left[\alpha\sqrt{x} + \beta\sqrt{y}\right]^{2} \leq \left(\alpha^{2} + \beta^{2}\right)\left(x + y\right) \tag{3.32a}$$

with equality when $\dfrac{x}{y} = \dfrac{\alpha^{2}}{\beta^{2}}$.

Proof:

$$\alpha^{2}x + 2\alpha\beta\sqrt{xy} + \beta^{2}y - \alpha^{2}x - \beta^{2}y - \alpha^{2}y - \beta^{2}x$$

$$= -\left(\beta\sqrt{x} - \alpha\sqrt{y}\right)^{2} \leq 0$$

with equality when $\beta\sqrt{x} = \alpha\sqrt{y}$ or $\sqrt{\dfrac{x}{y}} = \dfrac{\alpha}{\beta}$ □

As an implication of Equation (3.32a), we should mention in passing that if two partners work in combination $x/y = \alpha^{2}/\beta^{2}$, the combined output $(\alpha^{2} + \beta^{2})(x + y)$ of the two partners exceeds single outputs (standardized at unity $= x + y$), provided that:

$$\alpha^{2} + \beta^{2} > 1.$$

Table 3.2 Summary of modes of production

Types of production	Labour input, L	Capital input	Output	Function	Where
Writing	Writing time	K embodied in author	Q Pages written	$\min[L, K_0]$	(3.14)
				$\frac{1}{a}\ln(1+at)$	(3.15)
				$\frac{a}{2}L^2 - \frac{1}{3}L^3$	(3.18)
Research in established field	Time for reading literature and own research	Literature K_1	Papers	$f(L - R_1)$	(3.16)
Research as systematic search	Search time	Area A to be searched	Probability P of discovery	$q\frac{L}{A}$	(3.19)
Random search	Search time	Chance λ	Discovery	$1 - e^{-\lambda L}$	(3.24)

Table 3.2 Cont.

Types of production	Labour input, L	Capital input	Output	Function	Where
Pioneering research	Research time	Generated	Seminal publication	$\frac{1}{1+ae^{-t}}$	(3.26)
Individual research	Own research x	Reading literature y	Papers published	$x^{\alpha} y^{\beta}$	(3.31)
Publications in field	Number of active authors N	Stock of literature R	Current rate of publications	$bN^{\alpha} R^{\beta}$	(3.31)*
Co-authorship	Contributed efforts x and y	Embodied, not considered explicitly	Joint publications	$\left(\alpha x^{\rho} + \beta y^{\rho}\right)^{\frac{1}{\rho}}$	(3.29)
Academic performance	Teaching x and research y	Not considered explicitly	Scientific contribution	$\left(\alpha\sqrt{x} + \beta\sqrt{y}\right)^{2}$	(3.33)

Note: * The current rate of publications is assumed to be determined by the input of research labour time (N) and the funds allocated to research (R).

For purposes of maximization, it is useful that the linear homogenous Cobb–Douglas and CES functions:

$$f = x^{\alpha} y^{\beta} \quad \alpha + \beta = 1 \text{ and}$$

$$f = \left(\alpha\sqrt{x} + \beta\sqrt{y}\right)^2$$

are concave.

Table 3.2 summarizes the modes of knowledge production and their production functions, as reviewed in this chapter.

Input or Cost Functions for Multiple Outputs

The reverse of a production function – describing an output from several inputs – is an input function describing the input of a single resource that is required for combinations of various outputs. An example is the labour that is needed for the joint production of teaching and research. The function that corresponds to a concave CES production function

$$\left(\alpha x^{\rho} + \beta y^{\rho}\right)^{\frac{1}{\rho}} \quad \rho \leq 1 \tag{3.34}$$

is a convex input function with exponents reversed,

$$\left(\alpha x^{\frac{1}{\rho}} + \beta y^{\frac{1}{\rho}}\right)^{\rho} \quad \rho \leq 1. \tag{3.35}$$

Thus when $\rho = 1/2$, the labour (L) required for teaching (T) and research (R) is an input function:

$$L = \sqrt{T^2 + R^2} \tag{3.36}$$

and is the opposite of the production function:

$$Q = \left(\sqrt{x} + \sqrt{y}\right)^2 \tag{3.37}$$

$$= x + 2\sqrt{xy} + y.$$

For one unit of teaching ($T = 1$) and one unit of research ($R = 1$) to be performed separately by two professors, the total input is two labour units. A single professor would need just:

$$\sqrt{1^2 + 1^2} = \sqrt{2}$$

labour units for the same output, signifying a synergy in teaching and research. When multiplied by a given wage rate, the labour input function becomes a conventional cost function.

NOTES

1. 'Diversification versus concentration' was previously published in somewhat different form as Beckmann (2000).
2. An earlier treatment of 'the one-armed bandit' problem is given in Beckmann (1974).

4 Scientific Interaction and Organization of Knowledge Production

KNOWLEDGE NETWORKS

Although ideas may be conceived in isolation, knowledge production and distribution are social activities, as will be elaborated in this chapter. This social framework of science has been the subject of interest in recent sociology (Merton, 1968, 1969; Crane, 1972). In economic discourse the term 'knowledge networks' has emerged.

Scientific Interaction

Knowledge networks describe the set of knowledge producers and users (in a given knowledge field) and the communication links joining them. Three types of connection are easily recognized: the weakest one is citation, giving rise to a directed graph (directed from the citer to the cited). A strong one is collaboration resulting in joint publication, an undirected graph.

A third connection is that between teacher and disciple which in advanced graduate education also may involve collaboration and joint publication. In addition there is much informal exchange and communication among scholars and researchers in personal or in organized meetings and through correspondence. But this is not readily observed by outsiders. The term 'invisible colleges' (de Solla Price, 1961, pp. 62–91; Crane, 1972) has been proposed for groups whose links are particularly intense, though of limited duration (see next section).

In a well integrated field, the citation graph is connected (direction ignored). Every member is linked directly or indirectly to every other member.

The citation graph may however show three kinds of degeneracy:

1. Independent subsets of authors citing only members of the subset – forming a club of 'mutual admiration society'.
2. A subset of outsiders, not being cited by the insiders.
3. The combination of both resulting in non-overlapping subsets – a

division of the field into non-communicating subsets of sometimes hostile 'schools'.

Citation in written works and collaboration are slow processes. The spread of new knowledge through networks of personal acquaintances and through organizational channels as described later is a fast process. The disclosure of new basic knowledge is propelled by the need to assure priority. It is aided by channels of publication specifically designed to announce new results, such as *Physical Reviews* and *Physical Review Letters*. In some cases even the news media have been used.

By contrast, new applied knowledge, held as private property, is not freely disclosed or communicated. Allowing information on genes to be patented is said to have seriously hampered scientific progress in the Genome project of mapping the full set of human genes.

Knowledge networks of all types (citation, oral or written exchange, collaboration, teaching) may be usefully compared to transportation networks as shown in Table 4.1.

Table 4.1 Networks

	Transportation	Knowledge
Nodes	Origins/destinations	Scientists, scholars
Links	Roads	Meetings, fax, mail
Input	Trip demand	Scientific problems
Output	Trips made	Scientific progress
Dimension	Utility	Scientific worth
Proxies	Time, money	Papers published, citations
Observables	Traffic flows	Research activity, scientists on the move
Constraints	Flow equations	Time and money budgets
Objectives	Min. travel time/cost	Paper production
Medium	Vehicles	Ideas
Material aids	Signals, signs	Libraries, labs, computers
Routes	Long	Short
Variables	x_{ij}^{k}, z_{ij} Travellers	x_{ij} Interactions

One way of describing the nature and operations of existing knowledge networks is to trace the history of a scientific idea from its conception to its final enshrinement in handbooks or textbooks. This example is taken from economic theory.

Ideas are rarely born in discussion or discourse (although they may spring up while teaching). They are usually found in solitary study or thinking. But, as we all know, many of these flashes of 'insight' do not stand up or pan out. They must therefore be exposed at once to critical examination, preferably by knowledgeable and interested colleagues. Here is where serious discussion with one's fellow scientists in the next office or over the coffee table comes in. Politeness would be a disservice, unrestrained criticism is in order. To provide this opportunity is one good reason for having departments in a university. That they are also needed for teaching (knowledge distribution) will be considered below.

Sometimes the test of an idea is by a mathematical model, and the mathematics may be faulty; sometimes it is data that are needed, and always a check of the literature is needed. But discussion is at the core of it all, informal but relentless. If the first talks with colleagues prove encouraging, then the next step is to announce and prepare a presentation at an informal staff meeting. In the best organized research institutes and university departments, these are well attended (and hence, not overwhelmingly frequent) and are conducted in the spirit of 'anything goes'. The speaker is a target for uninhibited shooting, no heed being given to the niceties of academic rank and protocol.

Prior to the first staff meeting it is customary to draft and distribute an informal but reasoned short paper known as a discussion paper 'not for attribution or citation' although nowadays its purpose is often just that: in order to establish priority even before publication. In practice, discussion papers are rarely read before the staff meeting and help the speaker more than the audience.

If speaker and idea survive this 'free for all', the discussion paper may receive the department head's or research director's blessing and be released for presentation at one of the next professional conferences or specialists' workshops. Here a wider audience of outside experts can take a shot at it, sometimes in the role of official discussants. Assuming that speaker and paper survive once more, the contribution can then be submitted for publication in the conference proceedings or, for additional exposure, as an article in a professional journal. Once more the paper is screened by referees and an editor and may have to be rewritten.

Of the flood of papers published (even after one or several rejections a journal is usually found that will take it eventually), only a very small number are widely read or cited, let alone recognized as 'seminal' or even 'pioneering'. The ultimate triumph of an idea is to be embodied in the handbook and textbook literature, and not just as a reference or footnote, but as an actual part of the main text. Of course, as texts are revised, the idea may be dropped again; nobody can hope for permanence in a rapidly developing field. It is best to have been an early writer in a field.

Knowledge distribution does not aim at discovery but at disseminating existing knowledge to such interested parties as scientists, students, industrial users, and (sometimes) the curious public.

How adequate is the selection process of lectures and papers at national or international conventions or smaller workshops? The composition of the organizing committee means an orientation toward particular topics, often those currently in fashion. Departure from the main line of current research is not readily rewarded. This applies with even greater force to the editorial policies of scientific journals. One way out of this taken by the more enterprising of rejected authors, is to found a new journal. This has resulted in a spectacular increase in the number of scientific periodicals, since publishers have been willing accomplices in these enterprises. The proliferation of journals imposes a cost on the community, first in money to libraries and individual subscribers, but also in time. Who can read all this? 'Of the making of books there is no end' has been a universal complaint since the Middle Ages.

Book publication specifically is a business decision. When the expected audience is small, subsidies are expected, either drawn outright from research grants, or indirectly when university presses charge less than full cost and depend on the university's resources for covering their deficit. The expectation of subsidies removes an important incentive from writers, to treat their subject in sufficient breadth to make the book instructive and to write clearly and well enough or even with wit to sustain readers' interest.

Price policy makes a difference, too. Risk-averse publishers typically aim only at library sales at prices set high enough to recover cost from their limited sales, rather than looking for sales to researchers, students and even an interested public by setting an attractively low price. The book-buying habits of professors have been spoiled by publishers' presentation of free 'examination copies' or 'desk copies' for textbooks and potential 'recommended readings' for classes.

In sum, while there may be too much production of preliminary papers (urged on by prestige seeking and competitive pressure on young scholars) there probably is too little production of finished products for wider circulation.

Invisible Colleges

A type of knowledge network of particular intensity has been noted and described by de Solla Price (1963, p. 38) as 'Invisible Colleges'. It became a subspecialty in sociology after the seminal studies by Diane Crane (1972) (cf. also Chapter 8 'Expansion of knowledge and macroeconomic growth'):

> Probably during World War II pressure of circumstances forced us to form such knots of men and keep them locked away in interacting seclusion. We gave them a foretaste of urgent collaboration in nuclear physics and again in radar. These groups are still with us in the few hundred people who meet in the 'Rochester Conference' for fundamental particles studies, and in the similar number who congregate by imitation to discuss various aspects of solid state physics. ... Such activity is by no means confined to the two groups mentioned. Similar unofficial organizations exist in molecular biology, in computer theory, in radio astronomy, and doubtless in all sciences with tens of thousands of participants. ... they are inevitable, and not just a product of the war or the special character of each discipline. Conferences are just a symptom; it becomes insufficient to meet as a body every year, and there is need for a more continuous means of close contact with the group of a hundred.
>
> And so these groups device mechanisms for day-to-day communication. ... an elaborate apparatus for sending out not merely reprints of publications but preprints and pre-preprints of work in progress and results about to be achieved. In addition to the mailing of preprints, ways and means are being found for physical juxtaposition of the members. They seem to have mastered the art of attracting invitations from centers where they can work along with several members of the group for a short time. ... For each group there exists a sort of commuting circuit of institutions, research centers and summer schools giving them an opportunity to meet piecemeal so that over an interval of a few years everybody who is anybody has worked with everybody else in the same category (de Solla Price, 1963, pp. 84–85).

> … they confer prestige, and, above all, they effectively solve a communication crisis by reducing a large group to a small select one of the maximum size that can be handled by interpersonal relationships. … high-grade scientific commuting has become an important channel of communication… (de Solla Price, 1963, p. 85).

LOCATING THE NETWORKS OF INTERACTING AUTHORS[1]

One of the major challenges of bibliometrics and information science is to find the endogenous structure of science, by decomposing it into a set of research fields. Several attempts using citation analysis have been made during the years (Kessler, 1963; de Solla Price, 1965; Mullins, 1968; Crane, 1972; Small and Griffith, 1974; White and Griffith, 1981). A shortcoming of the methods used so far has been that they tend to rely on only one of three techniques – direct citations, co-citations or bibliographic coupling. In this section we propose a formalized approach combining all three of them.

In common with other production activities, science practices a division of labour. This means that at any one time, a scientist does active research in one particular field, mostly a specialty of his discipline. The grand system of scientific disciplines is common knowledge, but the subdivision of any discipline into scientific specialties is typically known only to experts in that discipline, since specialties tend to be subject to change. In fact the discovery of new specialties is itself part of scientific progress. As a challenge to bibliometrics there arises thus the following questions: how can scientific specialties be recognized without recourse to expert opinion (which might be biased), and how can the set of scientists active and interacting in such a specialty be determined?

Once a specialty and one practising scientist in it are known, our problem reduces to the second question and is considerably simplified: namely finding all scientists interacting in a given field and hence finding the scientists interacting directly and indirectly with the known scientist. It is this simpler question that we address in this section. The situation to be studied is not untypical: A field is often closely linked to a key person, who may (even) have started research in that area or else have acquired clear visibility in this field.

With focus on scientific interaction we should recall the types of scientific interaction that have been recognized in the sociology of science. Thus Crane (1972, note 4) distinguishes:

- Teacher–student relationship
- Being influenced in the choice of research topics
- Citation
- Collaboration resulting in jointly authored publications.

These interactions are not mutually exclusive but possibly overlapping and in any case correlated. It is this fact which opens up the possibility of discovery of scientific interaction among researchers constituting a given field through an analysis of citations.

'Invisible colleges' are usually defined as held together by informal interactions (de Solla Price, 1963). We do assume, in fact, that informal contacts are preceded by or followed with more formal interactions expressed in citations.

Model: Sets Defining a Field

We propose to cast a wide net in discovering all possible indications of interaction and then to cut the field down through more restrictive requirements as demanded by practical considerations.

In defining the various sets that make up a network of authors in a scientific field we hope to render somewhat more precise the terminology in the sociological literature. It is not clear for instance, whether 'circles' properly include all the members of a scientific specialty or whether the converse is meant. An 'invisible college' presumably refers to the core of the scientists constituting a specialty, but where is the periphery? Our approach would suggest that the peripheral members are most likely to be found in C_1, B_1 and A_1 while the core is concentrated in S_1 and S_2 (to be defined below).

A natural starting point is to list first all documents citing the (or a) key author's most authoritative document in the field. These documents constitute our first set:

$$S_1 = \{j | d_{1j} > 0\}. \tag{4.1}$$

Here d_{ij} is the frequency with which document i is cited by document j, that is:

$$d_{ij} = \begin{cases} 0 \\ 1 \end{cases}$$

according as i is cited by j or not.

We shall later convert this to frequencies c_{ij} with which author i is cited by author j, and here $c_{ij} = 0,1,\ldots,n$ can be zero or any integer. If in the citation of multi-authored documents, each citation is divided by the number of authors of the cited document, the c_{ij} may be fractional as well.

Next we must consider indirect interaction with key document 1 through citation of an intermediary i:

$$S_2 = \{j | d_{ji} d_{ij} > 0 \text{ for some } i\}. \tag{4.2}$$

Alternatively:

$$S_2 = \{j | d_{ij} > 0 \text{ for some } i \in S_1\}. \tag{4.2a}$$

In principle, n-stage interaction could be defined recursively:

$$S_n = \{j | d_{ij} > 0 \text{ for some } i \in S_{n-1}\}. \tag{4.2b}$$

But indirect interaction falls off rapidly after one intermediary so that the sets $S_3,\ldots,S_n$ can be ignored.

Moving backward again we must consider those documents, not necessarily by key authors, that have also influenced members of the set $S_1 \cup S_2$.

$$C_1 = \{i | d_{ij} > 0 \text{ for some } j \in S_1 \cup S_2\}. \tag{4.3}$$

In turn we must consider those other scientists (or rather their documents) who were influenced by the documents in C_1 (bibliographic coupling):

$$B_1 = \{j | d_{ij} > 0 \text{ for some } i \in C_1\}. \tag{4.4}$$

Finally we must move backward to discover those authors who through their documents have influenced the original key author and colleagues in C_1:

$$A_1 = \{j | d_{ij} > 0 \text{ for some } j \in \{1\} \cup C_1\}. \tag{4.5}$$

The grand set of documents G defining the field is then:

$$G = \{1\} \cup S_1 \cup S_2 \cup C_1 \cup B_1 \cup A_1. \tag{4.6}$$

While the description of a field in terms of citations among documents is interesting in itself, our principal objective is to discover the author set F constituting a scientific field and the matrix of citations $C = (c_{ij})$ linking them. There is thus a final step of assigning authors to documents and collating them. Joint authorship will serve to enlarge these sets, while production of more than a single document by any author will cause these sets to contract. To distinguish author sets from document sets we will use the hats (^) in their notation. After we translate documents into authors for each set the grand set of interacting scientists in this field is correspondingly:

$$F = \{1\} \cup \hat{S}_1 \cup \hat{S}_2 \cup \hat{C}_1 \cup \hat{B}_1 \cup \hat{A}_1.$$

Figure 4.1 shows how the various sets are generated. Arrows indicate the flow of citations from citer to cited. The direction of time is to the right since citation by its nature is a move backward in time.

The Citation Matrix

Since the construction of the sets is based on citation data d_{ij}, the end product is not only a set G of documents and a set F of authors representing a scientific field but a matrix of citations.

In the case of documents write:

$$D = (d_{ij}) \quad i,j \in G.$$

The Grand Field – F

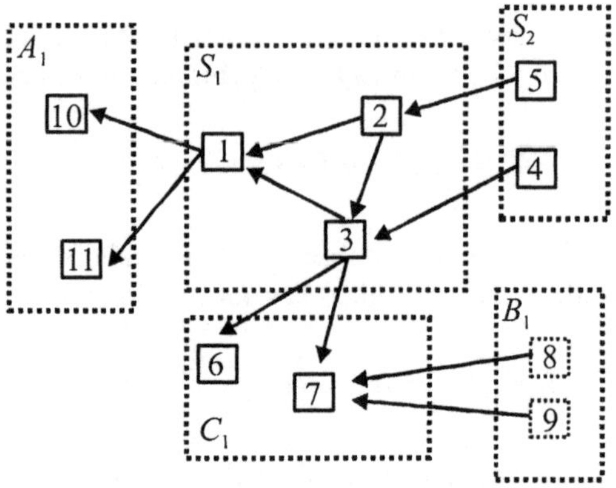

Note: 1 is the key-author, 2–3 are all citing 1; 4 and 5 are added since they are indirectedly connected to 1; 6 and 7 because they are co-cited with 1 by 3; 8 and 9 are included since they share a cited author with 3; 10 and 11 are added since they are cited by 1.

Figure 4.1 Illustrative flow of citations among a set of authors labelled 1,...11

In this matrix all components d_{ij} are either zero or one. If $d_{ij} = 1$ then $d_{ji} = 0$ for the cited document precedes the citing one. Also there would appear to be little point in mutual citation. (Occasionally one finds a reference to a paper listed as 'forthcoming', which amounts to citation forward in time, but this usually applies only to documents by the same author). For our purposes we must exclude self-citation by authors as well as by documents.

$$c_{ii} = 0 \text{ and } d_{ii} = 0$$

since documents never cite themselves. The diagonal of a citation matrix vanishes.

For all j in sets $\hat{S}_1, \hat{S}_2, \hat{B}_1$ there must exist an i with $d_{ij} = i$ so that their column vectors in the matrix cannot be zero. For all i in the sets $\hat{C}_1, \hat{A}_1$ there must exist a j with $d_{ij} > 0$ so that their row vectors in the D-matrix cannot be zero. In fact, for any k to be included in the set G, either the row or the column vector for k must be non-zero.

The row sums $\sum_j d_{ij}$ of the matrix give the frequency with which document i has been cited, an index of its impact. The columns sums $\sum_i d_{ij}$ gives the number of references (citations) contained in a document j, an index of scholarly zeal.

Consider also the total sum of entries in a document citation matrix D compared to the size of the matrix:

$$\frac{\sum_{i,j=1}^{n} d_{ij}}{n^2}.$$

This is an index of cohesiveness of the field.

In the author citation matrices $C = (c_{ij})$ the entries c_{ij} are all non-negative. Once more for any author k either the row or the column vector is non-zero meaning that the author is either cited or citing, as a requirement for being in the interacting set. An author's impact is shown by the number of citations $\sum_j c_{ij}$, and author j's learning is marked by the number of others citing $\sum_i c_{ij}$.

A matrix is said to be decomposable if (for authors, say) there exists subsets $M \subset F$ such that $c_{ij} = 0$ for all $i \notin M$, $j \in M$. The set M is then called an independent subset. It consists of authors who cite only others in this subset and ignore those outside the subset.

A row i in a citation matrix is said to dominate a row k if for all columns j:

$$d_{ij} \geq d_{kj}$$

and for at least one column $j = h$:

$$d_{ih} > d_{kh}.$$

Dominance establishes a partial ordering or ranking among documents or authors according to citations received, but such dominance relationships are rare.

A citation matrix (of documents or authors) may also be represented by a directed graph with arrows linking a citing document (or author) to the cited document (or author). This graph may consist of disconnected components each representing an independent subset (see Figure 4.2).

In the case of documents, citations should be acyclic. This means that their graphs should not contain any closed cycles; they must be (directed) trees. In the case of an author citation matrix such closed cycles, indicating a club or 'mutual citation society', cannot be ruled out. They can be discovered from positive elements in the diagonals of the power matrices C^n of an author citation matrix C. (Recall that the diagonal of C itself contains only zeros).

Application to the Field of 'Invisible Colleges'

Procedure in practice

It is perhaps appropriate that the first application of our model should be to a field defined itself as a study of science networks popularly known as 'invisible colleges'. Here a key author and a key document are clearly visible in the person of Diana Crane and her seminal publication *Invisible Colleges*, published in 1972. Over the years this book has been heavily cited; a search of the Social Science Citation Index™ database, retrieved no fewer than 400 articles citing it from 1972 to 1993. For our purpose it seems reasonable to restrict the time window to the first five years following the publication of *Invisible Colleges*.

In defining our data set the first step was to download all articles citing the book *Invisible Colleges*. We used the Social Science Citation Index™ for searching and downloading the citing articles used in this study. During the years 1972–76 there were 67 articles that cited *Invisible Colleges*. These citing articles constitute set S_1. Next we retrieved 60 articles citing the articles in S_1, forming the second set of citing articles S_2, S_3,...,S_n which would turn out smaller and smaller if only because tracking citations leads one out of the chosen time frame 1972–76.

The third set of citing articles would be set B_1, namely articles sharing references with the S_1 articles, but not directly citing S_1. However, we found that the B_1 set was extremely large with several thousand articles. The main reason for this is that the S_1 articles cite some documents that are heavily cited in the whole database. To reduce the B_1 articles set to a manageable size we need a minimum number of shared references as a required measure of association. This can be found by downloading all B_1 articles and then calculating the number of shared references with S_1. But that was considered too costly. Instead we decided to limit B_1 to articles citing the most frequently cited documents by S_1 and provided that these articles were published in the journal subject categories sociology or library and information science. The next step was to limit B_1 further by demanding at least two citations to documents in C_1. Finally we ended up with 28 articles in the B_1 set.

When all records were downloaded they had to be standardized in terms of author names and cited references.

The cited publications A_1 and C_1 were found via the reference lists of S_1. In order to work with sets of reasonable sizes, the C_1 was limited to documents being cited by at least three S_1 articles, and the A_1 set by at least five S_1 articles. Using these thresholds sets C_1 contains 32 and A_1 37 documents.

Sets and matrices found

We can now look closer to the matrix formed by the articles retrieved. Table 4.2 summarizes the citation matrix generated from $S_1 \cup S_2 \cup B_1 \cup C_1 \cup A_1$. It is a 225×225 matrix.

Table 4.2 The citation matrix of documents related to 'Invisible Colleges' 1972–76

	Citing articles						
Cited documents	S_1	S_2	B_1	C_1	A_1	Σ	N of rows
S_1	100	64	n.p.	n.p.	n.p.	164	68
S_2	6	11	4	n.a.	n.p.	21	60
B_1	1	4	6	n.a.	n.p.	11	28
C_1	153	27	73	n.a.	n.p.	253	32
A_1	317	18	55	n.a.	n.a.	390	37
Σ	577	124	138	0	0	839	225

Notes
S_1 = *Invisible Colleges* and all articles citing it 1972–76.
S_2 = all articles citing S_1 during 1972–76, but not *Invisible Colleges*.
B_1 = articles citing at least two of C_1 during 1972–76 and published in sociology journals or library and information science journals.
C_1 = documents published during 1972–76 and cited by at least three articles in S_1.
A_1 = documents published 1967–71 and cited by at least five articles in S_1.
n.p. means *not possible* for logical reasons.
n.a. means *not available* for practical reasons since most documents in C_1 and A_1 are too old to be in the database or books which are also not covered by the database.

The first step has been to apply some reasonable criteria for documents to be included in the field. Once these documents are found we can then list the authors belonging to the field, which is the aim set out at the beginning.

The documents in set S_1, S_2 and B_1 are all in the matrix because of their citation behaviour. Should all these be included in the field? What about documents that do not cite more than one document in the matrix? These are poorly related to the field: only citing Crane's book, only citing some of those who cited Crane's book, or only citing some of the documents co-cited with Crane's book. And what about the documents that did not get cited at all? Clearly, for whatever reason, such documents have not (yet) influenced the field and should not be included, at this stage. So the second criterion would be that the citing documents need also to be cited by at least another document in the field.

From the number of citations in each block of the matrix (Table 4.2) we can see that most of the citations tend to go to documents which are cited but not citing. Many of the C_1 documents were published in the same year as *Invisible Colleges* or shortly thereafter. This is probably the reason why they are not in the S_1 group. Therefore, it seems appropriate to select C_1 documents as relevant of the field, which are cited by at least three or more articles in S_1.

What about the documents, the A_1 set? Although these documents are not within the 1972–76 time window, several of them were published a few years before. Some of the authors of these documents appear as authors in the other sets. Others do not reappear as contemporary authors of the citing articles in our matrix, but should anyhow be included since they have published heavily cited documents a few years before 1972. Using a reasonable five-year time window backward, 1967–72, documents in A_1, not yet included in the previous sets, should be added to the field. These need also be cited by at least five of the S_1 articles.

Can we discover an 'invisible college' here? First of all this means that we have to turn from documents to authors. One straightforward way is just to list the first author of all documents qualified through the above criteria (Box 4.1). The authors are listed in author sets, on the basis of the document sets in which they first entered the matrix. We have also summed the number of times they are cited in the whole matrix.

In order to get a partial validation of this list we compared it to the authors listed in two reviews of the field made by Chubin (1976, 1985). One should not expect a perfect match with the subjectively composed lists in Chubin's review articles, based on 'clicks', but it is quite evident that the most cited authors are also in the reviews. We also checked for other documents listed by Chubin (1985, note 10) but not in our list. We found only three articles published during 1972–76 that could have been retrieved from the SSCI. Judging from the titles of these documents they all were of minor relevance to the field (Forman, 1974). So, it seems that our systematic approach not only retrieved most of the documents relevant for a review article but also identified a number of articles that ought to have been considered for reviewing.

The distributions of entrants by sets clearly shows the importance of indirect interactions, primarily via co-citations to contemporary papers, but also indirect citations and bibliographic coupling. The ancestors group is also very close in time and should be included, both for technical and substantial reasons.

Box 4.1 The invisible college as found by the model

Authors entered via document set S_1

Crane D (83), **Mullins NC** (45), **Hagstrom WO** (40), **Bendavid J** (30), **Mulkay M** (29), **Small H** (25), **Garfield E** (14), Lemaine G (10), **Law J** (9), Lin N (8), Peterson RA (7), Coser LA (5), **Gustin BH** (5), **Kadushin C** (5), Oromaner M (3), Dubiel H (2), Fox RC (2), Zaltman G (2), **Clark TN** (1), **Duncan SS** (1), **Edge DO** (1), Jones WT (1), Keller RT (1), Rose H (1), Tosi L (1)

Authors entered via document set S_2

Griffith BC (29), **Garvey WD** (14), **Allison PD** (13), Hirsch PM (8), Useem M (3), Cawkell AE (1), **Johnston R** (1), Line MB (1), Schroeder B (1), **Sullivan D** (1)

Authors entered via document set B_1

Blume SS (14), **Narin F** (9), Carpenter MP (5), **Mitroff II** (2), White HC (1)

Authors entered via document set C_1

Merton RK (53), **Cole JR** (37), **Zuckerman HA** (31), **Cole S** (27), **Barber B** (13), **Granovetter MS** (13), **Toulmin SE** (8), Barnes B (7), **Gaston JC** (7), **Krantz DL** (7), Blissett M (5), Heirich M (4), Langrish J (4), **Shils E** (4), **Fisher CS** (3), Ladd EC (3)

Authors entered via document set A_1

Price DD (58), Ziman JM (13), Ravetz JR (11), **Crawford S** (6), Greenberg DS (6)

Note: The authors appear as first authors of documents meeting the criteria discussed in the text. The number of citations in the grand matrix is given within brackets. Authors' names in bold indicate those who were listed with a pre-1977 publication in two review articles by Chubin (1976, 1985).

Turn now to the directed graph showing the interactions of the citing documents from S_1, S_2 and B_1 (Figure 4.2). All documents in the graph are connected to each other, via direct or indirect links. The major actors appear to be Mulkay, who has authored four, and Small three, of the citing papers and some of their papers are also frequently cited. Articles by Mullins,

Griffith and Law are also cited several times, but they do not appear as citers more than once. The more frequently cited papers may become key-papers for post-1976 research. The Small–74 paper is mostly cited by articles in the S_2 group, which means that it links to another subset of the grand field not directly linked to the Crane key paper, presumably bibliometric studies of scientific networks.

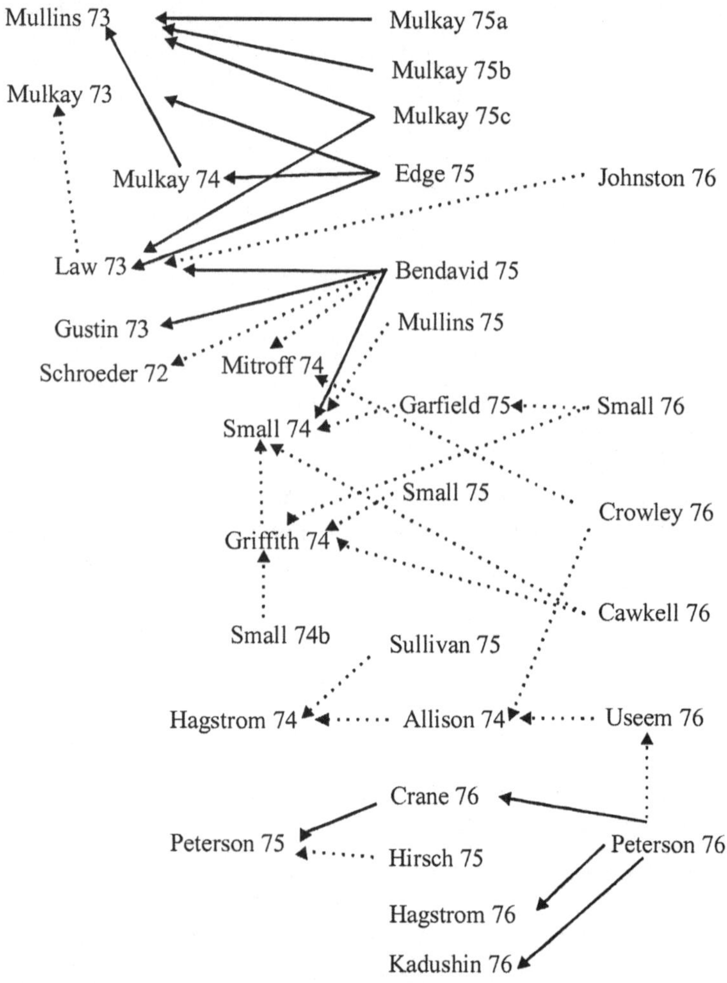

Figure 4.2 A graph showing direct citations between citing documents. Citations between documents in S_1 are indicated by lines and citations from S_2 or B_1 are indicated by dotted lines. Citations to Invisible Colleges excluded as well as self-citations.

The lower part of the graph is another indication of a split in the field. These articles, mostly written by American sociologists, are not citing articles in the upper part, obviously neglecting them. Judging from the titles these articles are rather on the sociology of culture than the sociology of science.

In Figure 4.3 we present an author citation matrix. The upper left quadrant shows an independent subset of the first twelve authors. The members of this subset cite only each other. This is a somewhat more restricted finding than that told in the graph of Figure 4.2. Within the independent subset there are also closed cycles (connecting different documents, however), for example Peterson–Crane–Peterson, Mulkay–Law–Mulkay, Small–Garfield–Small and Small–Griffith–Small. These authors may be considered to form the inner core of an invisible college.

Problems for Further Research

Can this approach be modified to discover fields or scientific specialities which are suspected to exist and for which no key author is known yet? Since a field has to be anchored somewhere, this may not be possible except by trial and error.

One line to pursue is to look for frequently cited documents and choose one of them as 'key document' on a trial basis. Alternatively one may look for a document containing a maximal number of citations, indicating that this is probably a review article, reviewing a scientific specialty. A key document may then be located among the documents cited as having a largest number of citations.

A related, but more difficult question is this: what are the consequences of starting with a document mistakenly thought to be a key document? Like all scientific documents, this document is in a special field and – if a key document exists at all – this like other documents in the field must be connected to a key document. The simplest case is that our mistaken key document cites the real key document. Then the mistaken document is in set S_1 and what was intended to be set S_1 turns out to be set S_2. More complicated shifts occur when the starting document mistaken for a key document falls into set C_2, B_1 or A_1. Clarifying these issues is another problem for the future.

One major problem in constructing a field from citations is that in an extended search too many documents may be unearthed. To guard against this flood of unwanted items, one should have a measure of the degree of connectedness of any document (or author) to a key document (or key author) and impose a threshold of minimum connectedness.

		1	2	3	4	5	6	7	8	9	10	11	12	13	14	15	16	17	18	19	20	21	22	23	24	25	26	Σ
Small	1		1	1						1													1	1				5
Mullins	2					4																						4
Griffith	3	3																						1				4
Law	4					1															1	1	1					4
Mulkay	5				1																2							3
Hagstrom	6							1	1																	1		3
Allison	7										1														1			2
Peterson	8											1															1	2
Garfield	9	1																										1
Useem	10								1																			1
Crane	11								1																			1
Kadushin	12								1																			1
Mitroff	13																						1		1			2
Schroeder	14																						1					1
Carpenter	15																		1									1
Oromaner	16																			1								1
Gustin	17																						1					1
Narin	18																											0
Line	19																											0
Edge	20																											0
Johnston	21																											0
Bendavid	22																											0
Cawkell	23																											0
Crowley	24																											0
Sullivan	25																											0
Hirsch	26																											0
	Σ	4	1	1	1	5	0	1	4	1	1	1	0	0	0	0	0	0	1	1	3	1	5	2	2	1	1	

Figure 4.3 Authors from S_1, S_2 and B_1 citing each other (based on Figure 4.2)

To construct such a measure one should first standardize the quantities of citations issued by the various citers. The simplest choice of a standard level is unity. The standardized citation frequencies for author j would then be defined as:

$$s_{ij} = c_{ij} \Big/ \sum_k c_{kj} \,. \tag{4.7}$$

But this should not apply to citations by documents in set S_1. For documents j in set S_1 we have by definition:

$$c_{1j} = 1$$

and we should also set their measure of connectedness equal to unity:

$$\mu_j = c_{1j} = 1 \qquad \forall_j \in S_1 \tag{4.8}$$

Consider S_2. For all $j \in S_2$ define the measure of connectedness as

$$\mu_j = \sum_{i \in S_1} s_{1j} s_{ij} \qquad j \in S_2 \tag{4.9}$$

$$= \sum_{i \in S_1} s_{ij} \tag{4.9a}$$

so that it is simply the sum of documents in S_1 cited.

Depending on the number of documents in S_1 that a document from S_2 is citing, the measure of connectedness of a document in S_2 may even exceed 1, although this is probably rare.

Now consider C_1. Here connectedness is established through co-citation. Thus, for any $j \in C_1$:

$$\mu_j = \sum_{i \in S_1} s_{1i} s_{ji} \tag{4.10}$$

$$= \sum_{i \in S_1} s_{ji} \,. \tag{4.10a}$$

This is just the sum of standardized citations by documents in set S_1.

Next for authors $j \in B_1$ the connection runs through both S_1 and C_1:

$$\mu_j = \sum_{j \in S_1} s_{1i} \sum_{k \in C_1} s_{ki} s_{kj} \tag{4.11}$$

$$= \sum_{i \in S_1} \sum_{k \in C_1} s_{ki} s_{kj} \,. \tag{4.11a}$$

The frequency of citation of a document k in set C_1 by a document j in B_1 is multiplied by the frequency of k being cited by a document i in S_1, and this is summed over all documents i in S_1 and all k in C_1. Since the s_{ki}, s_{kj} are fractions, the measure μ_j for documents in set B_1 will tend to have fractional values compared to C_1.

Finally consider A_1. By definition documents in A_1 are cited by 1 or S_1. In addition there may be citation relations also via C_1 as follows:

$$\mu_j = s_{j1} + \sum_{i \in S_1} s_{j1} \tag{4.12}$$

$$= c_{j1} + \sum_{i \in S_1} c_{ji}. \tag{4.12a}$$

It is the sum of the (non-standardized) citation frequencies for document j by key document 1 and by all documents i in set S_1. This measure will exceed unity if citation frequencies by documents S_1 are not standardized. In this exploratory approach no measures of connectedness were constructed and cut off is based on simple (not on multiplied standardized) citation frequencies for authors in sets C_1 and B_1.

Exploration and implementation of measures of connectedness constitutes another area for future research.

Finally, there are aspects of citation matrices that deserve further study. One example is their use for investigating impact of documents and prestige of authors beyond a mere count of the numbers of citations.

TWO-PERSON COLLABORATION

Interaction as considered so far has been through communication, manifest in citation. Whether cooperative or competitive, it stimulates productivity. The classical mode of scientific communication through the periodical literature can be enhanced through the circulation of preprints or discussion papers and through meetings in periodic conferences or workshops.

The most intensive type of scientific interaction is in collaboration for joint publication. This occurs by choice of free agents (who have met for instance at a convention) or as an organized effort in the setting of an organization. Although papers with multiple authors are not uncommon, particularly in the natural sciences, we will focus on two-author collaboration and consider research in larger groups later.

Collaboration for joint publication has been on the increase in science and in social science. This might be the result of increasing numbers of those

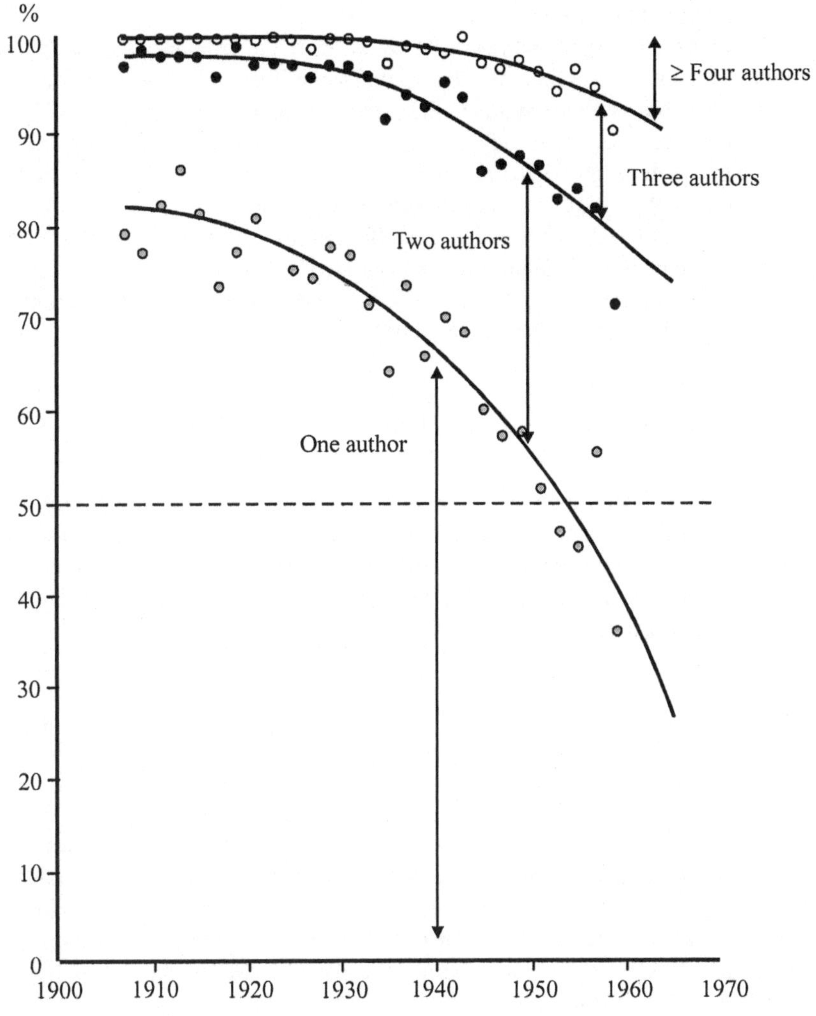

Figure 4.4 *Incidence of multiple authorship as a function of date (adapted from de Solla Price, 1963, p.88)*

active in research and of better communication among them. Successful collaborators tend to have different but complementary talents and harmonizing personalities.

In two-person collaboration it would be artificial to distinguish between communication time and working time, as we will in studying groups and teams. Work can take place in large part through an act of communication:

thinking out loud together.

Preliminary to organized research we consider the voluntary collaboration of two scientists, not necessarily in the same location. It may be interdisciplinary, but more often it is in the same specialty.

A first question is its advantage, what it depends on, and how it is perceived. Will credit be shared, and how? Can collaboration take place at a distance and still be rewarding? In any organization pair-wise collaboration may also be ordered. What is then the efficient allocation of partners to each other? Can pair-wise collaboration be expanded into teamwork?

The result of the contributions of efforts x and y by the two authors i, j may be described by a production function of CES type:

$$q = \left(\alpha x^{\rho} + \beta y^{\rho}\right)^{\frac{1}{\rho}} \qquad 0 \leq \rho \leq 1. \tag{4.13}$$

It is assumed that the partners may represent somewhat different abilities (competences) indicated by α and β. These productivity parameters represent qualitatively different types of embodied knowledge. The numerical values of α and β indicate the strength of these persons' abilities. This is revealed by the outputs achieved on their own:

$$q_1 = \alpha^{\frac{1}{\rho}} x \tag{4.14}$$
$$q_2 = \beta^{\frac{1}{\rho}} y$$

in their different specialties. Thus $\alpha > \beta$ need not mean superiority of talent, but productivity in different areas (which may differ in inherent difficulty). Assuming that doubling each contributor's input will double the output will make the CES function linear homogeneous, but each input by itself has diminishing returns for $0 < \rho < 1$.

In looking for a partner, an α person stands to gain more, the higher the productivity coefficient β of the β person, and vice versa. Collaboration is always more productive than isolated work even when contributed efforts are unequal in view of:

$$\left(\alpha x^{\rho}\right)^{\frac{1}{\rho}} + \beta\left(y^{\rho}\right)^{\frac{1}{\rho}} = \alpha^{\frac{1}{\rho}} x + \beta^{\frac{1}{\rho}} y < \left(\alpha x^{\rho} + \beta y^{\rho}\right)^{\frac{1}{\rho}} \tag{4.15}$$

provided the β partner is contributing some effort y. But how much will the two partners volunteer?

Presumably as much as to make his/her marginal product equal to opportunity cost $\alpha^{1/\rho}$ obtained by setting $y = 0$ in the production function, for solo activity (4.13). To simplify the mathematics let $\rho = 1/2$.
Compare once more joint output:

$$f(x,y) = \left(\alpha\sqrt{x} + \beta\sqrt{y}\right)^2 \tag{4.16}$$

with individual knowledge production:

$$= f(x,0) = \alpha^2 x \tag{4.17}$$

and:

$$= f(0,y) = \beta^2 y. \tag{4.18}$$

The return to the first party is:

$$g(x) = f(x,y) - f(x,0)$$
$$= 2\alpha\beta\sqrt{xy} + \beta^2 y.$$

A rational collaborator maximizing his/her return then maximizes within the limits of his/her capacity 1.

$$\max_{0 \le x \le 1} 2\alpha\beta\sqrt{xy} + \beta^2 y \tag{4.19}$$

achieved by the corner solution $x = 1$ provided $y > 0$ and yielding:

$$\alpha^2 + 2\alpha\beta\sqrt{y} + \beta^2 y. \tag{4.19a}$$

The same calculation applies to the other party, so that $y = 1$ and the total gain is:

$$g = 2\alpha\beta. \tag{4.19b}$$

Here it has been assumed that each party is credited with the full collaborative achievement.

If the credit must be split and is assigned in the fractions $a > 0$, $b > 0$ and not necessarily $a + b = 1$, the x contributor's net gain is:

$$\max_{0\le x\le 1} (a-1)\alpha^2 x + 2a\ \alpha\beta\sqrt{xy} + a\beta^2 y \qquad (4.20)$$

requiring:

$$0 = (a-1)\alpha^2 + a\alpha\beta\sqrt{\frac{y}{x}} \qquad \text{or}$$

$$\sqrt{\frac{x}{y}} = \frac{a}{1-a}\cdot\frac{\beta}{\alpha} \qquad (4.21)$$

and similarly:

$$\sqrt{\frac{y}{x}} = \frac{b}{1-b}\cdot\frac{\alpha}{\beta}. \qquad (4.22)$$

This is consistent only:

$$\frac{ab}{(1-a)(1-b)} = 1$$

or:

$$\frac{1-a}{a} = \frac{b}{1-b}.$$

The left side decreases with a and the right increases with b. The only solution is therefore when:

$$b = 1 - a \qquad (4.23)$$

implying shares must add up to unity. The resulting division of effort is:

$$\sqrt{\frac{x}{y}} = \frac{a}{b}\cdot\frac{\beta}{\alpha}. \qquad (4.24)$$

One's own contribution increases with one's share and decreases with one's productivity α.

When shares are equal, i.e. 1/2, then:

$$\frac{x}{y} = \left(\frac{\beta}{\alpha}\right)^2.$$

Knowing that one's own effort is matched in proportion (4.24) the return to partners x is:

$$(a-1)\alpha^2 x + 2a\alpha\beta\sqrt{\left(\frac{b}{a}\cdot\frac{\alpha}{\beta}\right)^2 x^2} + a\beta^2\left(\frac{b}{a}\cdot\frac{\alpha}{\beta}\right)^2 x$$

$$= \alpha^2 \frac{b}{a} x \qquad \text{using (4.20) and (4.23)}$$

which per unit effort is no more than for independent work when the credit share is $a = 1/2$, but the total effort required for the output, the paper, is shared.

SCIENTIFIC COLLABORATION AT A DISTANCE[2]

Consider two authors writing a paper. Let their contribution (effort) be x and y. We postulate a production function with two inputs, where only one is needed, $f(x,y)$. For a collaboration to be fruitful, one must have:

$$f(x,y) > f(x,0) + f(0,y) \tag{4.25}$$

or when working full time in this (for a while):

$$f(1,1) > f(1,0) + f(0,1),$$

denoting complementarity.

Let interaction at distance r take away time kr:

$$f[(1-kr)x, (1-kr)y] > f(x,y),$$

or with linear homogeneity and $x = y = 1$

$$[1-kr]f(1,1) > f(1,0) + f(0,1).$$

$$kr < \frac{f(1,1) - f(0,1) - f(1,0)}{f(1,1)} = u$$

where the right hand side is a measure of the advantage of collaboration.

Now let u be considered a random variable, normally distributed: many additive random elements are involved. The emerging probability of collaboration is then

$$P(\text{collab.}) = 1 - N(kr) \tag{4.26}$$

where N denotes the (standardized) normal distribution. Using the well-known approximation:

$$N_x \doteq \frac{1}{1+e^{-ax}} \tag{4.27}$$

$$P(\text{collab.}) = 1 - \frac{1}{1+e^{-ak}} = \frac{1}{1+e^{akr}} \doteq e^{-akr},$$

establishing an exponential distance effect (for longer distances), well known for other types of spatial interaction (Wilson, 1970).

LOCATIONAL ASPECTS OF KNOWLEDGE PRODUCTION

We may ask first: to what extent is scientific activity and its location governed by economic or rational principles at all, and to what extent is it set by seemingly arbitrary decisions of government and its agencies or by benevolent donors, for example foundations?

We shall take a Darwinistic position on that: universities and research centres may be founded by decree in various places; whether they flourish there is then a question in which economic principles will play at least some role.

It can be argued that historical accident still has a part to play: through sheer inertia traditions may linger. Great names like Bologna, Oxford, Cambridge, Leyden continue to fascinate and attract scholars; others in less accessible locations have faded from the European scene, like St. Andrews in Scotland and Trinity College, Dublin – and who has heard of Tromsø?

Research comes in many forms. The distinction between pure and applied research, however difficult to draw in some cases, is still fundamental. Here is the iron test: pure science produces nothing of market value, but rather a free public good. You cannot sell a theorem, and nobody will spend a nickel on any 'Golden Rule of Accumulation'. Applied research, if it lives up to its name, does produce a marketable result, even if only suitable for consulting. The locational implications are equally compelling: applied research should be market oriented, while basic research is essentially footloose. Ever since the Middle Ages have scholars been on the road, true to their footloose propensities.

Now applied research can be organized in two ways: as in-house production or for clients by independent research organizations. The economic advantage of in-house production is that its product is best tailored to the need of the customer. Also, it offers better protection against disclosure to competitors. In-house research is thus ideal for the attainment of a well-specified end. By utilizing consultants, the in-house facility can draw on wider professional experience and thus make up in part for the disadvantage of a too-narrow specialization.

Research organizations, of course, enjoy economies of scale and scope, and may pursue projects whose end results are not readily foreseen. When they do this on their own initiative, rather than on order from a client, they may face difficulties selling the results: too much disclosure will give the main part away, and too little will not be persuasive. Any seller of an uncertain product is faced with this. The most productive lines of applied research may also be the least predictable. No buyer may want to touch them, and they may have to go as free public goods. Government or foundation funding would then seem to be the logical answer, so that in practice, research institutes typically rely on government grants for a considerable part of their budget. To that extent, location decisions may be at the pleasure of government.

When business clients are the major customers, market orientation towards these is important. After all 'interaction decreases with distance' and face-to-face communication is particularly sensitive to distance, modern telecommunication technology not withstanding.

In locating facilities of any kind (army barracks, prisons, universities), questions of regional policy are sometimes dominant. In 1770 the good citizens of Göttingen were faced with the prospect of either a prison or a university in their walls. Some of them were sadly disappointed to see the prison go to Celle, another provincial town in the Kingdom of Hannover, but of course in the long run the Göttingers were the winners.

Proximity to government agencies is not necessarily an advantage for a research centre; on the contrary one may not want government agencies to be looking too closely over one's shoulders, a complaint sometimes heard from the University of Wisconsin in Madison, which is also the seat of the Wisconsin legislature.

Government financed applied research puts a centre more into the role of one doing basic research – a subject to which we now turn.

In the 17th and 18th centuries, basic research was a decentralized activity pursued by gentlemen scholars who interacted through academies of science, by correspondence or by reading papers to each other. The famous Royal Society was formed in 1660. It was the reformed universities of the 18th and early 19th centuries that were able to attract basic research back to the universities, where it entered into joint production with teaching. The economies of this joint production are well-known. Researchers are best qualified to teach subjects on the 'frontier of knowledge'. Moreover young brains are needed to take up new ideas, often against opposition from crusty traditionalists. These youngsters have less to lose compared to old-timers, who had once acquired laboriously and painfully the then state-of-the-art. Also teaching is a welcome change from research day in, day out, which sometimes runs into dry spells. It is comforting to know that one has done at least something useful when current research is not panning out. Also, a new outlook and different problems sometimes suggest themselves in the process of teaching, even at the undergraduate level, in spite of the adage that 'undergraduate teaching means casting false pearls before real swine'.

The combination with teaching imposes its own principles on the location of research. At the undergraduate level – and all universities (at least in Europe) combine graduate and undergraduate teaching – teaching institutions should once more be market oriented: to the population of potential students, and that is nowadays the population at large. No metropolitan area is thus without its university(ies). But not every university is also an active research centre.

In fact, the high cost of research facilities, particularly in the physical sciences, preclude their wide dispersal. The social sciences and the humanities are more readily decentralized, although access to libraries, particularly the current journal literature, is essential. These infrastructural considerations aside, there is a critical mass below which research, even pure basic research on any topic of one's fancy, does not come to flourish.

It requires interaction once more, this time with interested and competent colleagues close at hand.

Even thesis research, in the classical image from America's colonial days: teacher and student at either end of a log, benefits from critical discussion with someone other than the thesis advisor. Regarding that simile of teacher and student, George Stigler has remarked that it would sometimes be better if the teacher sat on the student instead of the log.

All of us who have done research, can agree on how important the exchange of criticism is at the early stage of an idea. That is what university departments are for, next to organizing an orderly teaching programme. To put it in economic terms, research activities are neoclassical: they show increasing and then decreasing returns to scale. Any new discipline should thus be concentrated in just one location in order to catch these increasing returns. Decentralization will follow later. Thus it was with mathematical economics in the 1950s and with regional science in the 1950s and 1960s. The point of origin of a new field is inevitably a major research university, where active research centres were established in other fields, preferably related ones. As the history of regional science shows, the neighbouring disciplines are not always welcoming, being reserved if not hostile to the newcomer. Still, research climate and facilities in place are needed to foster the young infants – some of whom are nevertheless thrown out with the bathwater, as well they should – for not all that is new is also good.

While economies of scope between different departments of a university or research institute exist, they generally are not strong enough to cause the best departments in the different disciplines to be located together. In fact, budget constraints often obstruct the cultivation of excellence in more than one field. For this reason, decentralization is still characteristic of the world of learning, unless forced into centralization through government planning.

How would one describe a location that a successful scholar in basic research would find ideal – and some pioneers have been in that lucky position to choose for themselves and their field.

Basic research being a footloose activity permits a wide choice. The research centre or department should be close to a major metropolitan area, although not in the core of it, but providing easy access to educational and cultural facilities. Another attractor is a benign climate. It does not have to be California and perhaps should not be if you are risk-averse to earthquakes. In a European context we do not perceive a migration of scholars to the sunny south, whose winters are hardly warm enough to compensate for underheated habitats, while distances to the rest of Europe remain large.

European research centres will be more strongly attracted to locations of culture and to places of grand tradition. Language remains an important locational factor. The Francophone region will foster its own set of centres, and perhaps the Mediterranean world as well. We see diversity in the new Europe rather than concentration of research activities in just a few places.

WHY ORGANIZATION?

Research by private scholars working on their own is rather exceptional. Today the normal scenario is that of researchers working as members of an organization. Collaboration in joint publications, viewed as a voluntary exchange of ideas or as an example of the division of labour, can be productive for all the reasons well-known in economic theory. What can the joining of scholars in organizations add to this?

First of all the sharing of overhead facilities such as laboratories, libraries and super computers. Second, in the theoretical sciences, the in-house availability of experts in the same field is valuable, particularly in the early stages when an idea has just surfaced and needs exposure to critical comment. This type of interaction, informal oral discussion, presupposes friendly personal contact at an intensity level somewhere between citation and collaboration and this is offered by today's research organizations.

Clearly, collaboration is arranged and kept going much more easily within the shelter of an organization rather than at a distance.

Third, funding, too, is more accessible to members of research organizations, when these organizations can show significant track records (some foundations like NSF give grants only to organizations). To sum up, research is another example of economic activities, in which organizations have outperformed individuals (Beckmann, 1978).

In organizations, voluntary exchange is replaced by command and control as the mode of organizing the division of labour. Its advantages are sometimes ascribed to lower transaction costs, greater reliability or faster delivery. Individual organization members may prefer the stability of employment and reduction of uncertainty, that is offered in exchange for the freedom of operating on one's own. When academic (or organizational) freedom in research is safeguarded by tradition or institutional rule, this attraction is reinforced. Moreover, the prestige of an organization may be a significant addition to the researcher's own prestige. It is thus not surprising that the private scholar is now extinct and organizations are triumphant.

TYPES OF ORGANIZATIONS PRODUCING KNOWLEDGE

Research organizations are basically of two types:

1. Those that do only research, often in different areas, for in view of riskiness some diversification is advantageous for economic survival
2. Those which utilize the synergy of research and teaching: institutions of higher learning, universities.

Organizations for research only include:

- Research laboratories or departments of business firms
- Independent research institutes and
- Think tanks.

Think tanks are a recent (about 1955) innovation. They allow scholars (typically university professors) time off from teaching, administration and routine research, to associate freely – or not at all – with likeminded scholars of noted distinction to explore fresh ideas and look beyond their narrow specialties. The idea has caught on and been applied to non-academic intellectuals as well. When a think tank provides patronage, i.e. offers financial support as well, membership (for up to a year) is by invitation only and eagerly sought.

In-house research has been a tradition of large corporate firms in the USA, such as the Bell Telephone Company, GM, GE, Ford and IBM. Monopolies such as Bell, have been generous supporters also of basic research that could promise no immediate payoff to the firm, but greatly bolster the firm's reputation. With the pressure of intensified competition under globalization, research departments have been directed to stick closer to the firm's business interests.

The internal organization of research departments corresponds to that of a corporation in general. Here management is organized on hierarchical lines. Scientific excellence does not often cohere with managerial ability, and selection for promotion is not usually based on scientific performance alone. Other rewards are needed, for example positions such as 'Fellow' have been created which absolve the successful researcher from managerial functions while granting greater freedom in scientific activity and other privileges. This counts as promotion by being placed in a higher position not based on authority.

Basic research should in fact not be the business of business firms, since they are reluctant to relinquish property rights in results paid for by the firm's research department.

Only monopolies or big oligopolies can afford in-house research departments. A regulated monopoly, like a national telephone company, may be allowed profits in proportion to its total costs. This enables and motivates them to keep a research laboratory which may engage also in basic scientific research. The excellence of the Bell Laboratories was due of course not only to generous funding but also to its management by outstanding scientists.

Industries in perfect or monopolistic competition may, in principle, organize research institutes as a cooperative undertaking through their respective trade associations.

Independent research institutes make research their business as a profit-making activity. This may include basic research which has no market value as a by-product or as the principal product when the client is a private foundation or the government acting as sponsors.

Research organizations face a difficult marketing problem: to persuade the client of its competence and ability, a research outline or first step towards the problem solution must be presented, but not enough to allow the client to walk off with it. An established firm can of course depend on its earned reputation. Some research institutes are in fact government agencies such as the Bureau of Standards. When secrecy is required in the national interest, i.e. research shading into the gathering of intelligence, or weapons' research, it should be done by a government agency.

Professional organizations, not considered here, do not themselves function as researchers or sponsors of research. Their main role is to facilitate communication by organizing periodic conferences or (larger) congresses. Election or appointment to presidential and other high offices always conveys and is (usually) based on prestige. Ostensibly professional organizations are charged with maintaining professional and ethical (civil) standards. Some also act as licensing agencies, admitting to membership only those with appropriate credentials, for example, diplomas.

Organizations engaged in both teaching and research can benefit from their synergy. This synergy arises from two basic causes. First, teachers enjoy research and researchers like teaching. Researchers often go through dry periods. Then it is comforting to have at least something to show for one's efforts: a course taught.

Good people become available when a combination of both activities is offered – particularly when the proportions can be varied according to individual preferences. Secondly, teaching is more productive at the higher levels by those acquainted with the latest developments through their own research. Again, creative teaching often generates new questions for research. Synergies thus arrive both from the product side and from preferences.

Research departments of business firms often allow their research workers to spend part of their time on pure basic research when their preferences are thus, for reasons of professional prestige or as a pleasant diversion from regimented project work. They sometimes encourage their staff to accept teaching invitations in their spare time.

The nature of a research organization is influenced by the type of research, whether pure basic or applied. The latter should be profit oriented and therefore more readily fitted in as part of a corporate business firm. Pure basic research has its natural location in universities and is less often performed by other types of private research organizations.

RESEARCH GROUPS

Besides organized teams with a designated or emerging team leader (to be studied in the next section) we must consider working groups without a leader, which may be small and no more than a temporary association between co-authors of a multi-author paper or they may be members of a university department composed of scholars with congenial research interests. In continuing groups of this type once more the gain of their combined (embodied) knowledge must be balanced against the time lost through communication. This can be formalized by means of a collective production function as follows.

Let x be the number of group members. Of a member's working capacity of unity we must subtract time $k(x-1)$ for communication with the $x-1$ other group members so that the available labour is:

$$[1-k(x-1)]\,x=(1+k-kx)\,x.$$

Substituted in a Cobb–Douglas production function this yields:

$$\left[(1+k-kx)x\right]^{\alpha}$$

with a productive contribution of group knowledge x^{β}, the group production function is then a modified Cobb–Douglas function:

$$q(x)=(1+k-kx)^{\alpha}\,x^{\alpha+\beta}. \tag{4.28}$$

If $\alpha+\beta=\eta>1$ it has initially increasing returns.

In order that the group's marginal product at $x=1$ exceeds opportunity cost unity it is sufficient that:

$$\eta>\alpha k \tag{4.29}$$

which is automatic for $k\leq 1$.

For large x the negative terms in the second derivative of q dominate so that the production function becomes negative after attaining its maximum at $x=x_2=(\eta/(\alpha+\eta)\cdot(1+k)/k)$. Returns are therefore initially increasing and then decreasing and show the production profile of Figure 4.5.

While the group's output is maximized at x_2 and each member's productivity at x_0, (the turning point) the optimal group size is x_1, when opportunity cost x is deducted from the working group's total product to determine largest net output. The tangent to the output curve at $x=x_1$ has slope 1. If a group can raise marginal product above unity, the opportunity cost, then $x_0<x_1$ as shown in Figure 4.5.

The simplest mathematical form of (4.28) results when $\alpha=1$, $\eta=2$ which also meets the criterion (4.29) for $k<1$:

$$q(x)=(1+k)x^2-kx^3. \tag{4.30}$$

This production function has been introduced by Frisch (1962) and also used by Puu (1997a) to study production with initially increasing and then decreasing returns.

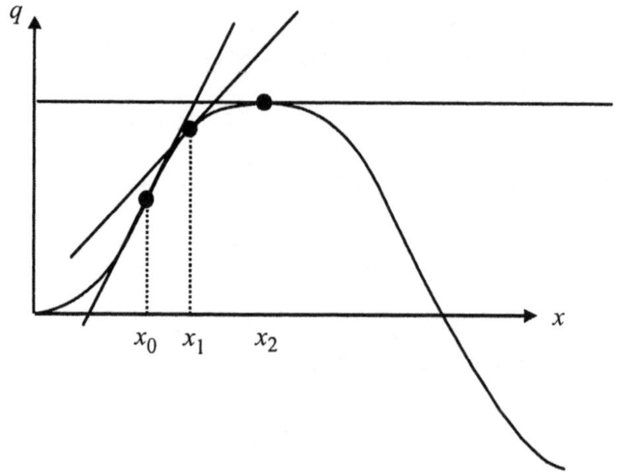

Figure 4.5 Output of working group

We now determine the points of interest x_0, x_1, x_2 for the Frischian production function (4.30). At the turning point $q''(x_0) = 0$:

$$x_0 = \frac{1+k}{3k}$$

At the point x_1 of largest net output:

$$0 = \frac{d}{dx}\left[(1+k)x^2 - kx^3 - x\right]$$

$$= 2(1+k)x_1 - 3kx_1^2 - 1$$

$$x_1 = \frac{1}{3k}\left(1+k+\sqrt{1-k+k^2}\right). \quad (4.31)$$

The output maximum is achieved at x_2:

$$0 = q'(x_2) = 2(1+k)x_2 - 3kx_2^2$$

or:

$$x_2 = \frac{2}{3} \cdot \frac{1+k}{k}. \tag{4.31a}$$

Table 4.3 lists the numbers for various communication levels k.

Table 4.3 Group size under various objectives

	k	$\frac{1}{2}$	$\frac{1}{3}$	$\frac{1}{4}$	$\frac{1}{10}$
Maximum of marginal product	x_0	1	4/3	5/3	11/3
Maximum net product	x_1	$1+\frac{\sqrt{3}}{3}$	$\frac{4}{3}+\frac{\sqrt{7}}{3}$	$\frac{5}{3}+\frac{\sqrt{13}}{3}$	$\frac{1+\sqrt{91}}{3}$
Maximum total product	x_2	2	$8/3 \approx 3$	$10/3 \approx 3$	$22/3 \approx 7$

For university departments, size is influenced more by the division of labour in teaching than by cooperation in research. Communication is handled by periodic department meetings, and the team model (to be considered next) seems more appropriate, with a department chair as its team leader.

Which of the possible objectives shown in Figure 4.5 will be realized?

When there is free entry into the group, successful research groups will have a bandwagon effect: others will want to join, until they are stopped at the point of zero marginal product for the last entrant. The result is a group size with maximal total product.

By contrast, assume that insider control insists on a group size that maximizes individual productivity as measured by marginal product. This is realized at point x_0, the turning point of the curve at which the slope (marginal product) is maximal. This point may be close to minimal group size, that is two-person collaboration (cf. section 'Two-person collaboration' above). It is easier to measure maximal per capita output x_3 (not shown) where a line from the origin touches the output curve. The socially optimal size x_1 where the value of output minus opportunity cost of the membership is maximized and marginal product is unity is not anybody's goal unless there is a group leader, that is, a team. (But a team production function is different.)

It may be noted that the Cowles Commission for Research in Economics, a highly productive research group at the University of Chicago, had approximately seven members in the 1950s, not all of them full-time.

TEAMS

Singling out a group member as a nodal point of communication is a device for reducing the communication load. It opens the chance of making the communication coordinator the source of leadership, thereby introducing hierarchical control at the root level. When a leader is designated or emerges, the structure of a working group is changed in two ways: the leader's input y should be considered qualitatively different from that of the x other group members, and communication is now (mainly) channelled through the leader resulting in a reduction of total communication flow as follows. We compare the time cost of inter-group communication for the following three scenarios.

Economies of Communication

Research group: anyone of the n members may initiate talk with the other $n-1$, each time involving two persons: in contact $2n(n-1) = 2n^2 - 2n$.
Staff meetings: called by anyone of n members, each using time of all n members: n^2.
Team leadership: talk initiated by each of $n-1$ members with the team leader plus talk by the group leader to anyone of the $n-1$ members: $2 \cdot 2(n-1) = 4n-4$.

In the order of communication effectiveness: team leadership ranges before staff meetings before pair-wise communication.

$$4n - 4 < n^2 < 2n^2 - 2n \quad \text{for } n > 2 \tag{4.32}$$

Teamwork is modelled as a CES production function, once more as in voluntary collaboration. The difference is in the introduction of explicit communication cost. Team members' inputs are x, team leader's y. For constant returns to scale, $y = 2$ should mean two teams operating separately. As before there are economies of scope, best seen in the case $\rho = 1/2$:

$$q(x,y) = \alpha^2 x + 2\alpha\beta\sqrt{xy} + \beta^2 y$$

exhibiting the gains $2\alpha\beta\sqrt{xy}$ over the opportunity costs $q(x,0) = \alpha^2 x$ plus $q(0,y) = \beta^2 y$.

Subtracting k for communication from the working time 1 of each team member and kx for the time of the leader, a team production function is constructed as

$$q(x,y) = \left[\alpha(1-k)^{\rho} x^{\rho} + \beta(y-kx)^{\rho}\right]^{\frac{1}{\rho}}$$

or simplifying $\rho = 1/2$.

$$\left[\alpha\sqrt{(1-k)x} + \beta\sqrt{(y-kx)}\right]^2$$

$$= \alpha^2(1-k)x + 2\alpha\beta\sqrt{(1-k)x(y-kx)} + \beta^2(y-kx). \tag{4.33}$$

Objectives

Allowing for opportunity costs of workers inputs $\alpha^2 x$ and leadership input $\beta^2 y$, the benefits of teamwork are reflected in the interaction term:

$$2\alpha\beta\sqrt{(1-k)x(y-kx)}.$$

Here we have neglected terms $k(\alpha^2 + \beta^2)x$ as small compared to the manpower terms x, y. Largest benefits (output) is achieved, given $y = 1$ for:

$$\max_x \; x(y-kx)$$

$$\text{yielding } x = \frac{y}{2k} \tag{4.34}$$

for a maximum of:

$$2\alpha\beta\sqrt{\frac{(1-k)(y-k)}{4k}} = \alpha\beta\frac{1-k}{\sqrt{k}} \qquad \text{given } y = 1. \tag{4.35}$$

Maximal output also requires a team leader's input at the maximum level $y = 1$. It is interesting to note that:

$$kx = 1/2 \tag{4.36}$$

means: half the team leader's time is taken up by communication with team members. The remaining half is devoted to other management tasks, for example, planning. When $\alpha < \beta$ the marginal product of management exceeds that of work as a member. Then a team leader should refrain from doing members' work.

In a team of one leader and three members, not uncommon in the social sciences, Equation (4.36) suggests $k = 1/6$ or an average of 80 minutes interaction time with the team leader per working day for each member.

TEACHING UNIVERSITIES

Turning now to larger organizations producing knowledge, we focus on universities as the principal distributors and producers of scientific knowledge. Here we find great variety. The main distinction for our purposes is that between teaching universities and research universities (although only the latter term is used, and as a mark of distinction in the USA).

Teaching universities come in two basic forms: specialized in a single subject or multidisciplinary. Examples of the first are: schools of mining, of commerce (business schools), of accounting, of law, theological seminaries and art academies. Some of these have been economically successful, even making a profit (in accounting or law). In China from 1947 to the 1980s when Russian influence prevailed, specialized schools of university status were founded, for example, in geodesy, meteorology and sports.

The prevailing model throughout the world is that of the university offering multiple fields of knowledge, besides the classical liberal arts. In antiquity and the Middle Ages the seven liberal arts were taught; which included grammar, rhetoric, logic, music and geometry.

As Savigny has eloquently stated: 'In them [German universities] is given a schema wherein every important educational talent finds its development and every susceptibility of the student its satisfaction, through which every advance of science finds easy and rapid entrance, by which is made easy a recognition of the highest calling of exceptional men, in which even to the poorer existence of more limited natures a higher sense of life is imparted' (Savigny, 1832).

The multidisciplinary university as a surviving institution captures synergies of several kinds. On the demand side it offers choice of subjects, as in a department store (invented much later), an attraction to those who are as yet undecided, thus capturing a larger market. On the supply side there is cross-fertilization between disciplines. Students are enabled and encouraged to look beyond their narrow disciplines. Philosophy, history, literature and fine arts offer diversion and stimulation without the strict requirements of the fields of concentration. Next there is the sharing of overhead facilities: libraries, computer centres, lecture halls and plant. Departments of mathematics or statistics provide teaching services to students of other departments, mainly in the natural and social sciences.

An unavoidable issue is the allocation of resources among departments in a teaching university. What should be the objective?

The object of teaching can be seen as the embodiment of existing knowledge in the graduates. In economic parlance this is accomplished by a production process with both students and teachers as inputs (cf. section 'Elitism versus egalitarianism' below). It has constant returns to scale. Doubling students and teachers (in double sessions) doubles the output. Academic rhetoric not withstanding, a teaching university simply produces graduates as human capital. An efficient allocation of resources maximizes this output across departments. In department i, a given number x_i of students is taught by y_i professors (measured in efficiency units) to become 'human capital' z_i (say):

$$z_i = F_i(x_i, y_i) = x_i F_i\left(1, \frac{y_i}{x_i}\right) = x_i f_i\left(\frac{y_i}{x_i}\right) \quad \text{(say)}. \tag{4.37}$$

We introduce the academic fiction that all branches of knowledge, i.e. all departments i are of equal importance and that teaching is essentially the same activity – at least within the compass of the humanities and the social sciences. Thus the production function is the same for all disciplines i:

$$z_i = x_i f\left(\frac{y_i}{x_i}\right). \tag{4.38}$$

Moreover we assume professors' salaries and other unit costs b_i to be the same. Department costs B_i are then proportional to the number y_i of teachers:

$$B_i = b y_i. \tag{4.39}$$

Output is then maximized by allocating teaching staff y_i within a total budget B:

$$\max_{y_i} \sum_i x_i f\left(\frac{y_i}{x_i}\right)$$

$$\text{subject to } \sum_i b y_i \le B. \tag{4.40}$$

This is achieved by:

$$f'\left(\frac{y_i}{x_i}\right) = \lambda b \tag{4.41}$$

implying uniform teacher–student ratios y_i/x_i and department budgets proportional to their students:

$$B_i = \beta x_i. \tag{4.42}$$

This is a budgeting policy widely advocated and practised in American universities.

The analysis reveals the several questionable assumptions on which this administration policy rests:

- Identical production functions for teaching in different fields
- Equal wages or opportunity costs for professors in different disciplines.

Assume instead that production functions are $a_i x_i f(y/x)$ and unit costs b_i may be different. Now:

$$\max_{y_i} \sum_i a_i x_i f\left(\frac{y_i}{x_i}\right)$$
$$\text{such that } \sum_i b_i y_i \leq B.$$

Then:

$$f'\left(\frac{y_i}{x_i}\right) = \lambda \frac{b_i}{a_i}. \tag{4.43}$$

Since the production function f is concave (for diminishing marginal product) raising b_i/a_i will decrease y_i/x_i. Departments with large productivity coefficients a_i, such as music, should have higher teacher–student ratios (up to one on one), ceteris paribus, and departments with more expensive teachers and facilities such as engineering, a lower faculty/student ratio, as economic intuition would also suggest.

Even a teaching university may afford the luxury of some research in order to attract better qualified faculty when its preferences run in this direction. In the context of this model this will raise the unit cost b_i of the departments in question and thus reduce the desired teacher/student ratio. This is usually accomplished by lowering teaching loads for researchers. Research itself and the higher qualification of a research-interested faculty will boost the a_i. But the net effect and the optimal amount of research time cannot be calculated from this simple model.

An entirely different issue is the effect of a reward system that recognizes research but not good teaching in academic advancement.

While prestige seeking is a mighty motor for activating university professors to do research and publish, will it not also lead to a neglect of teaching? Adam Smith chided his colleagues at Oxford for 'not even making the pretence of teaching' (cf. section 'Styles of university management' below).

While today, professors can no longer give up even the pretence of teaching, there remains the issue of the neglect of teaching in favour of research. A striking case is the observation that the most prestigious academics are those who apparently do the least amount of teaching. This observation is myopic since the type of teaching preferred and performed by research professors in research universities may fall under research.

Teaching doctoral or other research students is in fact inherent in the academic research process. In terms of total hours taught, the research seminars and advanced courses may seem to be less than the time involved in teaching and examining in introductory courses. One reason is the relatively small number of such advanced courses, another the limited capacity for absorption of difficult material by the students involved.

The fact remains that introductory courses are rarely taught by famous professors, while these were once sought after by them when the fee system gave teachers a monetary incentive.

It is an oversimplification to say that each college aims for the highest quality in students, given its own quality level of teachers and facilities. For that might restrict admissions to a single 'most qualified student'. After all it is quality and size that together define a university.

Selectivity is not inconsistent with profit maximization. In other businesses under monopolistic competition, a price is set and all demand is accepted. Prestigious universities use their admission rates, the ratio of acceptances x to applications z received as their strategic variable $u = x/z$. This admission rate u determines the market value $p = p(u)$ of an admission. In the short run, when application z is given, the profit objective would be to:

$$\max_{u} z \cdot up(u)$$

implying:

$$p + up' = 0$$

$$\frac{up'}{p} = -1$$

achieved at an admissions ratio where price, i.e. market value, is still falling with u, that is with the number x of admissions.

In the long run, the dependence of applications z on the admissions rate u, $z = q(x/z)$, must also be considered. At very low u a rise in admission makes applications more attractive, improving chances of success and lower price. At admission rates close to unity, chances do not improve much and the value of an acceptance is lowered, thus decreasing applications with respect to admissions. Profits thus have a maximum at some intermediate admission ratio u. Profit maximization now requires:

$$\max_u uq(u)p(u)$$

which requires:

$$\frac{d}{du}\left[q(u)p(u)\right] < 0$$

achieved at some $0 < u < 1$. Not all applications would be accepted.

ELITISM VERSUS EGALITARIANISM

We treat teaching as a production activity with teacher and student inputs measured in efficiency units. Efficiency units are the algebraic product of number and quality. We keep numbers fixed and focus on quality. An issue of great actuality is how to best pair students and teachers of different quality levels: egalitarians advocating to let poorer students be taught by better teachers while elitists demand pairing the best with the best. We examine the technology and economic effects of either and withhold any value judgements.

The term 'quality' stands here for the (algebraic) product of ability and effort (however difficult to measure in particular cases).

As before, let x and y be student and teacher numbers and let g and q be student and teacher qualities. The suggested production function for teaching is:

$$z = f(gx, qy) = f(u, v) \qquad \text{(say)} \tag{4.44}$$

in terms of efficiency units u for student input and v for teacher input. Without loss of generality we set $x = y = 1$.

In a first model we let standard quality be set at $g, q = 0$ and superior qualities at $g, q > 0$.

$$f(0,0)=0 \tag{4.45}$$

then denotes a standard output normalized at zero. This is consistent with the postulate of linear homogeneity in production. We also assume concavity that is decreasing returns to substitution. Concavity means:

$$\frac{1}{2}f(q,0)+\frac{1}{2}f(0,g)<f\left(\frac{q}{2},\frac{g}{2}\right). \tag{4.46}$$

Now:

$$f(q,0)+f(0,g)<2f\left(\frac{q}{2},\frac{g}{2}\right) \tag{4.47}$$

$$=f(q,g) \text{ by linear homogeneity}$$

$$f(0,g)+f(q,0)<f(q,g)+f(0,0) \tag{4.48}$$

using Equation (4.45).

The story of Equation (4.48) is that pairing the better and pairing the standard each together yields the higher return. This briefly is the economic justification of an elite system in education.

To bolster this argument consider also a CES production function and ability variables $g,q>1$ for superior and $g,q=1$ for standard quality:

$$\left(\alpha\sqrt{1}+\beta\sqrt{q}\right)^2+\left(\alpha\sqrt{g}+\beta\sqrt{1}\right)^2 \lesseqgtr \left(\alpha\sqrt{g}+\beta\sqrt{q}\right)^2+\left(\alpha\sqrt{1}+\beta\sqrt{1}\right)^2$$

or:

$$2\alpha\beta\left(\sqrt{q}+\sqrt{g}\right) \lesseqgtr 2\alpha\beta\left(1+\sqrt{gq}\right)$$

$$\sqrt{q}+\sqrt{g} \lesseqgtr 1+\sqrt{qg}.$$

Squaring:

$$q+g+2\sqrt{qg} \lesseqgtr 1+gq+2\sqrt{gq}$$

$$q+g \lesseqgtr 1+qg$$

letting $g=1+u$ and $q=1+v$:

$$2 + u + v < 2 + uv + u + v = 1 + (1 + u)(1 + v)$$

showing that:

$$f(g,1) + f(1,q) < f(gq,1).$$

The best should be paired with the best.

The model's specification of a single student and teacher was for convenience and is immaterial. It applies to classes equally well, when given class size x is called a unit.

The intuitive reason behind the argument from production theory is the complementarity of the two input qualities.

Our case for elitism is thus that of efficiency or effectiveness. Egalitarianism can still be advocated as a value judgement. But one should then admit that it comes at a cost.

RESEARCH UNIVERSITIES

Teaching can – and sometimes does – operate on a shoestring, while research requires a critical mass. This is due to its initially increasing (and then decreasing) returns and can be brought home by a highly simplified model of a research university.

For illustrative purposes once more we treat all departments as equal. Let the production function of a graduate department doing combined teaching and research have the form of a Frisch production function:

$$g(y) = by^2 - y^3 \tag{4.49}$$

where y is faculty. Each professor admits a certain number of graduate students with whom to work and thus teach (not shown explicitly here). The optimal research allocation turns out to hinge not on the question of how many departments a research university can afford to have but on how many universities should have a department of this discipline.

Allocation under Increasing/Decreasing Returns

This subsection examines the general problem of resource allocation under first increasing and then decreasing returns. For concreteness we consider y (homogeneous) workers to be assigned to n identical machines (departments). The problem is how many machines to use and at what level.

First we observe that no additional machine is to be used as long as any machines still operate under increasing returns. Secondly, all n operating machines i must be used at the same level $x_i = y/n$ and in the decreasing returns range. This means:

$$f''\left(\frac{y}{n}\right) < 0.$$

A transition from n to $n + 1$ machine in use occurs when (see Figure 4.6):

$$nf\left(\frac{y}{n}\right) = (n+1)f\left(\frac{y}{n+1}\right) \tag{4.50}$$

and:

$$\frac{d}{dy}nf\left(\frac{y}{n}\right) < \frac{d}{dy}(n+1)f\left(\frac{y}{n+1}\right)$$

implying:

$$f'\left(\frac{y}{n}\right) < f'\left(\frac{y}{n+1}\right)$$

is true when both $y/(n+1)$ and y/n are in the decreasing returns range. Geometrically this means that the total output curve for $n+1$ machines has the steeper slope at the intersection with that for n machines (as in Figure 4.6).

Table 4.4 shows the switching points y_n, meaning that n machines are to be used first when workers reach level $y = y_n$. We have calculated y_n for the Frischian production function $f = 2x^2 - x^3$.

For large n the switching points y_n approach $n - 1$ from below. The activity levels $x_n = y_n/n$ also increase with n and approach unity:

$$x = \frac{y_n}{n} \approx \frac{n-1}{n}.$$

They are well above the turning point $x = 2/3$ between increasing and decreasing returns even at the first switching point $x_1 = y_1 = 4/3$.

Table 4.4 Switching to n machines at y_n

n	1	2	3	4	5	n
y_n	0	$\frac{4}{3}$	$\frac{12}{5}$	$\frac{24}{7}$	$\frac{40}{9}$	$\frac{2n(n-1)}{2n-1}$

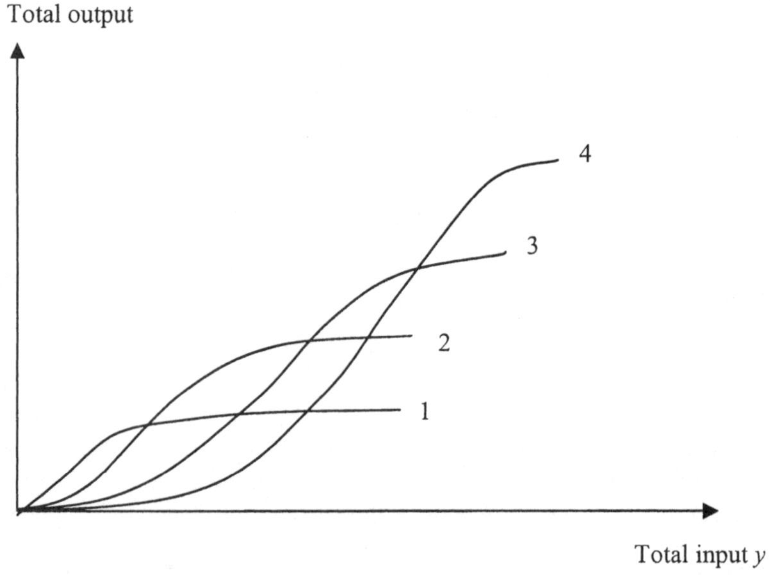

Figure 4.6 Production functions for n activities (machines)

Departments of Research Universities

All universities, including research universities, teach; research universities do so typically at both the undergraduate and graduate levels. Students can reach a doctorate only through research, under the guidance of a professor capable of and, one assumes, interested in doing research. The existing value system in academia rewards research, while downplaying teaching. In the same way research universities enjoy greater prestige than teaching universities.

A university's prestige is built up from its leading departments. Even the richest, best endowed, research university cannot afford to be leading in every field. How many research departments in a particular discipline should exist all together is a question for the machine model of the preceding section 'Allocation under increasing/decreasing returns'. That a Frischian production function may be applicable is shown in Equation (4.30) for working groups, here to be interpreted as departments. Not much can be said about which departments a research university should favour. Tradition may have given a university its profile of distinction based on the scholarship of one brilliant research department. On the other hand, graduate departments differ greatly in their production functions and their unit costs per professor. Building up a research university one might start with the least expensive department. When faced with a shrinking budget it is presumably the least prestigious (least productive) department that is the first candidate for being shut down.

STYLES OF UNIVERSITY MANAGEMENT

There are two extreme types of university management, the traditional academic self-government and the modern style of corporate management. The latter was in place at the University of Chicago in Veblen's time. His displeasure at the university operating as a business firm is eloquently voiced in his book *The Higher Learning in America* (1918).

Academic self-government depends on decision-making in committees whose work pace is slow. In fact it resembles real politics with horse trading, this is, the trading of favours. It has been said that compared to real politics 'the stakes are lower and the fighting is dirtier'. It is open to corruption, as Adam Smith pointed out citing the example of Oxford University in his days.

> If the authority to which he is subject resides in the body corporate, the college, or university, of which he himself is a member, and in which the greater part of the other members are, like himself, persons who either are, or ought to be teachers; they are likely to make a common cause, to be all very indulgent to one another, and every man to consent that his neighbor may neglect his duty, provided he himself is allowed to neglect his own. In the university of Oxford, the greater part of the public professors have, for these many years, given up altogether even the pretence of teaching (Smith, 1776, p. 871).

They would no longer get away with that today.

The modern corporate business style of university management is dominant in the research universities of the USA. But it is being copied now in Europe, notably in Germany. It has meant the introduction of bachelor and master degrees, the replacement of rectors by presidents and raising the power of the state ministry of education.

This is ironic since the American Graduate School, the distinguishing component of a research university, was itself modelled on the German university system in the late 19th century (Flexner, 1930).

In the corporate style, university administration is centred around the president who wields dictatorial power. She/he is selected and appointed by an outside board of trustees (themselves largely business owners or executives or state officials). While the president may have started out as a professor she/he is no longer an academic engaging in teaching or research but a professional manager, as are the team-members: provost, vice presidents and deans. The allocation of a universities' resources (the budget), often the principal business of the provost, is by command, though usually in consultation with the department chair persons. Thus positions and salaries may be adjusted to needs, as perceived in student enrolment in the various disciplines. Entire programmes or departments may be eliminated or newly created against the (possibly selfish) interests of the incumbents. When resources must be taken away, administration dictates and the teaching staff obeys; when new programmes are to be started, the faculty petitions. University departments are thus motivated to attract students.

At prestige-conscious research or teaching universities the quality of students is essential. Even ordinary run-of-the-mill schools prefer the better qualified candidates as students partly in expectation of their later success in economic life enabling them to play their role of generous alumni. In the prestige game of the research universities these students are also wanted as partners in research.

To attract students, money for scholarships or fellowships is essential. There is thus a positive feedback built into the competition of departments. Good performance now will loosen the funds (from the central administration) for good students and superior performance later. An initial decline may start an inexorable downward spiral to a department's extinction.

Faculty salaries are set by the administration so as to meet competition from other institutions and in some disciplines from non-academic employment opportunities. The growth of academia has generated a growth of incomes. The administration's salaries are an increasing function of the size of the university.

UNIVERSITY SYSTEMS

University Systems Centrally Controlled

Consider first a centrally, i.e. state, administered system of teaching universities, in which quality differences are not recognized and thus no ranking exists. Funds are allocated in proportion to student numbers. In the most rigid system students are also assigned to universities by the central authority. The assignment may be based on location, to minimize transportation cost, say, or on religion or some other attribute. To avoid invidious comparisons, income or test scores are excluded as assignment criteria, the aim being uniformity throughout the system.

When students are free to choose but universities' qualities are kept uniform through central control, attractions of location (cultural amenities, sports and recreational facilities, proximity to mountains or the sea and other external factors) may result in different sizes of teaching universities. With constant returns to scale in teaching, size will have no effect on quality (there is no gain from opportunities of further specialization).

What can teaching universities do to attract students and funds? One possible strategy would be a lowering of requirements in examinations. But such a reduction of standards, while perhaps initially successful, will lower a university's reputation and the value of its degrees.

A better strategy is to improve the quality of teaching. Once this is recognized, quality differences do emerge, even when the teaching talent has been equalized at the margin. To encourage better teaching, some incentive system will be needed. The fee system under which the teacher receives some part of the students' fees was once an effective way to motivate good teaching. But it has given way to equalization of professors' pay. Instead universities aim for a 'consumer-friendly' atmosphere, the meeting of student needs in all respects other than examinations.

As a complement to equality, governments may also aim at opening universities to a maximal number of potential students. To bring higher education within reach of the greatest numbers, two measures have been used: the opening of additional teaching universities in dispersed locations and the abolishment of any fees or tuition. The lowering of admission standards, another obvious method, has not been officially admitted, however.

While egalitarianism has often been the proclaimed democratic goal in centrally controlled university systems, as for example, in post-war West Germany, it need not be. Instead quality differences may not only be tolerated but planned and a corresponding ranking of universities set up. In 19th-century Prussia this was Greifswald, Köningsberg, Breslau, Bonn, Berlin where size and reputation went up with rank. University ranking in the Austrian Empire is neatly reflected in the university career of Josef Schumpeter: Cernowitz, Prague, Graz, but not Vienna which discriminated against Jews. (Thus Schumpeter went on to Bonn and eventually Harvard.) A ranked university system offers incentives and rewards for professors, but not for their institutions, when the ranking is frozen through central control.

Competition Among Universities

Consider now the operation of a system of state universities in different states under a federal system, or of independent private universities. The US will serve as our prime example. Some differences exist in admissions since state universities are usually required to accept any applicant from their state with a high-school degree. But they are free to dismiss failing candidates after one year. For all practical purposes both private and competing state universities can set their own admission standards.

Two different games may be played: either for prestige or for size and income. The latter is open to all and played by those institutions in lesser starting positions. They supply an ordinary education crowned with a standard degree to unambitious students seeking qualifications for regular jobs. Competition here is essentially for numbers of students. University administrators find rewards in size as would managers in business firms.

Although nominally non-profit, teaching universities behave in a profit maximizing or loss minimizing way aiming at size provided income tends to rise faster than costs. In fact, teaching can earn a surplus in certain disciplines, and some business and law schools in a university are indeed profitable.

More intriguing is the competitive scenario of the elitist universities, those concerned with prestige rather than just student numbers. Why should prestige matter to university decision-makers?

It matters to the teaching faculty, when they are in control of their university's policy, for two reasons: the quality and enjoyment of their job depends critically on the quality of the students attracted by a prestigious university, and their own career opportunities are strongly influenced by the prestige of their university. Time for and financing of research increase with the university's reputation, and a prestigious university is a better platform for a career move.

University presidents, provosts and deans like to luxuriate in the prestige reflected on them by their universities. Thus, the acquisition and furtherance of prestige is a rewarding goal for both administrators and professors as decision-makers in the elite game.

Prestige differentiation and ranking produces what Merton called the Matthew effect in resource allocation. 'For unto every one that hath shall be given, and he shall have abundance: but from him that hath not shall be taken away even that which he hath' (Merton, 1968, p. 59).

Since the product of universities is not homogenous, the market should be seen as one in monopolistic competition. How do price and quality operate here?

In the US, state universities are held by state governments to offer a decent college education at an affordable price. This price is in effect government controlled. There is no price competition among the state universities of different states and their prices are similar. Price discrimination exists, since state residents pay less, but only in the first year. After that, all students are also residents.

It is conceivable that private universities, e.g. some supported by religious institutions, might offer a college education at a lower price and without strict entrance requirements. But that has not been popular for the following reason. The principal cost being that of the teaching staff, low costs can be achieved only by hiring low-cost teachers, and these would have to be the least qualified so that the product would then also be of low quality.

A more promising strategy is the opposite. Offer a better college education at higher prices, and this has been the successful modus operandi of the private universities. Quality is not uniform however: there are many quality levels. The public (the parents of the aspiring college students) are well aware of the importance of a quality education for lifetime incomes. Thus students are induced to apply to the best their parents can afford and that they can be admitted to. As shown, the quality game can only be played through restricted admissions. Demand is rationed not by price alone, but importantly by perceived (and tested) student quality. Financial aid to students is a device to lessen the role of price and thus enlarge the pool of applicants – to the benefit also of the financial aid giver.

In view of admission restrictions, another market segment exists that has hardly been tapped yet: unrestricted admission to a high-priced college which would cater to a rich but untalented student population. Since such schools could offer good connections to rich circles, they might be attractive in spite of the small value of their education. It is reported that one school aiming in this direction has failed to gain certification, but only because too little was spent on the library.

State universities can compete for size with each other. Size is a worthwhile objective to university management since salaries and privileges tend to rise with size. Students will benefit from larger and more diverse facilities. Also the pool for dating and potential marriage mates is larger.

In the quantity game, perceived advantages rise similarly as with quality. Thus the incentives for strong competition are present both in the quantity and the quality game.

An interesting economic question is why higher education is nonprofitable. This should depend on the subject taught. The traditional liberal arts and the social sciences do not require substantial physical capital in the form of laboratories, animals, botanical gardens, and so on. On the other hand such subjects as law and business administration and economics have a high market value. Law, business and accounting schools have in fact been run as profit-making enterprises. Subsidies are mainly needed to provide the entire package of a multidisciplinary university. In the physical sciences, the vast expense of modern facilities is nowadays shifted to outside funding, largely as government grants for research projects.

The competition for quality in which universities set admission standards to attract students of a particular quality level, can be sustained only by a corresponding quality level of their professors. A simultaneous quality differentiation of teachers and students is efficient. It is elitism in contrast to egalitarianism. Here we find that elitism is also the outcome of monopolistic competition among universities.

Quality in teaching is dependent on the selection of professors by universities and of universities by professors. This raises the question of the role of markets in the allocation of knowledge and of its embodiments in professors as teachers and researchers.

Under the quality game, the market for professors leads to differentiation rather than equalization (say of marginal products).

Briefly, talented professors are attracted to elite universities, which maintain their elite status by having them. Professors being aware that they can achieve their full potential only at universities which offer the best conditions for research and teaching by means of superior facilities and the most talented students, aim for the best. Those professors who cannot enter this game are then relegated to the quantity game where higher salaries can compensate for lesser attractions of their universities. Elite professors are willing to sacrifice some salary advantage for the potential of excellence attainable only under the most favourable conditions offered by the leading research universities. That competition by the research universities for the best talent does not raise salaries to top levels may be traced in part to cartel-like collusion among the elite research universities. Exceptions occur in the case of a few star professors but generally salaries at prestige universities are below those of the large schools in the quantity game. This is particularly true for junior scientists of promise, for whom an elite school is the best platform for launching a career.

That the quality game pairing quality teachers and students results in greater efficiency as we have shown is a fortunate but unintended by-product of these competitive processes.

Since there is a natural association between scientific prestige and the ability to obtain research grants formalized for example in the bidding model of Chapter 5, there is now a deplorable reversal of causality, that is, to make success in attracting grants the basis of scientific prestige. This puts a premium on 'grantsmanship' i.e. promoting and ennobling the sometimes questionable practices of grant seeking to make this rather than scientific accomplishment the basis of scientific standing.

COSTS AND PRODUCTIVITY OF UNIVERSITIES – ECONOMETRIC ESTIMATES

The output of universities is meant to be contributions to knowledge, through its transmission by teaching, as well as its production as published research. For the working units of a university, its departments, there should thus exist production or their dual cost functions, waiting to be discovered.

Most contributions to this topic have focused on cost functions. Cohn et al. (1989) estimated a multiple-output cost function for institutions of higher education. They analysed economies of scale and scope for a sample containing a large number of institutions in the United States. De Groot et al. (1991) extended their research focusing on a subsample of 147 doctorate-granting universities. De Groot et al. (1991) also studied the sensitivity of their cost function estimates to different output measures.

The Swedish university system consists of a number of universities and colleges with a large variance in terms of sizes and composition of outputs. Some of the colleges are mainly oriented to undergraduate teaching, while a few institutions (for example The Karolinska Institute) are mainly focused on research.

An econometric cost study by Wibe (1988), based on cross-section data from the 1980s, provides the following cost function for the Swedish colleges and universities.

$$\ln C = -1.01 + 0.46 \ln R + 0.51 \ln E$$

$$(t = 2.22) \quad (t = 2.07) \qquad \text{R-square} = 0.94$$

C = total yearly cost of the university or college
R = research output in terms of published articles
E = number of full-time students.

The sum of coefficients is not significantly different from 1, implying constant returns to scale.

The Cobb–Douglas cost function is related by duality to a production function of a similar type.

We assume revenues of a university, Y, to be determined by the level of research activities, R, and by the level of educational activities, E. Furthermore, assume that there must at least be some positive amount of research as well as of education. The revenue function of a university could then be approximated by a Cobb–Douglas function:

$$Y = AR^{\alpha} E^{\beta} \qquad (4.51)$$

which can be maximized, subject to the cost function:

$$C = w_R R + w_E E. \tag{4.52}$$

At a maximum, research cost should be:

$$w_R R = \alpha/(\alpha+\beta)C \tag{4.53}$$

and education activity should be:

$$w_E E = \beta/(\alpha+\beta)C. \tag{4.54}$$

Inserting (4.53) and (4.54) into the production function (4.51) we get a relation between revenue and cost:

$$Y = (\alpha+\beta)^{-(\alpha+\beta)}(\alpha/w_R)^{\alpha}(\beta/w_E)^{\beta} AC^{(\alpha+\beta)}.$$

This implies that the total cost can be expressed as a log-linear function of research and education:

$$C = (\alpha+\beta)\left[A^{-1}(w_R/\alpha)^{\alpha}(w_E/\beta)^{\beta}\right]^{1/(\alpha+\beta)} R^{\alpha/(\alpha+\beta)} E^{\beta/(\alpha+\beta)}.$$

If the unit costs of research and education (w_A and w_E) are equal for all universities we have a simple log-linear cost function to be estimated econometrically:

$$\ln C = \ln a + \frac{\alpha}{\alpha+\beta}\ln R + \frac{\beta}{\alpha+\beta}\ln E + \varepsilon.$$

where ε is assumed to be normally distributed around zero.

The Swedish university system expanded considerably during the two decades after 1985. On the basis of this approach we have estimated a log-linear cost function with research activity, being represented by the number of full-time doctoral candidates and the number of full-time undergraduate students, representing educational output.

The estimated equation giving the expected cost of a university is:

$$\ln C = 6.25 + 0.14 \ln R + 0.76 \ln E$$

(t = 4.3) (t = 8.8) $R^2 = 0.95$

No. of obs. = 48

The sum of elasticities is 0.9, indicating some (weak) economies of scale.

A balanced size expansion of research and education by 1 per cent should thus be expected to increase cost by 0.9 per cent.

Including a significant dummy variable for the medical and technological institutes gives approximately the same estimates of the elasticities. A scrutiny of the statistical residuals indicates that increasing returns to scale are primarily concentrated to the smaller colleges with a limited size of doctoral programmes. The largest universities, Lund and Uppsala, have an observed cost in excess of expected cost, indicating an excessive size.

Our measure of research activity is number of effective doctoral candidates. Each doctoral candidate is expected to produce four to five publishable papers in three to four years. Some of these papers are written in collaboration with senior scientists. This implies that most of the research is represented by the measure of output chosen.

There is another advantage of this output measure. The number of published articles would be another suitable measure of research output. However, this measure of research seriously underestimates the research output from the large, multidisciplinary universities. In these universities with their large faculties of humanities, social sciences and law, most disciplines have concentrated research publication in monographs, published by each 'University Press'.

The implied dual production function of the Swedish university system is:

$$Y = AR^{0.18}E^{0.92}.$$

NOTES

1. This section, with Olle Persson, is reprinted from *Scientometrics* **33** (3), 1995, 351–66. 'Locating the network of interacting authors in scientific specialties'. Copyright 1995 Akadémiai Kiadó, Budapest. All rights reserved.
2. This section is reprinted from Beckmann (2008).

5 Knowledge and Society

THE FIVE ECONOMIC FUNCTIONS OF AN ORGANIZED SOCIETY

Frank Knight (1933) distinguishes five functions that the economic organization of any society must perform. These functions apply to knowledge as well as to goods and services. They will serve as our organizing principle for studying knowledge in relation to the scientific community and society. The five functions are:

1. Determining the ends of production
2. Allocation of resources
3. Distribution
4. Rationing in the short run
5. Maintenance and growth.

From the textbook *The Theory of Price* by Knight's student George Stigler (Stigler, 1947, p. 32), we paraphrase, using knowledge for 'goods and services':

1. Society must determine the ends – it must decide what goods and services (here, what new knowledge) – to produce and in what quantities.
2. Resources must be allocated among institutions and activities producing knowledge so as to satisfy the ends as fully as possible.
3. The production of knowledge must be distributed among the members of society.
4. Within short periods of time it may be necessary to adjust consumption to relatively fixed supplies – that is, to ration knowledge by appropriation.
5. Provisions must be made for the maintenance and expansion of knowledge.

AUTHORIZATION OF KNOWLEDGE

What knowledge to produce is also the question of what knowledge to recognize, maintain and distribute (teach), in other words, what knowledge society should have. Behind this has always been the issue of authorization, by religious organizations or the state. Negatively it is the issue of censorship. What knowledge is considered damaging and should be suppressed? At issue, even today, are matters such as child pornography, Nazi ideology, fundamentalism, and even the teaching of the theory of evolution. These are not matters of the economics of knowledge, but rather of the ethics or criminology of knowledge, not to be discussed further here.

In the last resort, politics decides whether to explore (and perhaps contaminate) Mars or dig up ancient graves for archaeology. On the other hand, the production of applied knowledge is the business of firms, whose decisions are guided by profit motives. But this in turn is, of course, activated by consumer demand. In this respect, applied knowledge behaves like all other economic goods and services and textbook economics need not be repeated here. But, here too, government policy may impose restrictions and prohibitions, for example on the use or trade of embryo tissues, body organs or genetically manipulated seeds.

Authorization of knowledge is reflected in the certification of schools and universities: what are the kinds of knowledge to be taught and researched with the use of public funds. These are political decisions which researchers and teachers may lobby for but not decide.

PLANNING VERSUS FREE CHOICE IN SCIENTIFIC RESEARCH

Given the authorized types of knowledge that are to be produced, the next question is how to allocate resources to these ends. In the matter of pure basic knowledge it is not politics or, as in the case of applied knowledge, economics, that figure prominently in making choices, but the scientists and scholars as producers themselves. Now, since scientific research is expensive, planning has again and again been advocated in order to channel research funds in the 'right' direction and avoid wasteful duplication (Brown, 1992). On the opposite side, the distinguished scientist Michael Polanyi has envisioned a 'society for freedom in science' (cf. Hodges, 1983).

Academic freedom is precious to the intellectual community. But do the intellectuals themselves respect it enough to rigorously defend it (Shils, 1972)? Consider the planners' side. Chairman George E. Brown Jr. (1992) of the Task Force on the Health of Research in his 'Report to the Committee on

Science, Space and Technology' is outspoken on the need for planning. While conceding that 'rugged individualism and unfettered competition led the US to world leadership in Nobel prizes, numbers of publications and numbers of patents', he nevertheless calls for 'setting government-wide research policy goals' and to 'link research programs explicitly to goals in a manner that would optimize the policy relevance of the research'. These remarks carry sufficient weight from the fact that 'for 1991 about 50 per cent of all basic research and about 30 per cent of applied research performed in the US was federally funded'.

Ideally, let the planner be a leading scientist or a committee, thoroughly familiar with the important problems in a scientific field and well informed about the abilities of expert colleagues, and confidently aiming at a maximum of scientific achievement. Formally, the job of science planning can then be described as follows:

Let $i = 1,\ldots,m$ be persons (scientists)
$k = 1,\ldots,n$ be problems
q_k be the level of research effort intended by the planner
c_i person i's capacity (available research time)
and a_{ik} the competence of scientist i in problem area k measured in 'efficiency units'.

The planner directs scientists i to spend x_{ik} units of time (effort) on problems k. In efficient planning, the objective would be to achieve the targeted output levels q_k at minimum costs when measured in time used by all scientists i. The planner thus seeks:

$$\min_{x_{ik} \geq 0} \sum_{i,k} x_{ik}$$

subject to:

$$\sum_i a_{ik} x_{ik} \geq q_k \quad k = 1,\ldots,n \tag{5.1}$$

$$\sum_k x_{ik} \leq c_i \quad i = 1,\ldots,m \tag{5.2}$$

which is a linear assignment problem (Koopmans and Beckmann, 1957).

This planning programme is feasible only if the targets are not too ambitious. Otherwise Equations (5.1) or (5.2) are violated. For instance, a programme is not feasible when:

$$\sum q_k \geq \sum c_i \quad \text{and} \quad 0 \leq a_{ik} \leq 1.$$

Assume that plans have been wisely scaled down to assure feasibility. The 'efficiency conditions' (Koopmans and Beckmann, 1957) or dual constraints of this linear programme are then as follows:

$$x_{ik} \begin{Bmatrix} = \\ \geq \end{Bmatrix} 0 \quad \Leftrightarrow \quad v_k a_{ik} \begin{Bmatrix} < \\ = \end{Bmatrix} 1 + u_i \tag{5.3}$$

in terms of the dual variables or efficiency prices u_i and v_k (per time) affiliated with persons and with problems, respectively. They have the dimension of 'scientific worth'. Notice also that:

$$u_i \begin{Bmatrix} = \\ \geq \end{Bmatrix} 0 \quad \Leftrightarrow \quad \sum_k x_{ik} \begin{Bmatrix} < \\ = \end{Bmatrix} c_i. \tag{5.4}$$

Condition (5.3) states that scientist i should not/should work on k if and only if the scientific worth of problem k times the productivity a_{ik} of i in k equals or falls short of the scientific worth of person i's time. The right side of Equation (5.3) implies:

$$1 + u_i = \max_k a_{ik} v_k.$$

A person's scientific worth is achieved only by seeking out his or her most rewarding problems. The question to be discussed is whether and how these efficiency conditions can be implemented through free choice by scientists intent on realizing their own potential of scientific worth and what influences might disorient them.

In a well-functioning scientific community the efficiency prices or dual variables as scientific worth are faithful reflections of the implicit values an omniscient planner would place on various problems. Rather than declare the amount of effort that should be directed to each problem, the planners may have announced this valuation and waited for the research efforts to be forthcoming by self-motivated researchers seeking to achieve their potential for maximum contributions as measured in the planner's valuation system.

Consider also the following implication of Equation (5.3):

$$v_k \geq \frac{i + u_i}{a_{ik}}; \qquad \text{with equality for some } i. \text{ Hence}$$

$$v_k = \min_i \frac{1+u_i}{a_{ik}}. \tag{5.5}$$

Interpreting $1 + u_i$ as scientist i's opportunity cost, Equation (5.5) states that the worth v_k of the scientific problem solution would be produced at minimum cost when scientists freely choose problems that realize their own potential $1 + u_i$.

When there is no planner, it is still possible for an agreed-upon valuation of outstanding problems within the scientific community to exist. The productivity of scientific effort in any field is only as good as the valuation system that assigns scientific worth to its scholarly problems and thus channels effort in the right directions. Such a valuation system cannot be taken for granted.

In the absence of such a well-defined and generally accepted valuation system, even a planner would be at a loss. By default it can happen that each problem, however trivial, is considered equally good and that research output is measured by simply counting papers or pages – as ignorant administrators sometimes do in their hiring decisions. One should not be surprised by the flood of trivial publications that is let loose by this type of incentive system.

This scenario represents what de Solla Price has called Little Science, in contrast to the Big Science carried on in modern laboratories, for instance in particle physics (de Solla Price, 1961). Big Science calls for a different formulation of a rational science policy, such as maximizing scientific payoff within a total budget. It is discussed in section 'Sponsorship and freedom'.

SCIENTIFIC WORTH

Not all scientific problems are equally important or worthwhile. What distinguishes the interesting from the trivial are factors such as:

- Degree of surprise engendered by the solution (or unpredictability)
- Starting point for further enquiries
- Closing of an unresolved issue
- Aesthetic qualities.

Interest often moves in waves, going up and down, thereby letting problems go out of fashion only to be resumed later. For scientific worth to be reasonably well-defined, some sort of agreement must exist on what are the important problems in a field. Here we observe wide differences between, say, mathematics and the 'exact sciences' on the one hand and some social sciences on the other. David Hilbert, in his famous address to the

International Mathematical Congress of 1900, could announce to wide acclaim what he considered to be the outstanding unresolved research questions of his day, including Fermat's last theorem, the continuum hypothesis, the Weierstrass conjecture and the four-colour theorem.

The scientific worth of a mathematical result is said to be based on (Borel, 1981):

1. Does it solve old problems
2. Does it have broad scope
3. Does it use simple and few assumptions yielding elegant results
4. Does it open new ways?

In general, an approximation to scientific worth may be inferred from the types of topics that have been considered worthy of publication in prestigious journals. But these of course do not yet contain the unsolved problems.

In economics, the new developments in econometrics as well as the new fields of game theory and mathematical programming determined research interests in the 1950s and early 1960s. These developments were followed by neoclassical growth theory. There seem to be no dominant themes in current economic research by which to gauge scientific worth.

However, in his 1985 Nobel Lecture, T.C. Koopmans did list the following problems as having the greatest relevance to economics: the future of energy, the environment and poverty. The Nobel awards themselves, including that for economics, tell at best a story of past research achievements but do not directly point in new directions.

PRESTIGE-SEEKING AND CIVILITY

The absence of direct monetary incentives prompts the following question: what motivates scientists to do basic scientific research and promptly disclose the results?

As they never fail to mention, it is first of all the sheer joy of discovery, the feeling to have found something new that is true. But to induce rapid publication, something more is needed: the recognition of priority. By being the first to communicate an advance in knowledge, the scientist thereby relinquishes the intellectual property rights for recognition of first discovery, that is, priority. Speed is therefore of the essence, since there is no payoff for rediscovery. The prestige incentive goes a long way to stimulate the production of the pure public good of knowledge (Stephan, 1996, p. 1203).

The race to publish is not compatible with leisured reflection and the patient working-out of the full story. It rather invites a flood of immature publications (Reif, 1961).

Prestige is a carrier of value that does not fit easily into economic thinking. To have great value it must be in short supply but great demand. It is both more elusive and more perishable than monetary value. It is real, however, and an important vehicle in the arts, and perhaps surprisingly, in the arena of knowledge.

In earlier eras, the very possession of knowledge – in particular magic knowledge – conveyed prestige. Learning as such does not bring much distinction anymore. Prestige as scientific reputation attaches to priority in discovery, to the generation of new knowledge. Prestige is diluted as further contributions are made, unless these enhance the insights of a pioneering one. To build or keep a scientific reputation in essence requires a virtually continuous stream of new contributions.

Sociologists of science have long argued that prestige-seeking is a mighty engine of research (Barber, 1952; Merton, 1970). The physicist Reif (1961) has made a similar argument. The latter contrasts the 'competitive world of the research scientist' with the idyllic picture of the ivory-tower scholar that inhabits the popular imagination. While the scientists themselves often disclaim any interest in fame or scientific reputation, the reality is otherwise, as is demonstrated by the severity of 'priority disputes' regarding scientific discoveries (Reif, 1961).

The view that prestige is the only reward for scientists (ibid.) may be an exaggerated one, but it is nevertheless true that prizes and distinctions such as membership in national academies, invitations, lectures, addresses at scientific conferences, positions in scientific organizations and of course, appointments at ranking universities are the coveted rewards of scientific prestige or reputation. While prestige may pave the way to monetary rewards, prestige-seeking is not equivalent to income-seeking (sometimes labelled rent-seeking) in the context of movements among universities (see Chapter 4).

The pursuit of knowledge, in research or teaching, is a privileged activity with valuable amenities. Above all, there is the incalculable satisfaction of a meaningful activity. In fact, it is remarkable to many of us that we are being paid for doing what we enjoy the most. Universities offer a pleasant environment and – after an early period of competitive struggle – job security. Whatever one's standing in the scientific community, a professor's job is prestigious in the world at large. It is one that allows for personal initiative as well as a great deal of freedom – with only a minimum of control. This is a world apart from the hierarchical organizations of the business world and government, which tend to rely on command and control. In addition, there is a sense of fellowship in the academy and a genteel lifestyle that is inherited from the past.

In view of these amenities, it should not be surprising that certain obligations must be observed. They are what Edward A. Shils has aptly called 'civility' (Shils, 1972) and impose some restrictions on an otherwise relentless pursuit of prestige. If freedom is to be preserved, then there must be a good deal of self-regulation that substitutes for command and control (the way business is done in other hierarchical organizations). This means in particular a willingness to serve as chair or on university committees.

In the role of being an advisor to students, more than a mandatory minimum of attention should be given. Time given to these duties is not rewarded (in money or scientific prestige) – but it is nonetheless expected. While the pursuit of scientific prestige through research may have become as goal-centred as profit-seeking or rent-seeking in the business world, it must not be allowed to dominate academic life, or its inherent quality is lost.

Civility extends beyond one's university or research organization to the greater scientific community. While refereeing and reviewing are not in themselves onerous and may even extend one's own knowledge, they are once again activities that are not rewarded by a gain in prestige. To alleviate the difficulty of finding competent and willing referees, some journals, for example the *Journal of Political Economy*, have been offering a fee for completing a referee report at an early date. Refereeing is generally treated as a burden. It may even be misused as a device for blocking early publication of results by authors who are considered rivals in one's field.

The practice of scientific research depends to a great deal on trust. But trust may be violated. The grossest violation of civility is cheating, such as withholding credit for results that have been gained from other persons' publications or communications. Its worst form is sheer plagiarism. Cheating can also mean polishing ('improving') or even inventing data. Civility is in danger because it must be practised in opposition to market forces. It is precious in that it creates a genteel climate that is entirely different from the cut-and-thrust of the business world.

ALLOCATION OF RESOURCES

Having first considered the fundamental question of 'who should do what', we turn to the institutional question of who should be 'where', which at first sight appears to be a formally quite similar question. But there is a deep problem hidden here. The basic criterion function, a_{ik} (the 'productivity' of individual i in institution k), also depends on who else is there – and this converts an otherwise linear assignment problem into a quadratic one (Koopmans and Beckmann, 1957) with little hope of an operational economic solution.

When a small number of vacancies are to be filled from a set of available candidates, a manageable assignment problem arises. Since the rest is in place, it can be treated as the optimal utilization of the productivity potentials a_{ik} – which only involves candidate i and institution k. The assignment problem:

$$\max_{x_{ik} \geq 0} \sum_{i,k} a_{ik} x_{ik} \tag{5.6}$$

$$\sum_{k} x_{ik} \leq 1 \quad i = 1, \ldots, n \tag{5.7}$$

$$\sum_{i} x_{ik} \leq 1 \quad k = 1, \ldots, n \tag{5.8}$$

originally formulated as 0/1 variables x_{ik} (of i going to k or not), may be shown to have 0/1 solutions even when relaxed to $0 \leq x_{ik}$ in order to generate a linear programme. The efficiency conditions describing optimal solutions now state:

$$x_{ik} = \begin{Bmatrix} 0 \\ 1 \end{Bmatrix} \Leftrightarrow p_i + r_k \begin{Bmatrix} > \\ = \end{Bmatrix} a_{ik} \tag{5.9}$$

where p_i and r_k are efficiency prices that are associated with persons i and institutions k, respectively. Equation (5.9) states that contributions p_i and r_k (credited to person i and institution k) can be earned only in an optimal assignment. This is apparent from the implications of Equation (5.9):

$$p_i = \max_{k} a_{ik} - r_k \tag{5.10}$$

$$r_k = \max_{i} a_{ik} - p_i. \tag{5.11}$$

Equations (5.10) and (5.11) are in effect statements of rent-seeking on the part of both persons and institutions, where 'rent' p_i means the value of person i to the institution and r_k means the value of the institution to the person (although neither are directly observable).

FINANCING: INSTITUTIONS OR PROJECTS

The funding of knowledge production (research) is one of the key economic issues in 'knowledge and society'. It is vital to pure basic research, since its product has no market value. Still, this type of research must be carried out as an economic activity in a market economy.

A traditional way of financing basic research has been by teaching. It may seem paradoxical that pure basic knowledge cannot be sold in the market but that some of it can be taught for profit. The demand for schooling has been discussed elsewhere (Chapters 2 and 6). Teaching and research are then carried out in the same organization, a university or, in concrete terms, a university department. Teachers and researchers need not be the same persons, but in practice they are. At an early stage in their academic career, assistant professors in the United States are expected to produce published research in order to qualify for promotion and tenure. After that, they may choose how to allocate their time between teaching, research and administration. Positive feedback operates in this context: successful researchers who are earning professional prestige are rewarded with smaller teaching loads that allow them to produce even more research. A successful chairperson has the option of pursuing an administrative career as dean, provost or perhaps president.

The prevailing system of rewards offers little encouragement to good teaching. A teacher's prestige is strictly local, unlike the scientific reputation that is earned through research or scientific entrepreneurship and which is recognized throughout the profession. To the extent that their research is financed by teaching, professors are in full control of the topics they choose for their research.

What is the alternative? For applied research, the natural agencies are private business firms. Sometimes such firms are spun off the university as firms started by inventive professors. Business firms can use the results for technological change in new processes or for new products (see Chapter 7). This type of research is typically pursued in in-house laboratories or by independent research institutes for business clients.

For pure basic research, the appropriate agencies are research universities that increasingly depend on outside funding from private foundations or the government. Basically, outside finance may be organized in two ways: by supporting institutions with unrestricted funds that function as additions to university endowments or by providing grants for specific research projects. In practice, the grants system has led to the expenditure of considerable effort on applications. This is a matter that tends to result in complaints by junior faculty (on 'grantsmanship', see the next section).

In the USA, grants in support of basic research are available from private foundations such as the Rockefeller Foundation, the Ford Foundation and the Sloan Foundation as well as from the government. In the United States, government grants are given by departments of the federal government such as Agriculture, Health, Environmental Protection, Housing and Urban

Development, and Transportation. However, the main source of American governmental grants is the National Science Foundation.

The underfunding of public goods has been a general issue in public economics. Underfunding may also be a problem for applied research that is normally undertaken by private business firms, for the results of applied research are highly uncertain and often available only in the distant future. Funding by teaching is now feasible only for theoretical research (that is, in Little Science) since Big Science is too expensive. Thus, government agencies appropriately are involved in Big Science research. Generally, government agencies can sponsor research on topics that are considered relevant from their perspective. Beyond the research interests of specific governmental departments, the support of research as a public good operates best through government-funded agencies that are independent of political influence. American examples of such agencies include the National Science Foundation and the Fund for the Humanities. The precursors of such foundations are the scientific academies, which are themselves mostly organized and sometimes financed by governments (the first such academy was the British Royal Institute, which was founded in 1799). Academies originally supported research by offering prizes for the solution of particular problems, such as the 'brachistochrone' or the question as to whether civilization had benefited mankind.

In a society of some wealth, private as well as government foundations can play an invaluable role as Maecenas for basic research. Grant dependence necessarily raises the question of who makes the funding decisions. In the case of scientific research, peer review within advisory councils has become the prevailing practice. These councils in turn consist of noted academics from the scientific community. In other words, they consist of scientists who are prestigious and highly visible in their fields. Having been successful in particular specialities, they tend to favour projects that continue research along lines that are similar to their own. The resulting phenomenon of 'main-lining' is not sympathetic to radically new ideas. This remains true if the scientific evaluation does not originate in advisory councils but from referees whose opinions are solicited by council members.

The co-existence of a number of foundations that compete in their support of worthwhile projects offers the best chance of overcoming referee biases, assuming that not every one of these relies on the same body of advisors. The fact that granting agencies tend to 'bet on a winner' (that is, support candidates with the best track records) has been called the 'Matthew effect' by the sociologist Robert Merton (1968, p. 59) – 'For unto every one that hath shall be given…'. This tends to generate more inequality among scientists than is warranted by the distribution of talent.

'GRANTSMANSHIP' OR BIDDING FOR RESEARCH FUNDS[1]

Introduction

Pure basic research produces nothing of value, that is of monetary value. Rather its product is a pure public good, not marketable, but freely available to any interested party. That at any rate, is demanded by the 'ethos of science'.

The economic implication is that researchers, unable to sell a marketable product, must seek financing elsewhere: from private sponsors, foundations, universities or, as a last resort (but in practice often the first resort) government agencies. What matters, however, is not the nature of the donor but the institutional arrangements that define the donor's influence over the topics and methods of the research thus financed. It varies between the two extremes of no influence whatever, that is complete freedom for the researcher and the fixing of the research objective as a research project, the common practice in applied research or development.

Historically, it was the learned societies and academies that sought to influence the direction of research by announcing prizes for the solution or best answer to a specific problem (the 'brachistochrone' or whether cultural development has improved mankind's happiness). Contemporary sponsors such as the NSF of the US will announce support to research in less specific but still well-defined areas, leaving the precise topic to be chosen to the applicant. In addition, there are sometimes government funds earmarked for topics of national concern.

The award decision by the sponsoring agency will depend on any of the following: competence in the research area as demonstrated by previously published research, importance and technical feasibility of the proposed programme and availability of resources and facilities at the research institution (NSF, 1998). It is conceivable but hardly ever admitted, that research grants are allocated according to ethnic or geographic quotas or even in a purely random fashion.

It is universal practice nowadays that a researcher seeking financial support must submit an application describing his/her plans, expectations, background and the relevance and importance of the proposed work. In doing so, he/she must decide how much effort to put into the application. Risk of failure and hence wasted effort is borne by the researcher.

It is an often-heard complaint that too much time is wasted, i.e. taken away from actual research in making grant applications, an onerous job often shifted to junior scientists in a university department, while the 'principal investigator' sometimes contributes little more than his/her prestigious name to the enterprise.

This risk is even larger when competing for a prize that will be awarded for completed research. In this section we consider the first alternative, i.e. how much effort to put into an application for a research grant. For concreteness we will assume that the number of competitors is known and begin with the case of only two applicants. The scenario is then that of a two-person non-cooperative non-zero-sum game.

The Pure Strategic Game

Following Gottinger (1996) we distinguish the case of a cursory from that of a thorough reading of the application by the funding agency or its referees. When read cursorily the chance of success depends on the funding agent finding something of appeal and interest in the proposal and this should be considered proportional to the length (quality) of the proposal which in turn would be proportional to the applicant's effort.

If x and y denote the two players' efforts, then player 1's chance of success $= x/(x + y)$ and his expected payoff is:

$$\frac{x}{x+y}v - x$$

where v is the research fund competed for. We assume this to be the same for both applicants. This game, which is structurally equivalent to some advertising scenarios (Funke, 1976) has a pure strategy solution.

$$\max_x \frac{x}{x+y}v - x \tag{5.12}$$

yielding:

$$\frac{y}{(x+y)^2}v - 1 = 0 \tag{5.13}$$

and for player 2:

$$\frac{x}{(x+y)^2}v - 1 = 0 \tag{5.14}$$

$$x = y = \frac{(2x)^2}{v}$$

so that:

$$x = \frac{v}{4}. \tag{5.15}$$

Thus each competitor puts in an effort worth one-fourth the prize, and the total equals half the intended research fund. Since each competitor has an equal chance in this game, choosing the winner at random would have produced the same result at no cost. Substituting the optimal strategies $x = y = v/4$ into the payoff function yields a value of $v/4$. Thus the opportunity of bidding for research funds v opening a one-half chance of winning v by spending $v/4$ on a proposal is worth only one-fourth of the grant offered.

What if proficiencies differ in the sense that a proposal of given length x requires an effort, ax, $a < 1$, while the rival's proposal y still needs an input y. Now:

$$\max_x \frac{x}{x+y} v - ax \tag{5.12a}$$

yields:

$$\frac{y}{(x+y)^2} v = a$$

and:

$$\max_y \frac{y}{x+y} v - y$$

$$\frac{x}{(x+y)^2} v = 1 \tag{5.14a}$$

so that:

$$\frac{x}{y} = \frac{1}{a} > 1 \qquad \frac{x}{x+y} = \frac{1}{1+a} > \frac{1}{2} \tag{5.16}$$

$$\frac{x}{\left[(1+a)x\right]^2} v = 1$$

$$x = \frac{v}{(1+a)^2}$$

$$ax + y = \frac{v}{(1+a)} > \frac{v}{2}. \tag{5.17}$$

While the chance of success is improved for the more proficient bidder, the total effort going into application is raised.

Suppose now that scientific reputation enters into the award process, perhaps by adding the length of the bibliography of the applicant (possibly with some weighting factor) to the length of the proposal in determining the chance of a favourable impression on the funding agent in the cursory review. Let a and b denote this quantification of an applicant's scientific reputation so that the chance of success for player 1 is now:

$$\frac{a+x}{a+x+b+y}. \tag{5.18}$$

Player 1's optimal strategy is then to:

$$\max_x \frac{a+x}{a+b+x+y} v - x \tag{5.12b}$$

yielding:

$$\frac{b+y}{(a+b+x+y)^2} v = 1 \tag{5.13a}$$

and for player 2:

$$\frac{a+x}{(a+b+x+y)^2} v = 1 \tag{5.14b}$$

$$\frac{y+b}{(a+b+x+y)^2} = \frac{1}{v} = \frac{x+a}{(a+b+x+y)^2}.$$

Effort plus reputation and hence probabilities are thus equalized through extra effort and hence are 1/2. From:

$$\frac{x+a}{4(x+a)^2}=\frac{1}{v}=\frac{y+b}{4(y+b)^2}$$

it follows that:

$$x+a=y+b=\frac{v}{4} \tag{5.15a}$$

$$x+y=\frac{v}{2}-(a+b). \tag{5.19}$$

Total effort decreases with the role of prestige.

Finally, suppose that the funds of v_1, v_2 sought by the two competitors are unequal. Player 1 now aims to:

$$\max_x \frac{x}{x+y}v_1-x \tag{5.12c}$$

yielding:

$$\frac{y}{(x+y)^2}=\frac{1}{v_1} \tag{5.13b}$$

while player 2 seeking:

$$\max_y \frac{y}{x+y}v_2-y$$

achieves:

$$\frac{x}{(x+y)^2}=\frac{1}{v_2}. \tag{5.14c}$$

From this follows that:

$$\frac{x}{y}=\frac{v_1}{v_2}. \tag{5.20}$$

Efforts are proportional to the amounts sought. When $v_1 > v_2$ the first player's chance of success:

$$\frac{x}{x+y}=\frac{\frac{v_1}{v_2}y}{\left(\frac{v_1}{v_2}+1\right)y}=\frac{v_1}{v_1+v_2}>\frac{1}{2}>\frac{v_2}{v_1+v_2}. \quad (5.21)$$

Asking for more and choosing one's effort accordingly will thus raise an applicant's prospects. Modesty never pays in science.

A Game in Mixed Strategies

Suppose now that the sponsor or referees scrutinize the proposals thoroughly, and award the grant to the applicant with the better proposal, i.e. the one prepared with greater effort. The payoff function for player 1 is then:

$$v\phi(x)-x \quad (5.22)$$

where:

$$\phi(x)=P(y<x) \quad (5.23)$$

describe the mixed strategy of player 2.

In a symmetric game, player 1's mixed strategy is the same:

$$\phi(y)=P(x<y). \quad (5.24)$$

For each active x, i.e. x chosen with positive probability, the expected payoff must then be the same, equal to the value u of the game for player 1:

$$v\phi(x)-x=u. \quad (5.25)$$

From (5.25) we obtain as the mixed strategy:

$$\phi(x)=\frac{u+x}{v} \quad (5.26)$$

with:

$$\phi(0)=\frac{u}{v} \qquad \phi(v-u)=1 \quad (5.27)$$

an equi-distribution over:

$$0 \le x \le v - u. \tag{5.27a}$$

Write now:

$$\frac{u}{v} = q \qquad \frac{x}{v} = t$$

$$\phi(x) = q + t = F(t) \tag{5.28}$$

To determine the value u of the game consider the expected payoff. With probability q^2 both players choose 0 and obtain a half chance of the prize v. When player 1 chooses x from (5.27a) the expected return is:

$$\int_0^{v-u} (v - x)\phi(x)\, d\phi(x) \tag{5.29}$$

$$= \int_0^{v-u} (v - x)\frac{u + x}{v}\frac{dx}{v}$$

$$= v\int_0^{1-q} (1-t)(q+t)\, dt.$$

Thus:

$$u = \frac{q^2}{2}v + v\int_0^{1-q}\left[q + (1-q)t - t^2\right] dt$$

$$q = \frac{q^2}{2} + q(1-q) + \frac{1}{6}(1-q)^3 \tag{5.30}$$

or:

$$q^3 + 3q - 1 = 0 \qquad q = \frac{1}{3}(1-q)^3.$$

Iterating yields:

$$q = \frac{1}{3} - h \qquad h \doteq \frac{1}{18}.$$

We shall use the approximations:

$$q \doteq \frac{1}{3} \qquad u \doteq \frac{v}{3}. \tag{5.30a}$$

Consider also the expected (average) cost of applications:

$$c = \int_0^{v-u} x d\phi(x) = v\int_0^{1-q} t dF(t) \tag{5.31}$$

$$= v\int_0^{1-q}\left[1-F(t)\right]dt = v\int_0^{1-q}(1-q-t)dt = \frac{v}{2}(1-q)^2.$$

With the approximation (5.30a), the approximate average cost is:

$$c \doteq \frac{2}{q}v. \tag{5.31a}$$

This is less than the effort (5.15) chosen for cursory reading, perhaps in view of the increased uncertainty.

With n competitors to player 1, i.e. $n+1$ contestants, the choice x of player 1 is described by:

$$v\phi_n(x) - x = u_n \tag{5.32}$$

$$0 \le x \le v - u_n$$

$$\phi_n(x) = \left(\frac{u_n + x}{v}\right)^{\frac{1}{n}}$$

$$\phi_n(0) = \left(\frac{u_n}{v}\right)^{\frac{1}{n}} \qquad \phi_n(v-u_n) = 1$$

$$q_n = \frac{u_n}{v} \qquad t = \frac{x}{v}. \tag{5.33}$$

The value u_n of the game is determined similarly by:

$$u_n = \frac{v}{n}\cdot q^{\frac{n+1}{n}} + \int_0^{v-u_n}(v-x)\phi_n(x)d\phi_n(x)$$

yielding:

$$q_n = \frac{n}{2n+1}\left(1-q_n{}^{\frac{2n+1}{n}}\right)+q^{\frac{n+1}{n}}\left(1-\frac{n^2}{n+1}\right) \tag{5.34}$$

which for large n means:

$$q_n \doteq \frac{1}{2n+1} \qquad u_n \doteq \frac{v}{2n+1} \tag{5.35}$$

which was also the approximate solution for $n = 1$.

Now in the active domain:

$$0 \le t \le 1-q_n$$

$$F_n(t) = (q_n + t)^{1/n}$$

increases with n and thus lowers the expected value of cost:

$$\int_0^{1-q_n} t dF_n(t) = \int_0^{1-q_n}\left[1-F_n(t)\right]dt \tag{5.36}$$

so that the more contestants $n+1$ the less effort each expends on his application (on average).

The game of seeking research funds, which should be just a preliminary to doing research, takes on a new face when getting grants is valued as an end in itself. Deplorably there is a recent tendency to attach prestige and measure a scholar's worth by his/her talent in obtaining money.

Just because modesty does not pay, we should give due recognition to those who succeed in research even without entering the game of getting money for research.

SPONSORSHIP AND FREEDOM

In this section we reconsider the topic of freedom of choice for researchers whose work depends on outside sponsorship. In the scenario of planning versus free choice, the cost of research is basically the opportunity costs of the researcher(s) themselves and the allocation problem that of their best utilization. Costs are those of human capital, and material capital is not important. Outside financing, if needed, is then sought for professional salaries in order to be released from teaching obligations.

This scenario represents what de Solla Price (1963) has called Little

Science, in contrast to the Big Science of e.g. modern physics laboratories. Big Science calls for a different formulation of a rational science policy such as maximizing the scientific payoff within a total budget. As before, let v_j be scientific worth and a_{ij} the productivity of institute i in research of type j:

$$\max_{x_{ij}\geq 0}\sum_{i,j} v_j a_{ij} x_{ij}$$

$$\sum_{i,j} k_{ij} x_{ij} \leq B \tag{5.37}$$

where k_{ij} is the (capital) cost of work by institute i on project j and B is the budget. At this point we must note that a marginal rate of scientific worth v_j is valid only within technical limits q_j of projects j:

$$\sum_{i} a_{ij} x_{ij} \leq q_j. \tag{5.38}$$

Adding this to the institutes' capacities (5.41) and the budget constraint, the planning problem becomes:

$$\max_{x_{ij}\geq 0}\sum_{i} v_j a_{ij} x_{ij}$$

$$\sum_{i,j} k_{ij} x_{ij} \leq B \tag{5.39}$$

$$\sum_{i} a_{ij} x_{ij} \leq q_j \tag{5.40}$$

$$\sum_{j} x_{ij} \leq c_i. \tag{5.41}$$

This linear programme is feasible and has the efficiency condition:

$$\hat{x}_{ij}\begin{Bmatrix} = \\ \geq \end{Bmatrix} 0 \;\Leftrightarrow\; v_j a_{ij} - mk_{ij} \begin{Bmatrix} < \\ = \end{Bmatrix} w_i + a_{ij} z_j \tag{5.42}$$

where m is a Lagrange multiplier reflecting the budget and converting money into units of scientific worth and z_j the Lagrange multiplier of Equation (5.40) and w_i that of Equation (5.41). Multiplying Equation (5.42) by $\hat{x}_{ij}$ yields the equation:

$$\left(v_j a_{ij} - mk_{ij}\right)\hat{x}_{ij} = w_i \hat{x}_{ij} + z_j a_{ij} \hat{x}_{ij}. \tag{5.43}$$

The value created by institute i working on project j to the extent $\hat{x}_{ij}$ is shared as scientific prestige $w_i \hat{x}_{ij}$ by institute i and as reputation earned $z_j a_{ij} \hat{x}_{ij}$ by the sponsor of j. Equation (5.42) may be rewritten:

$$w_i = \max_j v_j a_{ij} - mk_{ij} - z_j a_{ij} \tag{5.44}$$

$$z_j = \max_i v_j - \frac{mk_{ij} + w_i}{a_{ij}} = v_J - \min \frac{mk_{ij} + w_i}{a_{ij}}. \tag{5.45}$$

Institutes or scientists choose project j to maximize their prestige (per unit of effort) – after capital cost and allowing the sponsor his share $a_{ij} z_j$. Sponsors aiming for maximum credit share z_j from project j choose the least-cost institute i. Efficiency condition (5.42) may also be written as a cost–benefit test, using $k_{ij} > 0$:

$$\hat{x}_{ij} \begin{Bmatrix} = \\ \geq \end{Bmatrix} 0 \Leftrightarrow \frac{v_j a_{ij} - w_i}{k_{ij}} \begin{Bmatrix} < \\ = \end{Bmatrix} m \tag{5.46}$$

where benefits are scientific worth net of researcher's opportunity cost w_i, and m is the acceptable cost–benefits ratio.

We must remark that the efficiency conditions (5.42), (5.44) and (5.45) are difficult to implement since they require knowledge of efficiency prices (w_i and z_j) and pursuit of objectives ($v_j a_{ij} - mk_{ij}$) – that do not appeal to self-interest. Under self-selection, person or institute i would maximize the expression $v_j a_{ij}$ while disregarding cost rather than focus on the cost–benefit ratio in criterion (5.46). We propose to examine how these exalted recommendations (5.42 and 5.46) relate to current practice.

Like generals, 'big scientists' do not mind costs. The imposition of cost discipline can thus not be left to scientists' sense of self-control. Instead, it calls for some central agency such as the National Science Foundation. In the United States, Congress itself has in some cases stopped projects on account of their excessive cost. An example is the termination of the Superconducting Super Collider in 1992 (Weinberg, 1993, p. 283).

Call $v_j a_{ij} - mk_{ij}$ the 'social worth' – as distinguished from the purely scientific worth – of the research by institute or principal investigator i on project j. Here we must distinguish between research undertaken by internal decisions in university departments, invariably of the Little Science type, and research sponsored from the outside. Unsponsored internal research, involving as cost only the researcher's time off from teaching or administration, is left to individual initiative that is subject only to the consent of the department chair, which is usually easy to obtain. Since k_{ij} does not arise or is negligible, the free-choice scenario is what goes on in practice.

Current American practice regarding outside support of scientific research usually involves a three-stage decision process. Scientists choose a scientific problem and formulate it as a research project that they describe in an application. They submit the application to any one of a given set of foundations whose announced goal is the support of worthwhile scientific research 'for the benefit of humankind'. The foundation administrators then call on several consultants who are recognized expert scientists in the relevant field for peer review. This means an evaluation of both the scientific worth v_j of the project and the qualification a_{ij} of the applicant i. The foundation then performs a cost–benefit analysis, admitting projects with:

$$a_{ij}v_j/k_{ij} \geq m. \tag{5.46a}$$

How close does this procedure come to the recommendations (5.42) and (5.46) that were derived above? The difficulty of strictly applying Equation (5.46) instead of Equation (5.46a) lies in knowing the opportunity costs w_i. An exact calculation of these requires nothing less than solving Equations (5.37), (5.40) and (5.41) numerically.

An approximation to the w_i may be seen in the market worth of the principal investigator i, that is, his or her salary (plus other benefits which may be substantial). If the w_i are omitted all together, the net social worth of all projects is overstated, but so also would be the cut-off point m. These distortions may actually be small compared with the uncertainties about scientific worth v_j, particularly when comparisons are needed between various disciplines.

What then is the state of 'freedom of choice' in sponsored research today? In sponsored research the cost–benefit criterion appears as a restriction, but not as an a priori elimination, of the researchers' range of choice. Freedom of choice remains within these cost-imposed limits.

Of course, the decision process about what research is to be done and by whom is only as good as the estimates v_j (scientific worth) and a_{ij} (scientists' productivities). Peers may not be unbiased when asked to judge the intentions and qualifications of others who may be potential competitors. Moreover, the scientific community may be blind to truly innovative ideas and divided on issues of scientific worth. Still, reliance on peer review may be our best hope, in the sense of being preferable to arbitrary judgements by innocent or not so innocent administrators. It behoves us to remember John Stuart Mill's ([1859], 1975, p. 130) dictum that 'the price of liberty is eternal vigilance'.

DISTRIBUTION: KNOWLEDGE USED BY POLICY-MAKERS

The purpose of production is consumption, says Adam Smith. Is this true also for knowledge? After all, the use of knowledge never entails its consumption. Still, if knowledge production is to be more than *l'art pour l'art* it must be justified by the use of knowledge.

The users of knowledge are easily grouped as:

- Researchers
- Teachers
- Students
- Policy-makers
- Business firms
- The general public as consumers.

In the social sciences, applicants for grants are well advised to emphasize the social benefits of their research, in particular the potential improvements of social welfare. Concretely this mostly means usefulness to policy-makers.

From its beginnings, economics has been policy-oriented. Pure economic theory is policy-relevant, even when its conclusion is that no government action is called for. For example, neoclassical growth theory leads to advice on how to increase economic growth, while the economics of research and development implies measures that stimulate technological progress. Location theory, considered as pure economics, provides the foundation for regional policies. Welfare theory and sociology have much to contribute to policies that aim at improving the social welfare of the poor. Since Adam Smith, economics has targeted the wealth and well-being of nations and its citizens. To this encomium of economics, the unjustly called 'dismal science', we have little to add and thus turn to the business sector and general public as consumers of knowledge.

KNOWLEDGE AS INPUT IN PRODUCTION

In purely economic terms, the most important use of knowledge is as an input in production. Consider a representative business firm. Assume for simplicity a linear technology for a firm making products $i = 1,...,n$. Material inputs and labour are not considered explicitly, only profit margins g_i (before knowledge costs) and knowledge input coefficients a_{ik} for knowledge of type k required in the production of i.

The market for product i is limited to a fixed quantity (to be standardized at unity), within which the profit margin is g_i. In other words, we assume a rectangular demand curve. The generalization to an arbitrary demand function is straightforward. It leads to a concave non-linear programme with Kuhn–Tucker conditions in place of linear programming efficiency conditions.

Now knowledge use has two significant aspects. Knowledge items are 'lumpy', used either in full or not at all. Second, knowledge is non-rivalrous – that is, it can be used simultaneously in several activities. Moreover, knowledge is not used up but remains available, although that is irrelevant in this context.

Formally, this means that knowledge is a zero–one variable to the firm. Allocation of resources therefore becomes a mixed integer-linear programme. Assume that demand is given and standardized to be one unit. The firm chooses production x_i of products i and uses y_k of knowledge items k to maximize net profits:

$$\max \sum_i g_i x_i - \sum_k p_k y_k$$

with given knowledge costs p_k and restrictions:

$$0 \le x_i \le 1$$

$$y_i \ge \alpha_{ik} x_i .$$

This mixed integer linear programme can in fact be solved as a linear programme, with output and knowledge utilization variables x_j and y_k being treated as continuous non-negative variables. The Lagrange function to be maximized is then:

$$L = \sum_i g_i x_i - \sum_k p_k y_k + \sum_{i,k} \lambda_{ik} \left(y_k - a_{ik} x_i \right) + \sum_i \mu_i \left(1 - x_i \right) \quad (5.47)$$

and the efficiency conditions of the linear programme are:

$$x_i \begin{Bmatrix} = \\ \ge \end{Bmatrix} 0 \quad \Leftrightarrow \quad g_i \begin{Bmatrix} < \\ = \end{Bmatrix} \sum_k a_{ik} \lambda_{ik} + \mu_1 \quad (5.48)$$

$$y_k \begin{Bmatrix} = \\ \ge \end{Bmatrix} 0 \quad \Leftrightarrow \quad p_k \begin{Bmatrix} > \\ = \end{Bmatrix} \sum_i \lambda_{ik} \quad (5.49)$$

$$\lambda_{ik}\begin{Bmatrix} = \\ \geq \end{Bmatrix}0 \Leftrightarrow y_k\begin{Bmatrix} > \\ = \end{Bmatrix}a_{ik}x_k \tag{5.50}$$

$$\mu_i\begin{Bmatrix} = \\ \geq \end{Bmatrix}0 \Leftrightarrow x_i\begin{Bmatrix} < \\ = \end{Bmatrix}1. \tag{5.51}$$

The formulae (5.49) and (5.50) are in fact the Lindahl criteria for common use, here in terms of the production processes x_i. Statement (5.48) is the profitability test, with $\mu_i \geq 0$ as net profit. Mathematically, this is comparable to the (linear) 'assignment problem' (Koopmans and Beckmann, 1957), where an integer programming problem is reduced to a linear programme and yields an economic interpretation.

As an example, consider seven production processes, i, using three items of knowledge, k, in the seven possible combinations of Table 5.1, which lists the knowledge input coefficients, a_{ik}. In Table 5.2, the assessments λ_{ik} of product i for use of k are shown. They satisfy the profitability and Lindahl conditions (5.48) and (5.49), with $\mu_i = 0$. All products can be produced. There is no surplus since knowledge costs absorb all profits:

$$\sum_i g_i = 16 = \sum_k p_k$$

Any increase in the price of some k would eliminate not just the products i using this k, but all others as well – since all are needed for sharing their knowledge costs.

Table 5.1 Knowledge inputs a_{ik}

i \ k	1	2	3	g_i
1	1			1
2		2		2
3		1	2	3
4	1	2	1	4
5		1	2	3
6	1		1	2
7	1			1
p_k	4	6	6	

Table 5.2 Assessments λ_{ik} of products i and knowledge costs p_k

i \ k	1	2	3	g_i
1	1			1
2		2		2
3			3	3
4	2	2		4
5		1	2	3
6	1		1	2
7		1		1
p_k	4	6	6	

The given prices (p_k) of knowledge are either the licence fees or the costs of in-house knowledge production. In this case, knowledge production or acquisition is strictly business.

REFLECTIONS ON THE KNOWLEDGE CONSUMER

Knowledge is offered to the general public orally – in lectures and in the media – or in written form as books, magazines and newspapers. It is demanded for instruction or amusement and sometimes both.

Non-fiction comes in amazing variety. Examples include inspirational non-fiction (since Seneca and Thomas à Kempis) as self-help, advice on finance, health, nutrition, fitness, cooking, gardening, collecting, travel, biography and history as well as popular psychology, social science and economics. Interests vary widely: Sherlock Holmes ignored the solar system as having no relevance to the detection of criminals. Many of us pooh-pooh horoscopes and astrology or the 'new age' literature.

In fiction we find the classics of literature and an enormous outpouring of popular novels and stories including detective stories, adventure, romance, erotica, historical novels, science fiction and pure fantasy. Readers are drawn by their past experience to favourite authors (often bestsellers) or by the advice of critics, friends, helpful librarians as well as critical reviews (the blurbs on book covers always promise a masterpiece and are thus of little help).

The line between serious literature and entertainment is often hard to draw. Best-selling authors have usually found an appealing formula. Sexual explicitness helps and fantastic inventions trump realism. By contrast, classical literature has the appeal of worthwhile facts in combination with entertainment.

RATIONING OF KNOWLEDGE

There is a substantial literature on the economics of patents. Treating patents as the best proxy variable for new technical knowledge, the main theme of the economics of patents has been to establish and measure the relationship between knowledge (that is, patents) and the economic growth of firms, industries, markets, regions and nations (Mansfield, 1968; Scherer, 1984; Ernst, 1996; Brenner and Greif, 2006). Greif has developed and researched a comprehensive database on German patents. In particular, he has used the database to analyse the geography of patents and its relationship to the geography of firms (Greif, 2001).

MAINTENANCE OF KNOWLEDGE

The maintenance of ideas in persons means teaching them to successors. Ideas in documents are maintained by being worked over: reviewed, re-examined, revised, criticized – when not rejected completely, the documents may be qualified, specialized, exemplified, generalized, quantified and so on. The job of maintaining the documents themselves is entrusted to archives and libraries. Libraries thus fulfil several functions: preserving knowledge, making knowledge available for research and making knowledge available to the public for instruction and entertainment.

Research libraries should aim at completeness and accessibility. Completeness can never be one hundred per cent, since there is hardly enough storage space for an exponentially growing literature. The resulting selectivity means that libraries face difficult decisions that have to be taken under conditions of uncertainty. As Philip Morse (1968) shows, borrowing obeys a stochastic process in which future demand is raised by present borrowing. But a book may be a hidden classic while a current sleeper. Decisions to discard should thus not be made hastily on the basis of short-term lapses of demand.

Library fees charged per book do, of course, impose an obstacle to circulation more than period-based fees.

NOTE

1. This section is revised from Beckmann, M. (1999), 'Bidding for Research Funds', in U. Leopold-Wildburger, G. Feichtinger and K.P. Kirchner (eds), *Modelling and Decisions in Economics: Essays in Honor of Franz Ferschl*, Heidelberg: Physica Verlag.

6 Household Knowledge Investments

At the beginning of the 20th century most contemporary economically developed countries were only moderately industrialized. The general level of education was quite limited as can be illustrated by the following quote:

> In 1976 the average stock of formal education per person in these [industrialized] countries was 9.7 years, in 1950 it was 8.2 years. The evidence for a few countries suggests that in 1870 the average stock of education per person in these countries was about three to four years, with substantial sections of the population illiterate and with very little higher education at all (Maddison, 1982, p. 111).

In 1976, there was substantial variability in the formal education of the labour force, with the United States having the highest average level of education (11.6 years) while Italy's average education level was as low as 6.9 years of formal education. In 1992, the average level of education in the OECD countries had reached 11.3 years and the level of education of the US adult population was then 12.6 years. By 2005, the average level of education in the United States exceeded 14 years for the population between 25 and 64 years of age.

The financing of higher education has consequently become a major issue for most households in developed countries. However, in many countries some – or even most – of the educational funding requirements for households have been met by tax-funded provision of higher education.

The education distribution in 1900 was skewed – a small segment of the population had up to 18 years of schooling. The limited educational capacity was reserved for the prospective leaders of industry and the bureaucracy. The funding of their schooling was also seen as a limited problem. Education costs were normally out-of-pocket expenses for their well-to-do parents.

All of the industrialized countries have since then undergone a dramatic increase in the average number of school years of their populations. Meanwhile, the variability has been radically decreased – both in absolute and relative terms. The required duration of formal education for leaders of government and industry is still, in the first decade of the 21st century, around 18 years, while the average number of school years has risen to between 12 and 14 years in the OECD countries.

INVESTING IN EDUCATION

The importance of knowledge as an input in the economy was discussed already by Adam Smith in his *Wealth of Nations* (1776). The acquisition of knowledge by education was by Smith assumed to be regulated by the same mechanisms as the accumulation of material capital.

If we disregard the direct consumption utility of higher education, then the size of the voluntary educational effort is regulated by an ordinary household investment calculation in which the sum of discounted real income effects of investment in higher education is compared with the (almost immediate) cost of the education. Each potential choice of education would imply a different net present value and the informed consumer would choose the education giving the highest expected net present value.

A simple deterministic model can be used to illustrate the importance of the income and consumption (or direct utility-increasing) effects of education. In the model we assume that the utility of an individual is not only influenced by the prospective level of consumption but also by the level of education, within the aspired occupational career. We furthermore assume that the level of education is costly, but that it would also increase life-time income. For the moment we also disregard the problem of discounting future incomes as well as the uncertainty associated with the future. In the model the utility function is assumed to be concave and differentiable (at least twice). It is further assumed that income as a function of schooling exhibits diminishing returns. The problem is thus the following:

$$\text{Maximize } u = u(c,s) \tag{6.1}$$

$$\text{subject to } c + p_s s = y(s)$$

where

u = utility
c = consumption
s = schooling time
y = total life income.

The price of the consumption basket is for convenience assumed to equal one. Consumption is thus measured in the same dimension as income. The necessary conditions for an optimal choice of consumption, income and schooling is given by the following Lagrangian maximization:

$$\max_{\{c,s,\lambda\}} L = u(c,s) - \lambda\left[c + p_s s - y(s)\right]. \tag{6.2}$$

The necessary conditions for maximization, which under the assumptions made are also sufficient, are the following:

$$\frac{\partial L}{\partial c} = \frac{\partial u}{\partial c} - \lambda = 0 \tag{6.3}$$

$$\frac{\partial L}{\partial s} = \frac{\partial u}{\partial s} - \lambda\left(p_s - \frac{\partial y}{\partial s}\right) = 0 \tag{6.4}$$

$$\frac{\partial L}{\partial \lambda} = c + p_s s - y(s) = 0 \tag{6.5}$$

that is $\frac{\partial u}{\partial s}\Big/\frac{\partial u}{\partial c} + \frac{\partial y}{\partial s} = p_s$; $\qquad \frac{\partial u}{\partial s}\Big/\frac{\partial u}{\partial c} = -\frac{dc}{ds} \equiv W_s$

$$W_s + \frac{\partial y}{\partial s} = p_s.$$

These optimality conditions should be interpreted as follows:

1. The marginal utility of consumption must equal the implicit price of consumption, which is equal to the implicit price of income.
2. Substituting $\partial u/\partial y$ for λ in Equation (6.4) gives the second condition, implying that the marginal rate of substitution between income and years of schooling should equal the price of schooling minus the marginal income return to schooling.

If utility is only dependent on lifetime consumption the optimality conditions reduce to:

$$\frac{\partial u}{\partial c} = \lambda; \quad \frac{\partial y}{\partial s} = p_s; \quad \text{and } c + p_s = y(s).$$

If the only objective of schooling is to achieve maximum life income, then the optimality requirement would be to choose a number of periods (say months) of schooling at which the price of schooling corresponds to the marginal lifetime income return. Otherwise the marginal return to schooling plus the marginal willingness to pay for schooling (the marginal rate of substitution of schooling for income or consumption) should equal the price of schooling. With the assumptions made, this implies that formal education that exerts a direct positive influence on utility leads to an increase in the duration of schooling.

DYNAMICS OF RETURNS TO EDUCATION INVESTMENTS

Investments in higher education can be looked upon as any other investment decision problem. The simplification of the above model is obvious. The individual is there assumed to have a life plan which involves consumption and education. In reality the decision to invest in education is taken each year after the completion of high school. The decision to spend the next year at some college or university involves a cost; $C(0)$. The cost normally includes tuition, fees and the loss of income during the coming year. The revenue from an additional year of schooling is the real wage income increment that will accrue in future years. The increment must be large enough to compensate for costs incurred during the school year. The net present value of investing in an additional year of education can therefore be formulated as:

$$N(0) = -C(0) + \int_1^T \Delta W(t) e^{-rt} dt \tag{6.6}$$

where

$N(0)$ = net present value of education investment at time 0
$\Delta W(t)$ = annual real income increment of education (at cost C)
r = discount rate (= real opportunity rate of return)
g = expected rate of growth of annual real wage advantage
$C(0)$ = cost of education investment at time 0.

There is ample evidence that the annual real income increment from investments in education will be increasing over time. Assume that:

$$\Delta W(t) = \Delta W(1) e^{gt}; \quad \text{and } r > g. \tag{6.7}$$

The integral of Equation (6.6) has a value as shown in Equation (6.8):

$$N(0) = -C(0) + \Delta W(1) \frac{1}{r-g}\left(1 - e^{rT}\right). \tag{6.8}$$

Most higher education investment decisions are taken between the ages of 17 and 25. This implies that the duration of work will be no less than 40 years in most cases. With a reasonably high discount rate the exponential term of Equation (6.8) will be close to zero. Then:

$$N(0) \cong -C(0) + \frac{\Delta W(1)}{r-g}. \tag{6.9}$$

The internal (marginal) percentage return to an education investment with cost $C(0)$ is defined as:

$$r = \frac{\Delta W(1)}{C(0)} + g. \tag{6.10}$$

If, for example, the yearly real wage income increment of an additional year of education amounts to \$10 000, the cost of education is \$100 000, and the rate of growth of the yearly wage advantage is expected to be 2 per cent, then the percentage return to investing in one additional year of education is 12 per cent.

Let us now assume that the net present value of the first year of education after high school is positive. After the first year of 'higher' education the student can recalculate the net present value, and this can be done year after year as shown in Equations (6.7) to (6.10). Each year a decision can be taken to stay in education as long as the net present value of a further year of education is positive. The investment process will go on until the net present value of a further year of education equals zero. Proceeding with an education beyond the point of zero net present value indicates a pure consumption value from extending the years of studying. The decision problem can be illustrated in Figure 6.1,

where

a = duration of education in years
r = discount rate
g = expected real growth rate of the wage rate with an additional year of education
$N(a)$ = net present value of education
$\Delta W(a)$ = yearly wage increment with an additional year of education
$(1 + \alpha)W(a)$ = cost of an additional year of education.

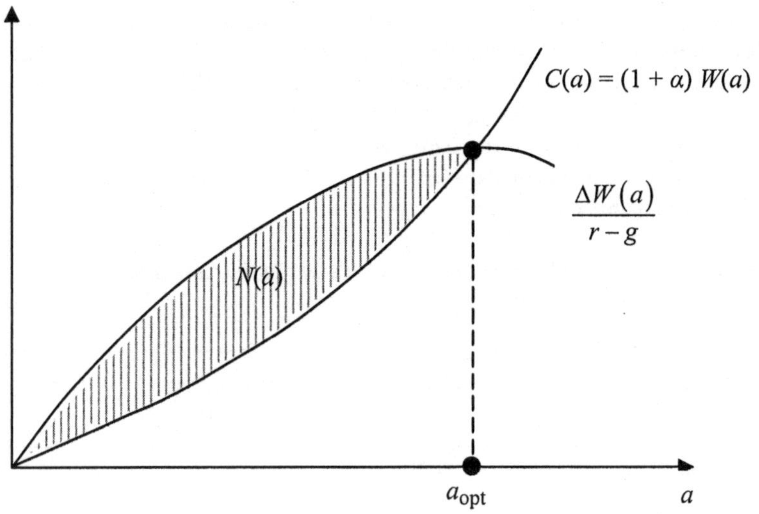

Figure 6.1 Development over time of the net present value of additional education

INTERNATIONAL COMPARATIVE STUDIES OF THE IMPACT OF EDUCATION ON INCOME

There have been a large number of studies of the empirical relationship between education and income. All support the conclusion that there is a strong positive association between personal income and the level of education (ceteris paribus). Explaining income as the effect of education duration while controlling for age and gender yields the following parameter estimates for Sweden in 1990 (Table 6.1). The estimation is based on census data for groups.

There is no self-evident way of deciding on a best functional form and therefore a number of different forms were tested. A popular form is the Becker–Mincer Equation in which log income is a linear function of education. The log–log equation used has the advantage of decreasing marginal returns to education and experience. The rate of return is approximately 10 per cent at the level of junior high school and decreases to approximately 5 per cent at the level of university education. The result is robust and in all cases the number of years of education has a much greater influence on the level of income than the age of the individual (which can be considered an approximate measure of work experience). Likewise, the influence of gender is stable over the various tested functional forms. This rather large gender effect can either be explained as a consequence of discrimination or by a possible preference for more interesting but less profitable work among women. Other empirical material from Sweden would suggest that both factors are at work in determining the lower returns to education for women as compared with men. A similar estimation based on household budget survey data for 1969 results in an elasticity of education of 0.7 with a t-value of 4.4.

Table 6.1 Personal income as a function of gender, age and years of education, Sweden, 1990

Variable	Coefficient	Standard error of estimate	t-value
Intercept	2.307		
Gender (female = 1, male = 0)	–0.248	0.026	9.615
ln of age (experience)	0.320	0.050	6.425
ln of years of education	0.727	0.050	14.689

Source: Statistics Sweden (1992).

These econometric results indicate decreasing returns to education. They also indicate that the impact of education is substantially greater than the returns from experience (or learning-by-doing).

In some of the studies that are based on micro-data it has been possible to separate private from public returns. In most of these studies, the return to education is calculated as the net return on investment under standardized assumptions regarding the investment cost of education and the discounted flow of net income (after deduction of taxes). Some studies also include the governmental investment cost and base their income calculations on gross income (including taxes). In many of the estimations an econometric procedure that was first proposed by Jacob Mincer (1974) has been used. In that proposed econometric equation the logarithm of income was assumed to be linearly dependent on the number of years of schooling. Table 6.2 provides a summary of estimated returns to education investments in different countries, as presented by the OECD.

As has been argued above, there are strong analytical reasons for expecting the returns to investments in education to vary among occupations as a consequence of differences in the volatility of salaries and other risks associated with the choice of an education and occupation – as well as differences in the consumption value of different educations and occupations.

Table 6.3 gives some indications of occupational differences in returns to educational investments.

Table 6.2 Returns to higher education (university education) by country and gender, 1992, per cent

	Male	Female
France	16	12
Finland	15	14
Germany	14	9
USA	13	12
Sweden	12	10
Denmark	11	8
Netherlands (1989)	10	8
Switzerland	8	5
Belgium (1989)	8	13
Average	12	10

Source: OECD (1995).

Table 6.3 Returns to investment in education by country and industry or occupation, percentages

Industry/ occupation	Canada (1985)	France (1971, 1975)	UK (1971, 1975)	Japan (1970)	USA (1978)
Private employment		12	9	19	9
Public employment		8	6	7	9
Commerce or law	13	14			
Engineering	14	n.a.			
Medicine	22	13			

Note: n.a. = not available.

Source: Psacharopoulos (1994).

The estimates in Table 6.3 indicate considerable differences in the returns to education across occupations. Public employment tends to give smaller returns than private employment, probably as a consequence of the higher risk of unemployment in the private sector.

Marginal returns to education tend to be a decreasing function of the level of education of the individual. It also tends to be a decreasing function of economic development. Table 6.4 illustrates the development effect.

Table 6.4 Returns to investment in education in countries at different levels of economic development, average returns in percentages, 2001

	Level of education	
Countries by per capita income	Secondary	Tertiary
Low income (≤ USD 755)	15.7	11.2
Middle income (USD 756 to 9265)	12.9	11.3
High income (≥ USD 9266)	10.3	9.5

Source: Psacharopoulos and Patrinos (2002).

Table 6.5, compiled from Psacharopoulos and Patrinos (2002), provides an overview of estimated returns to education in different developed economies. The table shows that an unweighted average return is 8.3 per cent. A number of economists have consistently estimated the returns to higher education investments to be around 10 per cent in the United States. According to Table 6.5, returns to investments in education have been substantially higher in the United States, Britain, Canada and Japan than in most parts of Europe.

Table 6.6 shows the returns to education as reported for men and women in studies from the 1980s and 1990s. Nine out of the twelve studies indicate somewhat higher returns to education for women with clear exceptions in Denmark and Sweden.

Table 6.5 *Estimates of returns to investment in higher education, percentages, 1980–95*

	1980	1981	1982	1983	1984	1985	1986	1987	1988	1989	1990	1991	1992	1993	1994	1995	Average
Japan									13.2								13.2
Britain			15.3		13.3			6.8									11.8
USA								9.8				10.0	10.0	10.0	10.0	10.0	10.0
Canada		8.5					8.8			8.9							8.7
Finland	9.1							7.0		8.2		8.8		8.2			8.3
Australia	7.9	8.4				10.9		5.4		8.0							8.1
Austria		11.6		7.9		7.6		7.4		7.6		7.4		7.2			8.1
Spain						7.7					9.0	7.1					7.9
Switzerland								7.9			7.5						7.7
Netherlands	10.9		7.0			7.2	5.2		5.7	7.3					6.4		7.1
Germany							5.5		7.7								6.6
Norway	5.5			6.1				5.4		4.9		5.4				5.5	5.5
Italy				5.5		4.5	4.6	2.7									4.3
Sweden		3.5			3.9						4.5	3.5					3.9
Denmark	2.6										4.5						3.6
Average																	8.3

Sources: See note 1.

Table 6.6 Returns to investments in education by gender

	Men	Women
All levels of education		
Austria (1981)	10.3	13.5
Denmark (1990)	5.1	3.4
Finland (1993)	7.8	8.3
Italy (1985)	3.5	3.9
Norway (1991)	4.2	5.3
Sweden (1991)	5.0	4.0
Switzerland (1995)	9.1	9.0
Tertiary education		
Canada (1985)	8.3	18.8
Denmark (1990)	3.5	5.2
Finland (1987)	6.6	7.7
Norway (1991)	4.0	4.2
Sweden (1991)	4.4	4.0

Source: Psacharopoulos and Patrinos (2002).

COMPARATIVE ANALYSIS OF PRIVATE RETURNS TO EDUCATION IN EUROPE

The comparative results reported above provide a rough overview of estimates of returns to educational investments in different parts of the world based on different approaches to the estimation problem. A weakness of this analysis is the heterogeneity of method, databases and time periods. This heterogeneity has to a large extent been avoided in a large study (PURE) by Asplund (2001). In that study, returns to higher education have been estimated for fifteen European Union member states based on data for the mid-1990s.

Figure 6.2 shows that the average real rate of return amounts to about seven per cent in Western Europe. However, the between-country variability is substantial. Labour markets in Portugal, Spain, Britain and Ireland generate much greater returns than in Denmark, Sweden, Norway and the Netherlands. These differences in returns point to the effect of differences in the degree of public funding of higher education. The Scandinavian welfare states employ extensive subsidies not only of students' tuition and fees but also of their living expenses. This has tended to encourage a longer period of enrolment in higher education. It has also encouraged educational orientations associated with occupations that have few opportunities of gainful employment, which has reduced the average real wage advantage of higher education and the average private rate of return.

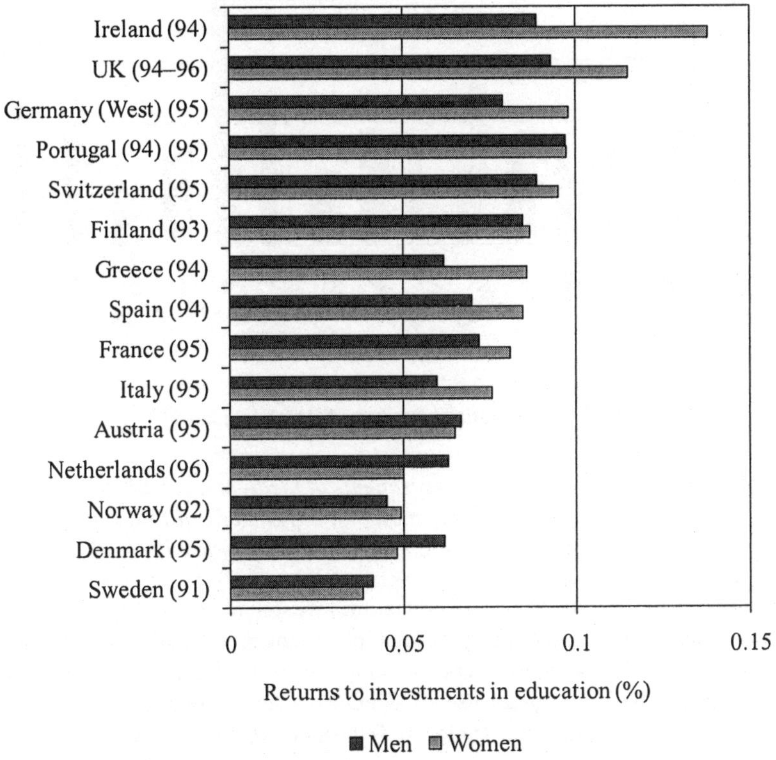

Figure 6.2 *Returns to investments in education by gender (Source: Asplund, 2001)*

The empirical studies also sometimes show non-trivial gender differences in the returns to higher education. Women have had much higher returns to education than men in Britain, Germany, Greece and Ireland. The opposite is the case in the Netherlands, Sweden and Denmark. The PURE study group has also shown that there has been a substantial decline in the real returns to education in the EU countries between the 1960s and the 1970s, and stabilization at around 6.5 per cent thereafter.

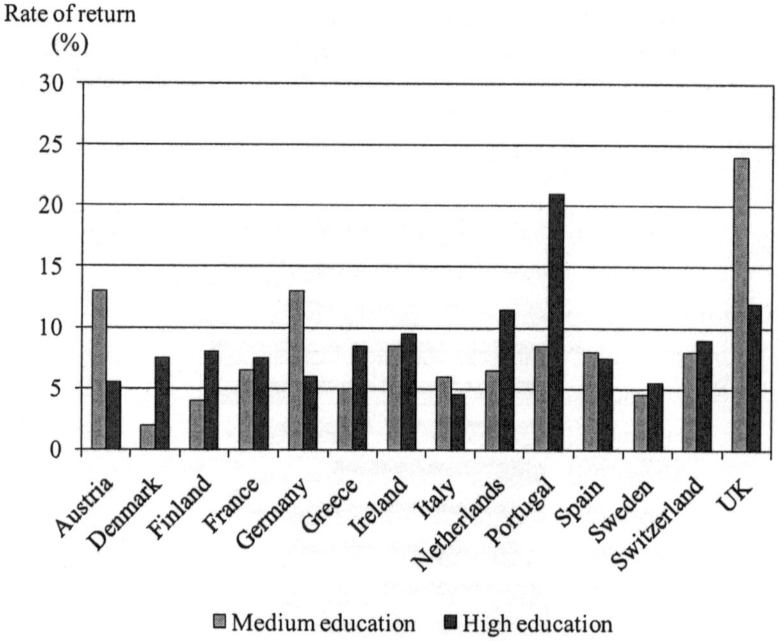

Figure 6.3 Rates of returns to investments in medium (secondary) and higher (tertiary) education, not adjusted for differences in unemployment, men (Source: Barceinas-Paredes et al., 2001)

In most studies, the return on education investments is estimated under the assumption that the probability of unemployment is independent of the level of education. This is an erroneous assumption in most countries – especially in Europe. The widespread use of egalitarian negotiation strategies in the labour market implies that (unionized) insiders in low education jobs will have wage rates that are well above equilibrium levels. As a consequence unemployment rates tend to decrease with increasing levels of education. According to Nickell (1979), the rates of return should be adjusted for expected unemployment. This implies that we should expect these unemployment adjustments to raise the returns to education in most European countries. Figure 6.4 gives the unemployment-adjusted internal rates of return to secondary and tertiary education in a number of European countries.

As can be seen from the diagram the adjustment is substantial, especially for secondary education. The unemployment adjustment is especially pronounced in Britain, Germany, Ireland and Portugal. The returns to secondary education in Britain are – after adjustment – approximately 30 per cent and for tertiary education almost 15 per cent. It is obvious that expectations of greater employability play a more important role in the decision to continue from compulsory to non-compulsory education as compared with the decision to proceed from secondary to higher education. The effect of improved employability exists but is quite small in Sweden, Finland and Denmark, which should be a reflection of generous unemployment benefits in the Nordic countries.

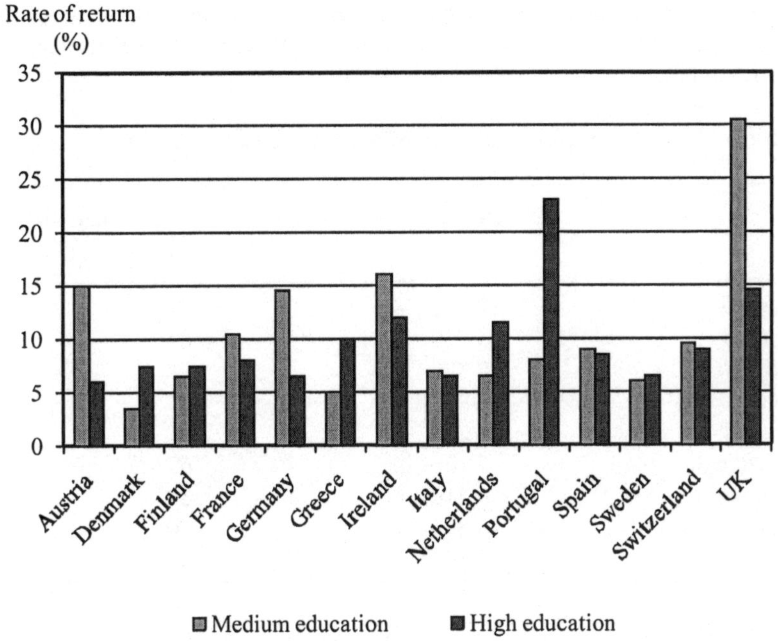

Figure 6.4 Unemployment-adjusted returns to investments in secondary (medium) and tertiary (high) education, men (Source: Barceinas-Paredes et al., 2001)

FINANCING HIGHER EDUCATION

There are considerable differences between countries in their public funding of higher education (universities and similar institutions). Table 6.7 provides some examples of these differences.

Public expenditure per student in the USA was (and still is) higher in absolute terms than in most developed countries during the 1990s, although the public share of expenditures was only 50 per cent of total expenditure per student. The major cost of living expenses and many years of foregone income remains a considerable financial burden, which is mostly addressed by student loans or parental subsidies.

At the Ph.D. level most countries have developed some combination of scholarships and part-time employment for students, which is not the case for the bulk of college and university students. For the early years of higher education there is in most cases a need for financing from loanable funds at some rate of interest. For the analysis of the optimality problem it is convenient to formulate optimization models that can highlight some of the important factors involved in the choice of an optimal educational strategy for the household.

Table 6.7 Public sector contributions to higher education, 1992

	Expenditure per student (USD)	Public share of expenditure
Canada	12 350	85
France	5 760	84
Britain	10 370	78
Netherlands	8 720	71
Ireland	7 270	67
Sweden	7 120	63
Denmark	6 710	62
United States	13 890	50
Japan	7 140	40

Source: OECD (2001a).

In the United States, a large part of the cost of higher education is shouldered by the student and his or her family. Tuition, fees and course material such as textbooks can amount to a very substantial part of the cost of higher education. This cost regularly amounts to $30 000 or more per year. Living expenses must be added to these costs.

In Europe the situation is quite different. In many countries such as Germany, the Netherlands and the Scandinavian countries, higher education is free from direct user charges. Other living expenses are usually covered by state subsidies, grants or loans. As an example, governments in Denmark and the Netherlands cover living expenses by offering grants that amount to two-thirds of the normal cost, while the remaining living expenses are covered by student loans. Many countries in Europe have however been changing their system from grants to loans. Norway, Sweden and Britain are examples of such a change of the financing of living expenses into a system of repayable loans. In 1999, Britain changed its system into 100 per cent loans to cover the cost of living. In Norway and Sweden the share of loans has increased to 80 per cent of the expected cost of living, with grants accounting for the remaining 20 per cent. In most countries, the interest rate on student loans implies that a portion of the risk is carried by the state. In the cases of Britain and Sweden, the risks of education-related debt are reduced for the student by income-contingent repayment rules.

Public policies such as subsidies to cover education investment costs and taxation of education-derived income obviously influence the private returns to education investments. Individual returns are thus in most countries influenced by the marginal taxation of income as well as by subsidies during time of schooling. Formally, the internal rate of return calculated at zero net present value, r_0, is:

$$r_0 = \frac{\Delta W}{C} \cdot \frac{1-\tau}{1-\sigma} + g \tag{6.11}$$

where

τ = marginal rate of taxation of income increments
σ = share of education cost that is covered by government subsidies.

This internal rate of return is calculated under the assumption that a fixed percentage share is deducted from the total cost and that taxes amount to a fixed percentage share of wages. It is furthermore assumed that the income increment will persist for a period that is sufficiently long to allow us to view the equation as an approximation of reality.

Some developing countries impose low rates of income tax, while costs of education are covered by government funds to a significant extent. One typical example is Hong Kong, where the internal rate of return to education, unadjusted for subsidies and taxes, was 12.4 per cent. The private return adjusted for taxes and subsidies, however, was at the same time estimated to be as much as 25.2 per cent (Psacharopoulos, 1994). By contrast, the average adjusted rates of return have been estimated to be about 2 per cent lower than the unadjusted rates in Belgium, Denmark, Netherlands, Norway and also in Sweden.

UNCERTAINTY OF RETURNS

As in any other type of investment, the returns to education are uncertain. Some jobs are associated with industries that are more susceptible to business cycles and other fluctuations than others. Examples of industries with an above-average exposure to fluctuations are stock brokerage, construction engineering, architecture and trade in information and communication equipment. In the same way that securities exhibit different combinations of expected return and risk, the young consumers (or their parents) are faced with a choice between different combinations of risk and uncertainty as illustrated in Figure 6.5.

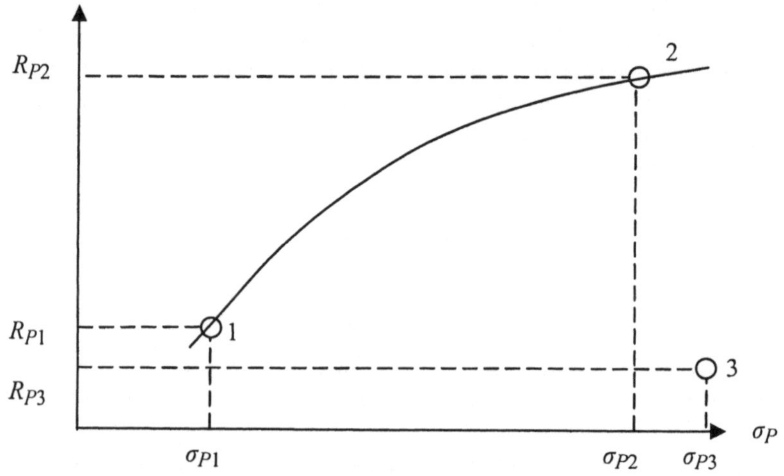

Figure 6.5 Expected returns (R) and risks (σ) of investment portfolios. (The curve from point 1 to point 2 indicates the maximum combinations of opportunities of different investment portfolios. All points below the opportunity curve are feasible but inefficient portfolios)

Point 1 in the diagram indicates the choice of an investment portfolio or – by analogy – an education that is associated with low returns and minimal risk. A realistic example is an education that qualifies the student for some well-established public sector position. The choice of education (and occupation) can therefore be seen as one investment within the overall household investment portfolio. A relatively low-risk portfolio of investment assets may also include a residential property in a safe neighbourhood and a set of government bonds rather than securities.

Point 2 indicates a different risk orientation in the choice of the household portfolio, which could for example consist of an education that leads to a job as a financial broker, a condominium on Manhattan and a set of high-tech securities. A high rate of expected return would then be combined with a substantial risk of negative returns or even bankruptcy.

Point 3 in the diagram indicates an inefficient point in the sense that a low rate of return is combined with a high risk. Such choices do occur quite frequently, but need not be an indication of irrationality or insufficient information about returns and risks. Point 3 could just as well correspond to a career choice that exhibits an inefficient combination of expected pecuniary return (but not expected utility) and risk as is found in the arts, humanities and professional sports. In these cases the empirical evidence suggests that the choice of such creative occupations is guided not only by financial returns but equally or even more by consumer preferences for the occupational activity itself. To the pecuniary returns one must therefore add the willingness to pay for an education that leads to an occupation that the prospective student considers intrinsically enjoyable. The willingness to pay for this type of work-as-consumption could be measured as the vertical distance from point 3 in the figure to the income opportunity frontier curve.

In a psychological study, G. Smith and I. Carlsson (1990) show that creative individuals in the arts and sciences are only weakly motivated by standard economic incentives. Recent statistics from Sweden also show that some creative workers such as architectural consultants have much lower returns to their education than, for example, management consultants and lawyers with similar education levels. One explanation could then be that many students perceive a career in law or business to be less attractive in its work-as-consumption sense than a career in architecture.

INCREASING INCOME INEQUALITY BETWEEN EDUCATION LEVELS IN THE UNITED STATES AND EUROPE

The development in the United States over the three decades after 1973 indicates a substantial change in the returns to education. In 1975, the real average wage rate difference between a college graduate and a high school drop-out was 116 per cent, which corresponds to an expected average gross return per school year of less than 9 per cent. In 2003 the real wage rate difference had increased to 192 per cent, or an expected average (gross) return per school year of close to 12 per cent. The widening real income gap between different education levels is further illustrated by Tables 6.8 and 6.9.

In Europe, the development of wage inequality by level of education has been somewhat different as is shown in Figure 6.6.

There are two main causes of the increasing real wage gap between workers with different levels of educational attainment:

1. The increasing global division of labour, with outsourcing of low education jobs to newly industrialized countries.
2. The increasing focus on knowledge-intensive goods and services in the United States and other advanced economies.

Table 6.8 Development of hourly wages by highest educational qualification in 2003 US dollars, United States, 1975–2003, (100 = less than high school in 1975)

	Less than high school	High school	Some college	Bachelor's degree	Advanced degree
1975	100.0	116.5	125.6	168.7	215.8
1980	104.2	116.6	126.3	166.4	202.3
1985	96.4	114.3	126.5	175.5	220.3
1990	90.5	111.0	126.8	179.0	229.7
1995	83.5	110.5	123.6	183.4	241.9
2000	86.8	116.8	132.8	204.0	258.0
2003	90.0	120.7	135.5	208.5	263.2
Wage increase by level of education, 2003		+34.0%	+12.2%	+53.9%	+26.2%
Gross return from one additional year of education		+11.0%	+12.0%	+27.0%	+9.0%

Table 6.9 Average annual change of real wage rate, percentages, United States

	Less than high school	High school	Bachelor's degree	Advanced degree
1975–1984	–0.4	–0.2	+0.4	+0.2
1985–1994	–1.4	–0.3	+0.4	+0.9
1995–2003	+0.9	+1.1	+1.6	+1.1

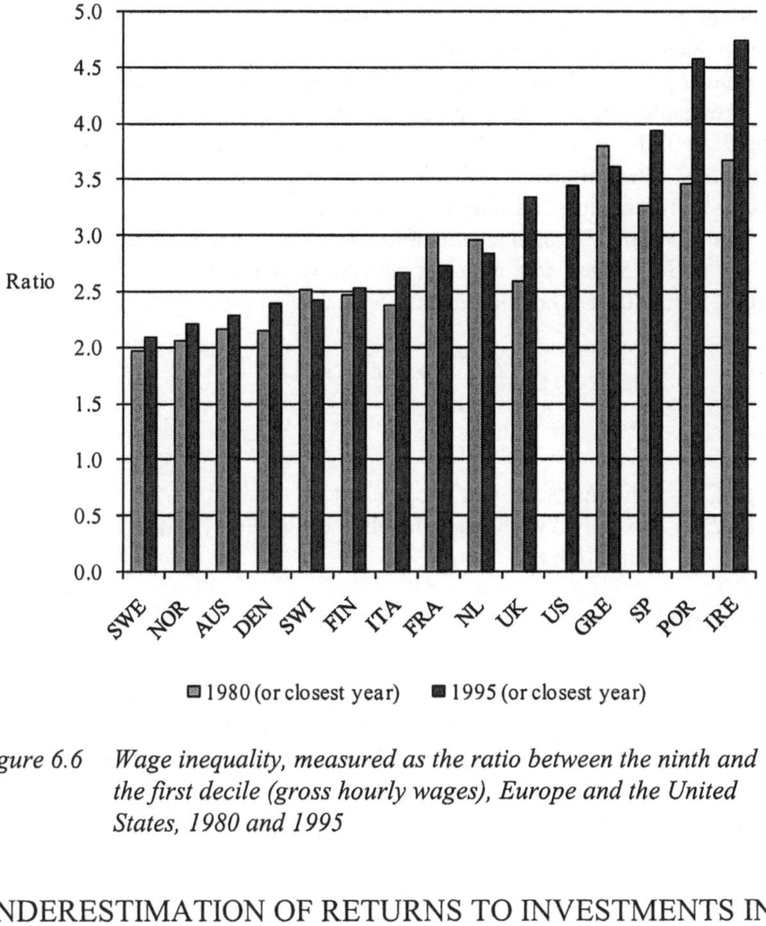

Figure 6.6 *Wage inequality, measured as the ratio between the ninth and the first decile (gross hourly wages), Europe and the United States, 1980 and 1995*

UNDERESTIMATION OF RETURNS TO INVESTMENTS IN EDUCATION

Reduced Transaction Costs

Conventional estimates of economic returns are based on simplified assumptions. Although it is common to refer to non-pecuniary benefits, it is much less common to estimate or indicate such benefits in the discussion of econometric results. (However, see Barasinska et al. (2008)).

An obvious consequence of most kinds of higher education is the reduction of many types of transaction cost that result from learning skills in subjects such as mathematics, languages, information retrieval and communication technology. We can illustrate such benefits from investments in education with a model of consumer decision-making. The model takes account of the impact of education on effective prices of consumer goods, which includes transaction costs. Let $p_i = p_i(E)$, where p_i is the price of consumer good *i*. We assume $p_i = p_i(E)$ to be a monotonously non-increasing differentiable function with respect to increasing level of education. Thus $\partial p_i / \partial E \leq 0$. To simplify matters, *E* is assumed to be measured in years of schooling. The following analysis can easily be extended to encompass a vector representation of different types of education.

The consumer is assumed to maximize the (remaining lifetime) utility, $U = U(x, F)$; where *x* is a vector of consumer goods, $(i = 1,...,n)$, and *F* equals leisure time. The function is subject to the following constraint:

$$\left[p(E)\right]^T x + C(E) = w(E)(T - F) \tag{6.12}$$

where

$p(E) = [p_1(E),\ldots,p_i(E),\ldots,p_n(E)]$
$C(E)$ = cost of education as a function of the level (or duration) of education (E).

Assumption:

$$\frac{\partial C}{\partial E} > 0. \tag{A1}$$

$w(E)$ = wage income per unit of time as a function of the level of education.

Assumption:

$$\frac{\partial w}{\partial E} > 0. \tag{A2}$$

The Lagrange function to be maximized is

$$H = U(x, F) - \lambda\left\{\left[p(E)\right]^T x + C(E) - w(E)(T - F)\right\}$$

which yields the following necessary conditions for maximization:

$$\frac{\partial H}{\partial x_i} = \frac{\partial u}{\partial x_i} - \lambda p_i(E) = 0; \quad (i = 1,\ldots,n) \tag{6.13}$$

$$\frac{\partial H}{\partial F} = \frac{\partial u}{\partial F} - \lambda w(E) = 0 \tag{6.14}$$

$$\frac{\partial H}{\partial E} = \lambda \left[\sum_{i=1}^{n} \frac{\partial p_i}{\partial E} x_i + \frac{\partial C}{\partial E} - \frac{\partial w}{\partial E}(T-F) \right] = 0 \tag{6.15}$$

$$\frac{\partial H}{\partial \lambda} = \left[p(E) \right]^T x + C(E) - w(E)(T-F) = 0 \tag{6.16}$$

$$\frac{\partial H}{\partial E} = 0 \Rightarrow \lambda \neq 0 .$$

Thus:

$$\frac{\partial w}{\partial E}(T-F) - \sum_{i=1}^{n} \frac{\partial p_i}{\partial E} x_i = \frac{\partial C}{\partial E}.$$

The term $\partial w / \partial E(T - F)$ corresponds to the conventionally measured financial returns to investments in education. Since $x_i > 0$ and $\partial p_i / \partial E \leq 0$, it follows that the term $\sum_{i=1}^{n} \left(\partial p_i / \partial E \right) x_i < 0$.

Conventionally measured returns to investments in education thus underestimate the true returns, which should include the reduction in consumer transaction costs.

Education and Efficiency of Consumption

Hicks (1956), Morishima (1959) and Lancaster (1966) all propose a production function approach to consumer analysis. The main argument is that consumer goods are used as inputs by the household in order to generate outputs of utility-enhancing service characteristics to the household members. Becker and Michael (1973) and Andersson and Lundqvist (1976) have proposed to include education in the household production function, assumed to influence the productivity in generating household services. The household decision problem is thereby subdivided into an objective production decision part – on how to efficiently purchase and use goods – as well as a subjective part on how to trade off different services against each other in order to maximize the utility of the household. The production functions can be formulated as:

$$Z_j = Z_j \left(x_{1j}, \ldots, x_{ij}, \ldots, x_{nj}, E \right) \tag{6.17}$$

where

Z_j = the output of household service j
x_{ij} = the input of good i into the production of service j
E = level of education.

Assumption:

The marginal productivities are positive and diminishing. For simplicity we assume the utility function to be additive:

$$u = \sum_{j=1}^{m} w_j z_j \left(x_{1j}, \ldots, x_{ij}, \ldots x_{nj}, E\right). \tag{6.18}$$

The utility is to be maximized and is subject to the following budget constraint:

$$\sum_{i=1}^{n} p_i(E) x_{ij} + C(E) - w(E)\left(\overline{T} - \overline{F}\right) = 0.$$

Labour time = $(\overline{T} - \overline{F} = \overline{L})$ is assumed to be given. The corresponding Lagrangian to be maximized is:

$$H = \sum_{j=1}^{m} w_j z_j \left(x_{1j}, \ldots, x_{ij}, \ldots, x_{nj}, E\right)$$

$$-\lambda \left[\sum_{j=1}^{m} \sum_{i=1}^{n} p_i(E) x_{ij} + C(E) - w(E)\overline{L} \right].$$

The necessary conditions for equilibrium are:

$$\frac{\partial H}{\partial x_{ij}} = w_j \frac{\partial z_j(E)}{\partial x_{ij}} - \lambda p_i(E) = 0 \tag{6.19}$$

$$\frac{\partial H}{\partial E} = \sum_{j=1}^{m} w_j \frac{\partial z_j}{\partial E} - \lambda \left(\sum_{j=1}^{m} \sum_{i=1}^{n} \frac{\partial p_i}{\partial E} x_{ij} + \frac{\partial C}{\partial E} - \frac{\partial w}{\partial E} \overline{L} \right) = 0$$

$$\frac{\partial H}{\partial \lambda} = \sum_{j=1}^{m} \sum_{i=1}^{n} p_i(E) x_{ij} + C(E) - w(E)\overline{L} = 0.$$

This implies:

$$\sum_{j=1}^{m}\left(\frac{w_j}{\lambda}\right)\frac{\partial z_j}{\partial E}-\sum_{j=1}^{m}\sum_{i=1}^{n}\frac{\partial p_i}{\partial E}x_{ij}+\frac{\partial w}{\partial E}\bar{L}=\frac{\partial C}{\partial E}.$$

(b) (c) (d) (a)

The level of education should thus be adjusted until the marginal cost (a) corresponds to the sum of weighted marginal household productivities from education (b), in addition to transaction cost reduction (c) and the marginal income returns to education (d).

We should thus expect consumer demand for different goods to be dependent on education, ceteris paribus. This is also empirically the case, as is shown by Table 6.10.

*Table 6.10 Consumption elasticities of education (measured in years) estimated on household budget survey data for Sweden, 1969**

Type of consumption good	Educational elasticity
Social interaction services	+2.1
Education	+1.7
International travel	+1.4
Restaurants and hotels	+1.2
Childcare	+1.1
Telecommunications	+1.0
Housing	+0.5
Books and magazines	+0.4
Toys	+0.3
Interior decoration	+0.3
Domestic travel	–0.3
Clothing	–0.4
Alcohol	–0.4
Television and radio	–0.8
Tobacco	–2.0
Entertainment	–2.7

Note: * The estimates control for the effects of age, income, household size and location. All estimates are significant at the 1 per cent level and there is no significant multicollinearity.

The negative education elasticity of tobacco as well as alcohol probably indicates that education (already in the 1960s in Sweden) contributed to knowledge of adverse health effects associated with the consumption of these goods.

An empirical separation of the transaction cost effect from the household productivity effect is of course impossible for the demand for consumption goods that are associated with positive education elasticities. However, it seems reasonable to assume that education raises the household productivity in services attributable to education, books, magazines and international travel.

CONCLUSIONS

This chapter focuses on the analysis of private knowledge acquisition through formal education. We show that the choice of education is similar to other investment choices that households face. In the case of a household that exclusively regards education as a means to improve its income standard, we conclude that the basic optimality condition boils down to a requirement that the marginal lifetime income (properly discounted) should be equal to the marginal cost in terms of the direct education costs and the loss of income.

However, substantial differences in the net returns to education between different occupations indicate that other factors than future real incomes also influence households' educational choices. An obvious example is the choice of pursuing an artistic education, where financial returns are notoriously small. This is compatible with rational decision-making with the proviso that the educational capital itself enters the household's utility function. With this additional assumption, it becomes necessary to consider the marginal rate of substitution between knowledge and consumer income as well as the real income effect, which can be used to explain the demand for education that prepares students for occupations with minimal expected pecuniary returns.

Although much of the analysis can proceed within a deterministic framework, there are also considerations of risk and uncertainty that may affect educational and other investment decisions. As with other long-term financial decisions, returns may have to be traded off against risk. A typical example is different returns and risk in public as opposed to private sector occupations in most countries. Many private sector jobs offer much higher expected returns to education than corresponding jobs in the public sector; consider the differences between a defence attorney and a public prosecutor or a judge. Similarly, an economic consultant normally earns much more than a tenured professor with a similar or higher level of knowledge and skills. But the exposure to income volatility and other financial risks are in this case much greater for the business consultant or lawyer, making the choice an issue that concerns differences in risk aversion. Many long degree programmes do not accommodate any choices between different combinations of risk and returns after graduation. The trade-off between risk and returns has then to be made already in conjunction with the initial educational choice.

Financial problems are central to the choice of education. Increasing the number of years of schooling implies that the cost of education and forgone income opportunities increase as well. For most students, higher education entails borrowing at some positive real rate of interest that is to be covered by future incomes. Households' planning of higher education investments consequently requires a lifecycle perspective.

Most empirical studies of the returns to education substantiate that households base their decision-making on a rational calculation of long-term financial returns. Substantial deviations from the (financial) rationality postulate can mostly be seen in the educational preparation for careers that are looked upon as inherently enjoyable or subjected to extremely skewed returns such as is common in the performing arts or in professional sports. The comparative analysis of returns to education investments indicates substantial differences in returns between countries. The 'welfare states' of Scandinavia – with their substantial subsidies to students – produce a pattern of returns that are systematically lower than returns in countries where most of the costs have to be covered by the students themselves (or their families). A reasonable interpretation is that there is a systematic loss of incentives to choose education with high expected future returns if current costs are covered by government subsidies.

NOTE

1. Australia: Miller, Mulvey and Martin (1995), Patrinos (1995), Cohn and Addison (1998); Austria: Psacharopoulos (1994), Fersterer and Winter-Ebmer (1999); Canada: Patrinos (1995); Denmark: Christensen and Westergard-Nielsen (1999); Finland: Asplund (1999); Germany: Ichino and Winter-Ebmer (1999), Cohn and Addison (1998); Italy: Brunello, Comi and Lucifora (1999); Japan: Cohn and Addison (1998); Norway: Barth and Roed (1999); Spain: Cohn and Addison (1998), Alba-Ramirez and Segundo (1995); Sweden: Arai and Kjellström (1999), Isacsson (1999), Palme and Wright (1992); Switzerland: Psacharopoulos (1994), Weber and Wolter (1999); UK: Patrinos (1995), Harmon and Walker (1995, 1999); USA: Psacharopoulos (1994, 2000), Rouse (1999).

7 Information and Knowledge in the Decision-Making of Firms

Information and data are building blocks in the formation of knowledge. Information in the form of statistical data is a key input in the evaluation of firms in financial markets. Profit and sales figures and information concerning new products and changes in the leadership of publicly listed firms often have immediate impacts on shareholders' evaluations. In addition, information on the administrative practices of firms has always been considered important. The role of macroeconomic conditions in the determination of stock prices, on the other hand, was rarely discussed before the 1970s.

In the 1960s, Sharpe (1963, 1964), Lintner (1965) and Mossin (1966) proposed the use of the Capital Asset Pricing Model (CAPM) as a way of predicting the returns on the financial capital of firms, as traded in the stock market. Their model postulated that the percentage return of a firm would be determined by a statistical constant, β_i, multiplied by returns in the capital market as a whole, which was typically represented by the returns to a market-index portfolio. A β_i that equals one indicates that the individual share i would have the same risk as the market index.

In the 1970s, Stephen Ross (1976) proposed a generalization of the CAPM model of the valuation of firms in the stock market – so-called 'Arbitrage Pricing Theory' (APT). Ross's idea was quite similar to an information-theoretic approach. He made a distinction between firm-specific and macroeconomic information. The assumption was that the general development of demand, as represented by the GDP growth rate, inflation, export growth and other macroeconomic variables would influence different firms and their returns to different degrees. For each such variable a separate β_{ik} should be estimated, which would then indicate the elasticity of returns to firm i with respect to information on macroeconomic variable k. Using arguments that are similar to information theory, information in the APT model is defined as measuring the degree of surprise regarding changes in various macroeconomic variables. If, for example, the GDP growth rate is greater than expected, then this would impact share prices and thus expected returns. Share prices would remain unchanged if there is no new information (that is, no surprises).

The distinction between information and knowledge can be highlighted in the context of the APT model. The flow of information is important for pricing and returns, but only if analysts have substantial knowledge about the macroeconomic factors that constitute the explanatory variables in the model. Knowledge is necessary for the formation of reasonable expectations. It is thus useful for the modelling and formation of expectations, which are activities that are exogenous to the APT model. Information can be seen as an aggregate measure of deviations from established knowledge that indicates the unreliability of such knowledge.

THE OPTIMAL USE OF EDUCATED LABOUR IN FIRMS

A firm's most basic decision on the use of knowledge concerns its employment of labour. Each firm has to decide on its desired level of knowledge and skills. For simplicity, we can assume that there are only two kinds of labour that are available for employment. The first kind of labour – unskilled labour – has no education above the compulsory level, which has been acquired in childhood, during which we assume that there are no alternative employment opportunities. Consequently, there is no need for the employer to compensate for the education investment costs. The employment of unskilled labour gives rise to a per-unit cost that is proportional to the minimum wage rate.

The other kind of labour – educated labour – is educated beyond the compulsory level, and its wage rate must compensate for the additional educational investment. This implies that educated labour must command a wage rate that is the sum of the rate for unskilled labour and a wage premium that compensates for the cost of additional education. If the level of education of educated labour is uniform, then its wage rate will correspond to a constant percentage addition to the wage rate for unskilled labour. For example, United States data show that averaging of educated labour implies a wage rate that is about three times greater than that for unskilled labour.

The following simple model illustrates optimal hiring conditions for different educational categories. We assume that the firm faces a labour market with a fixed wage rate, w, for unskilled labour. The wage rate for the educated category is equal to a constant percentage, α, above the wage rate of unskilled labour; α depends on the equilibrium rate of return to an investment in education of a specific duration. At given cost and given return-to-education requirement, the marginal productivity of the different categories of labour would have to be adjusted until differences in marginal revenue product equal the required rate of return, which compensates for the cost of education.

Although the growth of knowledge in its technological sense has often been regarded as exogenous to the firm, it is still possible for the firm to pursue a knowledge strategy: the firm can decide on the optimal educational composition of the labour force.

We assume that the amount of educated labour (E) represents the input of knowledge in the production process. The production function, Q (E, L) thus includes educated as well as unskilled labour (L). We further assume that the production function is concave and differentiable:

$$\max_{(E,L)} V = pQ(E,L) - \omega(1+r)E - \omega L \tag{7.1}$$

where

p = product price
ω = basic wage rate
r = returns to higher education.

The optimality conditions are:

$$\frac{\partial V}{\partial E} = p\frac{\partial Q}{\partial E} - \omega(1+r) = 0 \tag{7.2}$$

$$\frac{\partial V}{\partial L} = p\frac{\partial Q}{\partial L} - \omega = 0 \tag{7.3}$$

$$\frac{\partial Q}{\partial E} \cdot \frac{1}{1+r} = \frac{\partial Q}{\partial L} \tag{7.4}$$

that is, the use of educated labour should be adjusted, so that the marginal productivity of unskilled labour equals the marginal productivity of educated labour, which is discounted by the returns to education (above the standard wage rate).

This model shows that the optimization criterion is the same as for any other factor input. The marginal value of the services provided by a certain educational category should equal the marginal cost of that category of labour.

SCIENTIFIC RESEARCH AND KNOWLEDGE INVESTMENTS IN THE FIRM

The infrastructural conditions of industrial organization have changed since the days of Adam Smith and later classical analysts of the industrial organization of the manufacturing firm. During early industrialization, transport and communication modes were notoriously slow and sparsely distributed in space. The labour force had little or no formal education and 'tinkerers' rather than organized scientific research caused technological progress in production processes. Massive inputs of raw materials, unskilled labour and energy were responsible for the attained reliability and other desirable characteristics of manufactured goods. Production recipes such as blueprints were at a low level of complexity, with limited education requirements of foremen and workers. This does not imply that manufacturing work did not require skills. In the process of 'learning-by-doing', occupational skills most certainly developed – but without any substantial inputs of formal education.

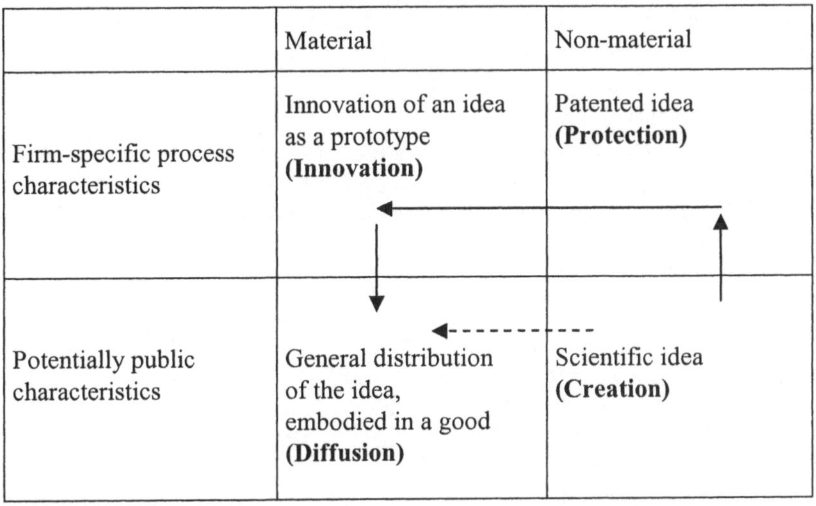
Material
Non-material
Firm-specific process characteristics
Innovation of an idea as a prototype (Innovation)
Patented idea (Protection)
Potentially public characteristics
General distribution of the idea, embodied in a good (Diffusion)
Scientific idea (Creation)

Figure 7.1 *The dynamic and conceptual relations between creative scientific ideas, patenting, innovation and diffusion*

The first economist to address firms' use of scientific knowledge was Joseph Schumpeter (1912). In Schumpeter's theory, independent scholars in academia are the producers of knowledge; curiosity and prestige rather than expected profits drive such knowledge acquisition. As 'scavengers' for profitable by-products from the ivory towers of learning, entrepreneurs exploit scientific findings and peddle profitable investment opportunities to capitalists. Figure 7.1 illustrates this Schumpeterian framework, with its process interdependencies between science, technology patenting, innovation and the diffusion of ideas.

There is a necessary causal sequence from the creation of an idea to the diffusion of a good that results from the new idea. There are also uncertainties that are associated with the different stages of the process – from the scientific creation of a new idea to the marketing of a new product.

The speed of diffusion differs between ideas and their embodiment in tangible goods. Tangible goods with complex designs are harder to imitate than, for example, embodiments of simple food recipes such as hamburgers.

THE INNOVATION AND DIFFUSION OF SCIENTIFIC KNOWLEDGE

Firms' adoption of scientific knowledge and their R&D-driven adaptation of such knowledge into new technologies are the two aspects of innovation. The innovation process has been extensively studied since the 1950s. Zwi Griliches (1957) and Edwin Mansfield (1968) conducted two of the most influential studies of innovation.

Griliches (1957) analysed the innovation-diffusion process of hybrid corn, where the new type of corn was the outcome of genetic research. His analysis shows that the innovation process followed an elongated s-curve (see Figure 7.2).

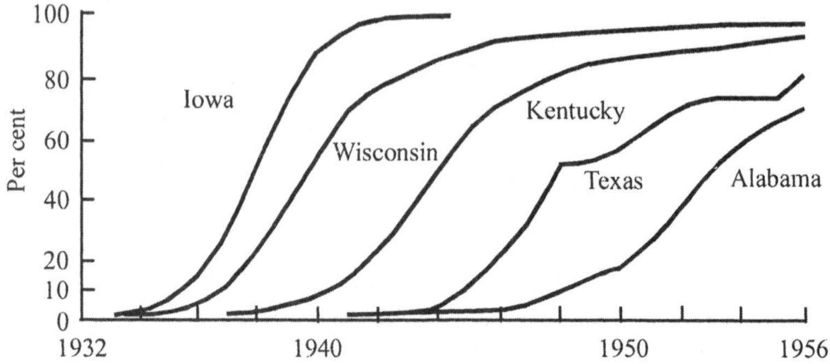

Figure 7.2 Percentage of total acreage planted with hybrid seed (Source: Griliches, 1957)

The innovation processes of Figure 7.2 illustrate the same type of dynamic process, but with different times of introduction and different speeds of innovation in different parts of the United States.

Mansfield (1968) tracks innovations of agricultural machinery with similar results. The simplest dynamic model consistent with these findings is the logistic differential equation model:

$$\dot{Z}_i = \alpha_i Z_i (B - Z_i) \tag{7.5}$$

where

$\dot{Z}_i$ = growth in the number of firms that adopt knowledge of type i (that is, innovation of type i)
Z_i = number of firms that have already adopted knowledge of type i
B = total number of firms capable of adopting knowledge of type i.

Equilibrium requires $\dot{Z}_i = 0$, which can occur if $Z_i = B$ or $Z_i = 0$; $\dot{Z}_i = 0$ represents an unstable equilibrium, whereas $Z_i = B$ is stable.

The classical logistic equation is a quadratic differential equation which shows how growth increases towards a maximum and how it subsequently declines towards zero in a monotonous fashion. The total adoption of a new type of knowledge thus approaches the predetermined maximum level of its use. Two parameters determine the shape of the logistic innovation curve, where α denotes the speed of innovation/diffusion and B denotes the maximum number of firms that can adopt the new type of knowledge.

As it stands, this dynamic model of innovations does not account for any economic interactions. A simple way of introducing economic interdependencies is by assuming that α is a function of relative prices. If the innovator has monopolistic control over the new knowledge – for example by patent protection – then demand will be a negatively sloped function of the price of the new knowledge. In the simple case of a linear demand function, the logistic equation that describes the innovation process would become a third-degree differential equation (see Equation 7.10):

$$\alpha_i = \alpha_0 + \alpha_1 p_i \tag{7.6}$$

$$p_i = a_0 + a_1 Z_i \tag{7.7}$$

$$\alpha_i = \alpha_0 + \alpha_1 (a_0 + a_1 Z_i) = A_0 + A_1 Z_i \tag{7.8}$$

where p_i = reactive price of knowledge of type i. Assuming $A_0 > 0$ and $A_1 < 0$:

$$\dot{Z}_i = (A_0 + A_1 Z_i) Z_i (B - Z_i) \tag{7.9}$$

$$\dot{Z}_i = A_0 Z_i (B - Z_i) + A_1 Z_i^2 B - A_1 Z_i^3 \tag{7.10}$$

$$\dot{Z}_i = A_0 B Z_i + (A_1 B - A_0) Z_i^2 - A_1 Z_i^3 \tag{7.11}$$

$\dot{Z}_i = 0$ implies that:

$$A_1 Z_i^2 - (A_1 B - A_0) Z_i - A_0 B = 0. \tag{7.12}$$

This second-degree equation has one stable equilibrium solution, Z_i^* with $0 < Z_i^* < B$.

With this formulation, the dynamic (stable) equilibrium will be reached at a level below the full saturation point *B*. It is not in the interest of the patent-protected monopolist to let the number of users of the new knowledge exceed *M* in Figure 7.3, where *M* denotes the temporary monopolistic saturation point. Since the related knowledge acquisition represents a sunk cost, it follows that *M* corresponds to a price at which the marginal revenue is zero and the price elasticity of demand is minus one. After a specific period of time has elapsed, however, the protection of the monopoly ceases (usually after 10 to 15 years) and the third-degree part of the differential equation (7.11) becomes applicable. Equation 7.11 exhibits the classical shape with competitive equilibrium at full saturation (that is, at the stable competitive equilibrium point *B*).

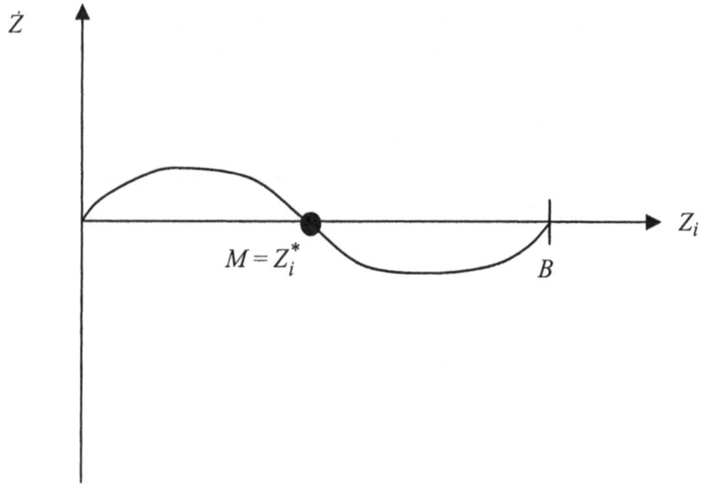

Figure 7.3 Rate of innovation of technology i with pricing feedback from the market

There are many examples of such dynamic innovation processes with an initial period of patent or copyright protection, which gives the inventor a temporary monopoly (or, alternatively, gives the monopoly to the firm that has acquired the exclusive rights to the knowledge from the inventor). One recent example is the extensively used allergy drug Loratadin, which was initially monopolized under the name Claritin (or Clarityn). As soon as the patent rights expired, a number of firms started marketing the drug as Loratadin. Loratadin is sold at prices that are as low as one fifth of the monopoly price.

THE NET PRESENT VALUE OF RESEARCH AND DEVELOPMENT

An investment in new knowledge is to some extent similar to any other investment, such as in machinery and other capital goods. It is similar in the sense that the investments have to be based on an evaluation of future income as compared with early (or even immediate) costs. However, it is different from material capital investments because of the public nature of knowledge, which refers to the risk of competitive imitation by firms that have not paid for acquiring the new knowledge that makes it possible to adopt the associated production technology.

For simplicity of exposition, we assume that a firm (for example, a pharmaceutical corporation) can acquire scientific research findings from medical and technological schools at the rate R. This knowledge will then be permanently available, generating increased production revenues that corresponds to a knowledge-induced increment, ΔQ. The net present value of a given scientific research input is:

$$N = -C(R) + \int_1^T \Delta Q(R) e^{-rt} dt. \quad (7.13)$$

Assuming the impact of the purchased research to be valuable far into the future (that is, as $T \to \infty$), the net present value is simply:

$$N = -C(R) + \frac{\Delta Q(R)}{r} \quad (7.14)$$

where $C(R)$ = cost of acquiring knowledge R, $\Delta Q = \Delta Q(R)$ = increase of revenue as a function of R, and N = net present value of R.

The firm should continue buying scientific knowledge until the net present value approaches zero for the last amount of new knowledge purchased:

$$\frac{dN}{dR} = -\frac{dC}{dR} + \frac{d(\Delta Q)}{dR} \cdot \frac{1}{r} = 0 \quad (7.15)$$

$$\frac{d(\Delta Q)}{dR} = r\frac{dC}{dR}.$$

Assume:

$$\frac{dC}{dR} = p = 1,$$

where p is the price per unit of knowledge:

$$\frac{d(\Delta Q)}{dR} = r. \tag{7.16}$$

The marginal growth impact of increased new knowledge should thus equal the internal (required) rate of return.

UNCERTAINTY, RISK AND KNOWLEDGE INVESTMENTS

Research and development projects are inherently uncertain. It is impossible to know beforehand what will be found at the end of a research process. The theory of statistical hypothesis testing is based on this fundamental uncertainty and consequently all hypothesis testing is formulated in probabilistic terms.

The organization of research and development at the industrial level also reflects fundamental uncertainty. Research-oriented firms tend to develop various strategies that help them cope with uncertainty. One of the most important management problems in such firms is the choice of a research portfolio that is large and diversified enough to attain an optimal combination of expected returns and risks. Many research projects are necessarily long-term commitments and, additionally, require indivisible resources. Some projects require collaboration with university departments, as is for example the case in the biotechnology and information technology firms. Relationships that extend beyond the boundaries of the firm often increase the uncertainties even further.

An example of uncertainty is bio-medical research, which Figure 7.4 illustrates. The research effort is a multi-stage process where P_i denotes the probability of success at stage i. These stages are irreversible and thus imply cumulative sunk costs. Each one of the ten stages offers a choice between continuing and terminating the process. Assuming a 0.8 probability of continuation at each stage ($P_i = 0.8$) implies a success probability of about 10 per cent ($0.8^{10} = 0.1074$). A 0.5 probability at all stages would imply a project success probability of less than 0.1 per cent ($0.5^{10} = 0.00098$).

The only efficient way of dealing with very low success probabilities is by increasing the scale of firms, so as to increase the number of uncertain research projects. Such scale economies have been most evident among research-intensive firms in the pharmaceutical industry.

P_1	Scientific research: Identification of potential treatment
	↓
P_2	Preclinical testing
	↓
P_3	Phase 1: Clinical trials (first testing on humans)
	↓
P_4	Phase 2: Clinical trials (small-scale testing for efficiency and safety)
	↓
P_5	Phase 3: Clinical trials (large-scale testing)
	↓
P_6	FDA application
	↓
P_7	FDA approval?
	↓
P_8	International applications and approvals
	↓
P_9	Profitable marketing and sales
	↓ ↑
P_{10}	Side-effect studies

Figure 7.4 The probability structure of a pharmaceutical R&D project

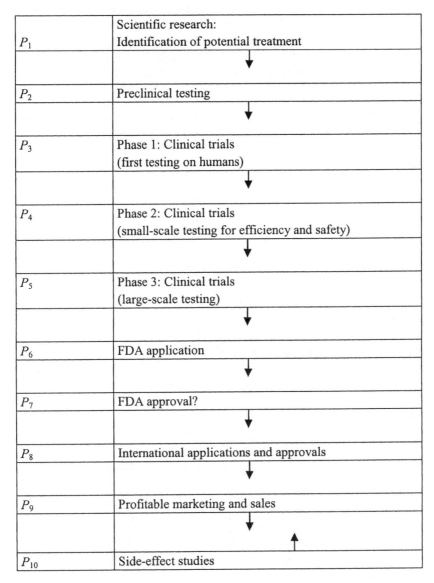

NET PRESENT VALUE, RISK AND DISCOUNT RATES IN R&D PROJECTS

It is well known that there are great uncertainties associated with investments in knowledge by most industrial firms. As shown by Edwin Mansfield et al. (1977), there is – on average – an approximate fifty–fifty chance of technological success in research and development projects. However, the economic success probability for R&D projects in the market is much smaller – of the order of less than 20 per cent. Knowledge-based firms can accommodate the sluggish nature of returns from different new products in two different ways. One way is to introduce a measure of return volatility into the net present value calculation as shown in the following model.

Let us assume that we want to calculate the one period present value V, which is:

$$V = \frac{CEQ}{1+r_\tau} \tag{7.17}$$

where

CEQ = certainty equivalent revenue flow
Q = revenue
r_τ = risk-free rate of interest
$1 + r$ = QV^{-1}.

According to the capital asset pricing model:

$$r = r_\tau + \beta(r_m - r_\tau) \tag{7.18}$$

where

r = rate of return and discount of a given firm
r_m = rate of return to a fully diversified market portfolio

$$\beta = \frac{\text{covariance}(r, r_m)}{\text{variance}(r_m)} = \frac{\text{cov}\left(QV^{-1}, r_m\right)}{\text{var}\left(r_m\right)} \tag{7.19}$$

where β is a measure of the relative risk of investments. The revenue flow, Q, is uncertain, but V is not. Thus:

$$\beta = \frac{\text{cov}(Q, r_m)}{V \cdot \text{var}(r_m)} \tag{7.20}$$

$$\frac{Q}{V} = r_\tau + \frac{\text{cov}(Q, r_m)}{V} \cdot \frac{(r_m - r_\tau)}{\text{var}(r_m)} + 1 \tag{7.21}$$

$$V = \frac{Q - \text{cov}(Q, r_m) \cdot (r_m - r_\tau) / \text{var}(r_m)}{1 + r_\tau}. \tag{7.22}$$

Alternatively, one may use the capital asset pricing model (CAPM) directly in order to determine the risk-adjusted discount rate, r_i.

$$r_i = r_\tau + \beta_i (r_m - r_\tau) \tag{7.23}$$

where

r_i = rate of discount (or return) of project i

$\beta_i = \frac{\text{cov}(r_i, r_m)}{\text{var}(r_m)}$

r_τ = risk-free rate of interest

r_m = rate of return to the market portfolio.

That rate is used for the discounting of future revenues into its present value.

The elasticity β_i shows the percentage return to project i that is associated with a 1 per cent increase in the return to the market portfolio. Estimates of β_i for R&D-based firms are normally well above one, indicating that investments in such firms are more volatile (or risky) than investments in a representative market portfolio.

Figure 7.5 illustrates the use of β_i in determining the risk-compensated discount rates and net present values of research and development projects.

For a knowledge-based firm such as Ericsson – with a β_i estimate that roughly equalled two in the first years of 21st century – the risk-compensating discount rate would be about 16 per cent. That figure implies a risk compensation that corresponds to an additional 12 or 13 per cent above the risk-free real rate of interest, as determined in the financial markets.

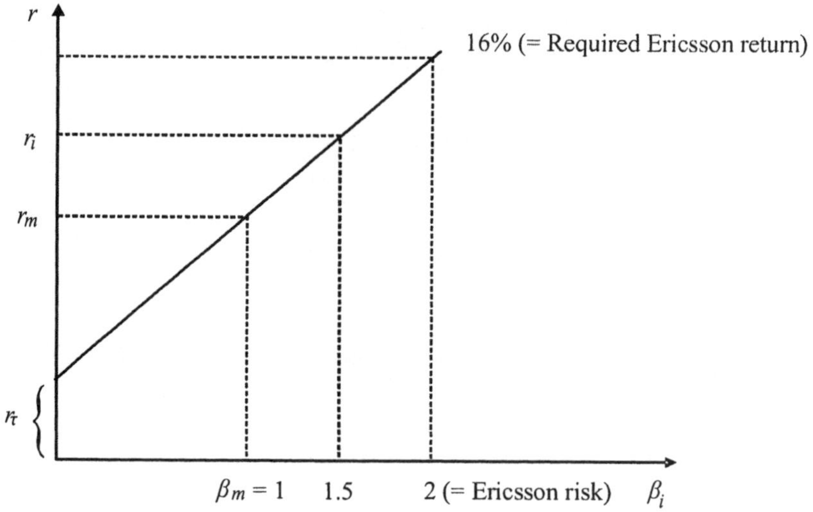

Figure 7.5 Risk and expected return of different projects

COMPARATIVE ANALYSIS OF ESTIMATES OF PRIVATE RETURNS TO INDUSTRIAL RESEARCH PROJECTS

Mansfield et al. (1977) is an early and sophisticated study of private returns to research investments, which included 36 industrial research and development projects in the United States. The projects ranged from new products and processes to new control systems. The mean of the calculated returns was 39 per cent while the median was 28 per cent, indicating highly skewed returns.

The estimation of returns to investments in research is often based on some simple econometric production function. The relation between private rate of returns and the production function is straightforward: Assume a Cobb–Douglas production function that includes the impact of R&D capital:

$$Y_{it} = A_{it} L_{it}^{\alpha} K_{it}^{\beta} \bar{R}_{it}^{\gamma} \varepsilon_{it} \qquad (7.24)$$

or:

$$\ln Y_{it} = \ln A_{it} + \alpha \ln L_{it} + \beta \ln K_{it} + \gamma \ln \bar{R}_{it} + \ln \varepsilon_{it}$$

where

Y_{it} = output of firm i at time t
L_{it} = labour input in firm i at time t
K_{it} = material capital input in firm i at time t
$\overline{R}_{it}$ = knowledge capital input (equal to accumulated R&D investments) in firm i at time t.

The estimated private return to knowledge capital is thus:

$$\gamma Y_t / \overline{R}_{it}.$$

Later estimates of private returns to R&D investments are seldom substantially different from Mansfield's et al. (1977) estimates (see Table 7.1).

Table 7.1 Estimated rates of returns to R&D investments

Study	Private rate of return
Griliches and Lichtenberg (1984b)	0.34
Hall (1995)	0.33
Griliches and Lichtenberg (1984a)	0.30
Scherer (1982)	0.29
Terleckyj (1980)	0.25
Sveikauskas (1981)	0.17

Jeffrey Bernstein and Ishaq Nadiri (1997) estimated private rates of return on physical capital as well as R&D investments for a number of knowledge-based manufacturing industries for the period 1964 to 1991 (see Table 7.2).

Table 7.2 Private rates of return on physical and R&D capital 1964–91 (%): manufacturing industries, United States (estimated means and standard deviations (in parentheses))

	Physical capital	R&D capital
Chemical products	0.208 (0.037)	0.219 (0.028)
Non-electrical machinery	0.174 (0.050)	0.212 (0.044)
Electrical products	0.167 (0.038)	0.202 (0.037)
Transportation equipment	0.182 (0.064)	0.178 (0.040)
Scientific instruments	0.199 (0.034)	0.254 (0.052)

Source: Bernstein and Nadiri (1997).

SOCIAL RETURNS TO INVESTMENTS IN R&D

Knowledge is – at least potentially – a public good. Private optimization of knowledge investments, based on private returns to R&D investments, would thus be socially sub-optimal. The importance of knowledge capital accumulated elsewhere is obvious if the production function has the form:

$$y_j = y_j\left(K_i, \bar{R}_1, \ldots, \bar{R}_i, \ldots, \bar{R}_n\right) \text{ with } \frac{\partial y_j}{\partial \bar{R}_i} > 0.$$

Maximizing the sum of profits would then require that:

$$\sum_j \frac{\partial y_j}{\partial \bar{R}_i} = r \tag{7.25}$$

where r = required rate of return, y_j = output of firm j and R_i = knowledge capital of firm i.

The discrepancy between social and private returns is the main rationale for subsidizing investments in research. These subsidies are at their greatest in universities and other institutes that engage in basic scientific research. However, a number of empirical studies of discrepancies between private and social returns to industrial research indicate a need for increased subsidies also to applied research.

Mansfield et al. (1977) estimated the mean and median social returns to R&D to be approximately 100 per cent and 80 per cent, respectively. The social rate of return would thus be 2.5 to 2.9 times the private returns. Table 7.3 reports the estimated ratios between social and private returns from a number of empirical studies.

Table 7.3 Ratio of social to private returns on R&D investments

Terleckyj (1980)	3.29
Scherer (1982)	2.55
Griliches and Lichtenberg (1984a)	1.37
Bernstein and Nadiri (1997):	
Chemical products	2.29
Non-electrical machinery	3.88
Electrical products	1.59
Transportation equipment	3.02
Scientific instruments	2.60

These studies indicate that the expected social returns are in the order of 2.5 times greater than the private returns. According to the analysis of Jones and Williams (1998) (which was based on similar data), the optimal allocation of research resources should be increased to four times the current level of R&D in the United States.

KNOWLEDGE ACQUISITION AND OPTIMAL QUALITY AND QUANTITY

In the three decades after 1980, research and development investments have assumed ever-greater strategic importance in the decision-making of firms. Instead of regarding new knowledge as a means of improving efficiency in the production of an unchanged set of goods and services, there is an increasing channelling of investment resources to R&D of new products and production processes. In the jargon of R&D economists, product R&D has been given priority in strategic decision-making. The term 'high-tech industry' is strongly associated with a high share of investments, profits or value-added going to this type of knowledge investments. The attendant reorientation of investment strategies implies a shift from quantitative growth to qualitative product improvement.

The measurement of quality is quite amenable to strict economic analysis according to ideas developed by several prominent economists (for example, Morishima, 1959; Hicks, 1956; Lancaster, 1966). However, the basic idea goes back to Johann Heinrich von Thünen (1826) and his analysis of the impact of location quality on the equilibrium price of land.

Each good or service can be represented by an n-dimensional vector of characteristics. Characteristics such as normal speed, energy requirement and comfort may for example represent a certain type of bicycle. A different configuration of the same characteristics may offer a serviceable representation of a car. In Baumol's terminology, concrete means of transportation are transformed into abstract modes. Technological changes may then be represented by Pareto-efficient increases of the characteristics of abstract modes or by the introduction of a completely new abstract mode with a new positively valued characteristic. It can further be assumed that the accumulated level of knowledge – in terms of R&D investments – influences each such new value of a characteristic.

In Thünen-type models, location is a part-determinant of the willingness to pay for a location-specific good such as housing. One may therefore assume that the accessibility, such as time distances to work or service locations determine the price of a unit of housing services. However, accessibility is only one of many important characteristics of 'abstract modes of housing'.

The quality of the neighbourhood (Å. Andersson and D. Andersson, 2006) and characteristics of the housing unit itself can also be introduced as factors influencing the willingness to pay in terms of bid prices. As the willingness to pay must necessarily increase with improved accessibility, an investment into improved infrastructure should under normal conditions imply an increase in the willingness to pay for housing of all those households that benefit from the improved accessibility. In the same way as various housing characteristics influence the price of housing in Thünen-type models, it is also possible to model other goods and services as consisting of a vector of product characteristics for which consumers offer bid prices.

In order to simplify matters, we now assume the existence of a knowledge and information-based firm that produces a new knowledge output with the help of knowledge and information inputs. We assume the knowledge input to be proportional to labour time of employees with appropriate knowledge. Examples of this type of firm are university departments, research institutes, software developers and consulting firms.

We further assume that we can either use an increase in the input of labour for increasing the quantitative output of the knowledge firm or for improving the quality of the output. Quality improvements refer to measured increases in one or more of the valuable characteristics of the product. For instance, increasing the speed of execution of some computer software would require an increased input of knowledge that is necessarily reallocated from other important quantitative tasks. The allocation of knowledge labour between quantitative and qualitative tasks therefore constitutes a problem. To make the argument clear, we assume that a knowledge firm has a given amount of knowledge labour, L, to be allocated between qualitative and quantitative activities. It is further assumed (in line with our earlier discussion) that the work on improved product quality will influence the bid price, p, of product users, while the directly productive work will only influence the quantity that is produced. As usual, we assume a profit-maximizing firm, which leads to the following optimization problem:

$$\max y = p(\rho\ell)q(\theta\ell) - \omega\rho\ell - \omega\theta\ell \qquad (7.26)$$

where $\rho, \theta \geq 0$ and $\rho + \theta = 1$ and

- $\rho =$ the percentage share of total labour allocated to quality improvement tasks
- $\theta =$ the percentage share of total labour allocated to quantitative production
- $\ell =$ total available knowledge labour
- $p =$ bid price for the product
- $q =$ quantitative output.

For simplicity we assume the total amount of labour to equal unity. The p- and q-functions are assumed to be r-differentiable and concave. The maximization conditions are the following:

$$\frac{\partial y}{\partial \rho} = \frac{\partial p}{\partial \rho} q - \omega \ell = 0 \tag{7.27}$$

$$\frac{\partial y}{\partial \theta} = p \frac{\partial q}{\partial \theta} - \omega \ell = p \frac{\partial q}{\partial (1-\rho)} - \omega \ell = 0 \tag{7.28}$$

$$\frac{\partial p}{\partial \rho} q = p \frac{\partial q}{\partial (1-\rho)} \quad \text{or}$$

$$\frac{\partial p / \partial \rho}{p} = \frac{\partial q / \partial (1-\rho)}{q}. \tag{7.29}$$

This condition implies that the optimum percentage share of knowledge labour that is allocated to quality improvement should be:

$$\rho = \frac{\varepsilon_{p,\rho}}{\varepsilon_{p,\rho} + \varepsilon_{q,\theta}}. \tag{7.30}$$

The optimality conditions further indicate that the gradient of the bid-price function should be set equal to the marginal cost of labour divided by the scale of the operations of the knowledge firm. The allocation of labour to quantitative tasks is the conventional requirement that the marginal productivity of labour should equal the marginal cost.

COMPLEXITY, KNOWLEDGE AND THE VALUE OF GOODS

Improving the qualitative characteristics of many goods – for example computers, cameras or cars – requires not only the use of more capital and knowledge in the production of the goods. Increasing the computational speed of a computer, the pictorial precision of a camera or the energy efficiency of a car also requires new blueprints and associated production instructions. In an abstract sense, blueprints and other production instructions are similar to computer programs; such programs are more or less complex (Kolmogorov, 1965; Chaitin, 1966). The shortest possible program that generates all natural numbers is less complex than the shortest possible program that generates all prime numbers. The complexity of a program for solving a given problem can be defined as:

> the minimal number of primitive instructions that solves the problem.

It is possible to apply this definition to the production of goods. The following simple example illustrates the problem. In some intuitive sense most people would agree that the object 1, 'pancake', is less complex than the object 2, 'bouillabaisse'. The definition of complexity would then say that object 2 is more complex than object 1, because the minimal length of the recipe for cooking bouillabaisse would be much longer than the minimal length of a recipe for cooking pancake. Obviously, a more complex object would entail greater accumulated effort, ceteris paribus, and would not be viable in the market, unless it could be sold at a higher price than the less complex object. Thus, increasing complexity should imply increasing value (increasing willingness to pay).

Unfortunately, computer program (or mathematical theorem/proof) definitions of complexity are not enough for defining the complexity of goods. A computer program is a symbolic recipe for the production of a symbolic output from symbolic inputs. Any physical output is a set of physical and symbolic attributes produced by a set of physical inputs according to a symbolic recipe. The complexity of a good is thus at least three-dimensional:

1. The number of physical and symbolic output attributes that is compatible with a given unit value of the output to the user.
2. The number of different inputs that are needed to produce a unit of the output at given value to the user.
3. The minimal length of the recipe for production according to requirements 1 and 2.

Thus, there must be at least a three-dimensional representation of complexity in production theory.

Let us assume that the value of (that is, the willingness to pay for) a given good, υ, is an increasing function of all the three types of complexity:

$$\upsilon = \upsilon\left(C_U, C_I, C_R\right). \tag{7.31}$$

We assume that observable factors determine each kind of complexity. Output complexity (C_U) and recipe complexity (C_R) are obviously related to the consumer's and the producer's knowledge, respectively. Moreover, we assume that C_U is constant and that $C_R = C_R\left(\psi\right)$, where ψ is knowledge that we measure, somehow, on the real line. An additional assumption is that the quantity produced per unit of time is an *r*-differentiable concave function, q, of the input of labour, ϕ_L, at the location of production. In this simple model, we disregard the input complexity, C_I.

Assuming a price of knowledge, $(1+r)w$, and a profit-maximizing strategy, it becomes possible to calculate the optimal use of knowledge:

$$\max_{\{\psi,\phi_L\}} V = \upsilon\left[C_R(\psi)\right]\cdot q(\phi_L)-(1+r)w\psi - w\phi_L \tag{7.32}$$

$$\frac{\partial V}{\partial \psi}=\frac{\partial \upsilon}{\partial C_R}\cdot\frac{\partial C_R}{\partial \psi}q-(1+r)w=0 \tag{7.33}$$

$$\frac{\partial V}{\partial \phi_L}=\upsilon\frac{\partial q}{\partial \phi_L}-w=0.$$

The term $\partial \upsilon/\partial C_R$ is obviously of a subjective nature, while $\partial C_R/\partial \psi$ is of an objective nature in the sense that inputs of knowledge lead to a higher level of complexity. There are economics of scale in the use of knowledge as a factor that increases with its *R*-complexity.

Let us now assume that the increase in value that derives from an increase in *I*-complexity necessitates a greater use of inputs from other regions and a greater number of delivery regions. Formally, we assume:

$$\upsilon=\upsilon\left[C_R(\psi),C_I(Z_N)\right] \tag{7.34}$$

where Z_N = use of transport services on the given networks.

The profit maximization conditions are determined as follows:

$$\max_{\{\psi,Z_N,\phi_L\}} \quad V = \tag{7.35}$$

$$\upsilon\left[C_R(\psi),C_I(Z_N)\right]q(\phi_L)-(1+r)w\psi - wZ_N - w\phi_L$$

$$\frac{\partial V}{\partial \psi}=\frac{\partial \upsilon}{\partial C_R}\frac{\partial C_R}{\partial \psi}q-(1+r)w=0 \tag{7.36}$$

$$\frac{\partial V}{\partial Z_N}=\frac{\partial \upsilon}{\partial C_I}\frac{\partial C_I}{\partial Z_N}q-w=0 \tag{7.37}$$

$$\frac{\partial V}{\partial \phi_L}=\upsilon\frac{\partial q}{\partial \phi_L}-w=0. \tag{7.38}$$

There are thus in this model two ways of increasing the value of a unit of the commodity. Either the input of knowledge will increase the R-complexity by a more sophisticated combination of a given set of inputs or the I-complexity is increased by adding a number of new 'gadgets', that are attached to a product of given R-complexity.

QUALITY, INFORMATION AND RESEARCH CONTACTS

As argued elsewhere (Å. Andersson, 1985, 2003), the quality of a good – as measured by consumers' willingness to pay and production quantity – determines the profitability of a firm. The use of different inputs is the primary determinant of the quantity of the product (at some given willingness to pay). Inputs include labour and other energy, information for controlling the production process, capital services as well as different types of material, which may be produced locally or imported from other regions of the world. Equalizing the value of the marginal productivity of each of these resources with the marginal cost of acquiring the resource ensures an optimal combination of resource inputs. This principle corresponds to the well-known marginal productivity conditions of the profit-maximizing firm, which has formed the basis of the microeconomic theory of production for more than a century. The principle provides the necessary conditions for optimizing the management of production units.

These conditions are, however, not satisfactory for analysing the optimal behaviour of the information-dependent and research-based firm. Such firms, which are becoming increasingly important, must include quality aspirations among their optimality conditions. The quality of the material inputs – as well as a host of other factors – determines product quality and consumers' willingness to pay. In this context, we shall focus on necessary knowledge and information inputs that aim at increasing the internal complexity of the product. Much of the creative process of researchers and designers substitutes information and knowledge for conventional energy and other material inputs. The primary reason for increasing the use of information and knowledge is to produce (otherwise unattainable) consumer-relevant product characteristics. Successful attainment results in a higher willingness to pay. A relevant example of this substitution of complexity for traditional material resources is the evolution of automobiles. Consequently, we should expect the willingness to pay for a given commodity to be a direct function of the complexity of the product and an indirect function of the information and knowledge inputs.

In most technology-intensive industries, the research and development efforts are geographically dispersed and not concentrated in a single creative centre. Countries such as Switzerland and Sweden have targeted substantial portions of their research resources on biomedicine. Even so, they have a joint share of the research output in that field that is less than 4 per cent of the global output. Most of the knowledge of any country tends to be generated in other parts of the world, at least in the long run. This fact has important implications for the theorizing about interregional, international and global interdependencies. The following model of knowledge and information interdependencies indicates the structure of an improved theory of optimal research management.

In the model, we explicitly assume that the willingness to pay for a unit of output of firm i (that is, located in region i) is determined by the information I_{ji} and the knowledge R_{ji} that it receives from region j; $(j = 1,\ldots,n)$. We further assume that knowledge only affects product quality. The P and Q functions are both assumed to be concave and r-differentiable:

$$\underset{\{I,L\}}{\text{Maximize}}\; G_i = P_i\left(I_{1i},\ldots,I_{ni},R_{ni}\right)\cdot Q\left(L_i,I_{ii}\right)$$

$$-\sum_j \tau_{ji}I_{ji} - \sum w_{ji}R_{ji} - w_i L_i - \tau_{ii}I_{ii} \tag{7.39}$$

$$\left.\begin{aligned}\frac{\partial G_i}{\partial L_i} &= P_i\frac{\partial Q}{\partial L_i} - w_i = 0\\ \frac{\partial G_i}{\partial I_{ii}} &= P_i\frac{\partial Q}{\partial I_{ii}} - \tau_{ii} = 0\end{aligned}\right\}\quad \text{Marginal productivity conditions} \tag{7.40}$$

$$\left.\begin{aligned}\frac{\partial G}{\partial I_{ji}} &= \frac{\partial P_i}{\partial I_{ji}}Q_i - \tau_{ji} = 0\\ \frac{\partial G}{\partial R_{ji}} &= \frac{\partial P_i}{\partial R_{ji}}Q_i - w_{ji} = 0\end{aligned}\right\}\quad \text{Marginal interactivity conditions} \tag{7.41}$$

Let us further assume the following approximations:

$$\tau_{ji} = \alpha_i + \beta d_{ji} \tag{7.42}$$

$$w_{ji} = w_i + bd_{ji} \tag{7.43}$$

and:

$$\frac{\partial P_i}{\partial I_{ji}} = Q_j^{\gamma} I_{ji}^{-\lambda};\quad \frac{\partial P_i}{\partial R_{ji}} = Q_j^{g} R_{ji}^{-\ell}. \tag{7.44}$$

Then:

$$Q_j^{\gamma} I_{ji}^{-\lambda} Q_i = \alpha_i + \beta d_{ji} \tag{7.45}$$

and:

$$Q_j^{g} R_{ji}^{-\ell} Q_i = w_i + b d_{ji}. \tag{7.46}$$

Thus:

$$I_{ji} = \frac{Q_i^{1/\lambda} Q_j^{\gamma/\lambda}}{\left(\alpha_i + \beta d_{ij}\right)^{1/\lambda}} \qquad (j = 1, \ldots, n) \tag{7.47}$$

$$R_{ji} = \frac{Q_i^{1/\ell} Q_j^{g/\ell}}{\left(w_i + b d_{ji}\right)^{1/\ell}} \qquad (j = 1, \ldots, n). \tag{7.48}$$

In this theory of the networking firm there are not only the marginal productivity conditions of each input, which influence the optimal resource combinations and regulate the scale of operations. There are also the quality-oriented marginal interactivity conditions that must be observed in the search for an optimal management strategy. The extent to which a firm should achieve interaction through direct contacts or through the transmission of information by communication links is an empirical issue. It depends on the degree of substitutability between knowledge and information in the creation of product quality and consumers' willingness to pay.

Information and knowledge transfers thus decline with distance between source and destination (i.e. between the location of information/knowledge generation and the firm). As a result, the marginal interactivity conditions tend to generate gravity-like interaction behaviour in space. This analysis leads to the following conclusions:

1. Interactivity is necessary for efficient scientific and industrial research.
2. The interactivity conditions exhibit increasing returns to scale.
3. Interaction between units of equal size is more favourable than between units of different size.
4. Increasing distance between research units is associated with diminishing returns to interaction.

There have been few empirical studies of R&D spillovers between firms in different locations. Bernstein and Nadiri (1997) is one of the few studies that offer estimates of the benefits from international R&D spillovers (see Table 7.4).

R&D spillovers obviously decline with distance and increase with the size of the economy. A multiple regression estimate of the role of distance in determining spillover benefits – based on the data in Table 7.4 – shows that the distance elasticity of spillover benefit flows is –0.495 (t-value = –4.350).

Table 7.4 Balance of international R&D spillover benefit flows in seven OECD countries, mean values, 1964–91, (US$ billion, current prices)

To \ From	USA	Japan	France	Germany	Italy	UK	Canada	Total
USA		4.03	0.60	1.35	0.60	1.02	4.52	12.12
Japan	8.69		0.63	1.25	0.47	0.65	1.58	13.27
France	1.62	0.62		3.79	2.23	1.36	0.16	9.78
Germany	1.64	0.93	2.57		1.95	1.37	0.20	8.66
Italy	2.44	0.76	5.55	7.65		1.90	0.31	18.61
UK	2.06	0.86	1.49	2.52	0.90		0.48	8.31
Canada	10.20	0.89	0.22	0.39	0.19	0.51		12.40
Total	26.65	8.09	11.06	16.95	6.34	6.81	7.25	83.15

Source: Bernstein and Nadiri (1997).

8 Expansion of Knowledge and Macroeconomic Growth

MACROECONOMIC ACCOUNTING FOR GROWTH

In the early 1960s, Edward Denison (1967) initiated an extensive discussion about the relative role of different factors of production in determining the rate of growth of different national economies. The starting point was the observation by Robert Solow (1956, 1957) that the long-term rate of growth of per capita income in the USA could only to a very limited extent be explained by the growth of the stock of material capital and the increases of quantitative labour supply. In an econometric estimation of the rate of growth of the national product per capita, Solow estimated that the contributions by growing capital stock and labour inputs accounted for no more than one-third of the total rate of growth. The remaining two-thirds of the rate of growth of the USA was a 'residual factor'. A number of economists beside Denison proceeded to explain the different components of the residual factor of economic growth accounting.

In the important contributions by Angus Maddison (1982, 1995) the macroeconomic accounting data by Kuznets (1966) has been extended to cover a very long historical record for a large number of industrialized nations. This database has increased our possibilities of explaining the relative importance of the growth of different inputs contributing to the rate of growth of real national products.

If we assume that the national product (GDP or GNP) could be explained by the use of different inputs according to a Cobb–Douglas macro production function (corresponding to the idea that the net output of the economy would be determined by a weighted geometric average of different inputs) we have the following growth accounting equation:

$$\frac{\Delta Y}{Y} = \alpha_1 \frac{\Delta R}{R} + \alpha_2 \frac{\Delta K}{K} + \alpha_3 \frac{\Delta H}{H} + \alpha_4 \frac{\Delta L}{L} + \alpha_0 \tag{8.1}$$

where

$\frac{\Delta Y}{Y}$ = rate of growth of GDP

$\frac{\Delta R}{R}$ = rate of growth of knowledge, in which ΔR = investments in research and development (R&D) and R = the stock of knowledge (equal to the accumulated investments in R&D)

$\frac{\Delta K}{K}$ = rate of growth of the material capital stock

$\frac{\Delta H}{H}$ = rate of growth of human capital

$\frac{\Delta L}{L}$ = rate of growth of the number of working hours

α_0 = residual growth rate.

The parameters α_1,..., α_4 could be estimated by the factor shares in GDP, if $\alpha_i > 0$ and $\sum_i \alpha_i$ equals 1, corresponding to an assumption of constant returns to scale. If material investments are constrained by savings, Equation (8.1) can be rewritten as (8.2). Thus:

$$\Delta K = S = \left[s_H + s_M + n + (t-g)\right]Y = s_T Y \tag{8.2}$$

where

S = savings
s_H = household savings ratio
s_M = firm savings ratio for material investment
n = net import surplus ratio
$t-g$ = net government taxation surplus ratio
s_T = total net savings ratio.

Further $\alpha_2 = \frac{\partial Y}{\partial K}\frac{K}{Y}$. Thus:

$$\alpha_2 \frac{\Delta K}{K} = \left[s_H + s_M + n + (t-g)\right]Y \frac{\partial Y}{\partial K}\frac{K}{Y} \Big/ K = s_T \frac{\partial Y}{\partial K} \tag{8.3}$$

where

$\dfrac{\partial Y}{\partial K}$ = marginal productivity of material capital

ΔR = research and development investments = $s_R Y$

s_R = savings rate for R&D.

$$\alpha_1 \frac{\Delta R}{R} = s_R \frac{Y}{R} \alpha_1 = s_R \frac{Y}{R} \frac{\partial Y}{\partial R} \frac{R}{Y} = s_R \frac{\partial Y}{\partial R} \tag{8.4}$$

where $\partial Y / \partial R$ is the marginal productivity of research and development investments.

The accumulation of human capital is primarily determined by government spending and forgone earnings. The elasticity α_3 has been estimated for the US to be of the order 1/3 (Mankiw et al., 1992).

Equation (8.1) can be rewritten as (8.5).

The most important explanatory variables accounted for in Maddison (1982) are capital investments, knowledge accumulated by an increased number of school years and the role of international trade in the supply of material capital investments. In addition to the national supply of savings from household income and profit retention ratios of firms, the economy can also support a high rate of capital accumulation by an import surplus (or international credits). This is reflected by the following growth accounting equation:

$$\frac{\Delta Y}{Y} = s_R \frac{\partial Y}{\partial R} + s_T \frac{\partial Y}{\partial K} + \alpha_3 \frac{\Delta H}{H} + \alpha_4 \frac{\Delta L}{L} + \alpha_0 \tag{8.5}$$

Assume s_R to be in the range of 3 per cent, $\partial Y / \partial R$ to be in the order of 0.25, s_T to be in the order of 0.20, $\partial Y / \partial K$ equal to 0.10, α_3 equal to 0.3, $\Delta H / H$ equal to 0.015 and α_4 and $\Delta L / L$ to be zero. Then the rate of growth of the economy would be in the order of 3.0 per cent per year, which would also be the rate of growth of income per working hour.

As the rate of national growth of labour supply is often close to zero in mature economies the main factors determining growth are:

- Marginal productivities of material and knowledge capital
- The propensity to save of households, firms and government and
- The rate of growth of human capital by investments in education.

The growth of human capital by education has been substantial in all of the industrialized economies. According to Maddison (1982) the average level of education of the labour force of most OECD countries was close to three years of formal education around 1900. Currently the average level of formal education of the labour forces of Europe, USA and Japan is close to 12 years. This corresponds to an average increase of the supply of educational capital per capita of 1.5 per cent per year since 1900.

The contribution to the growth of the national product from material capital is determined by the product of the savings rate (as influenced by national savings and import surpluses) and the marginal productivity of investments. The marginal productivity of investments can essentially be influenced by two factors only. The first factor is the capacity to reallocate capital from inefficient to efficient firms and the second factor is the capacity to develop and use new technologies of production. The development of new technologies of production is closely related to the accumulation of knowledge by research and development investments.

The data on the long-term growth of the supply of labour as provided by Maddison show that the total number of working hours per unit of labour is steadily decreasing with the rate of growth of income per capita. This indicates that leisure time is a complement to consumption of goods. Table 8.1 summarizes the development of the per capita working hours.

Table 8.1 Annual hours of work per capita of the labour force in different OECD countries 1870–1979

	1870	1900	1929	1950	1979
Australia	2 945	2 688	2 139	1 838	1 619
Belgium	2 964	2 707	2 272	2 283	1 747
Canada	2 964	2 789	2 399	1 967	1 730
Denmark	2 945	2 688	2 279	2 283	1 721
France	2 945	2 688	2 297	1 989	1 727
Germany	2 941	2 684	2 284	2 316	1 719
Netherlands	2 964	2 707	2 260	2 208	1 679
Norway	2 945	2 688	2 283	2 101	1 559
Sweden	2 945	2 688	2 283	1 951	1 461
United Kingdom	2 984	2 725	2 286	1 958	1 617
United States	2 964	2 707	2 342	1 867	1 607

Sources: Different sources as given in Maddison (1982).

Estimating the dependence on working hours upon real income indicates an income elasticity of working hours per capita of approximately –0.2 to –0.3 for the different OECD countries (Table 8.2).

Table 8.2 Estimates of real income elasticity of working hours for a selected set of OECD countries based on time series observations, 1870–1979

	Income elasticity	t-value	R-square
Australia	–0.38	12.3	0.93
Belgium	–0.23	20.8	0.97
Canada	–0.23	25.5	0.98
Denmark	–0.22	29.3	0.99
France	–0.19	10.0	0.89
Finland	–0.18	13.5	0.95
Germany	–0.19	29.8	0.99
Netherlands	–0.23	19.9	0.97
Norway	–0.22	31.6	0.99
Sweden	–0.23	25.4	0.98
United Kingdom	–0.33	26.5	0.98
United States	–0.26	23.1	0.98

Source: Maddison (op.cit.) for the data.

The effect of the increasing number of persons employed and the decline of working hours per employed has implied a fairly constant supply of labour in many of these countries. This means that growth is primarily dependent upon *three forms of capital accumulation*, investments in material capital, in human capital by education investments and in other knowledge capital by research and development investments.

There has been a common assumption that the American labour productivity has been growing more rapidly than the labour productivity in the European Union (EU). This assumption has been disputed by the MIT economist Oliver Blanchard. One of his empirical results is given in Table 8.3.

Expressed in absolute rather than relative terms, US GDP per capita increased by 64 per cent between 1970 and 2000. During the same period working time per capita increased by 21 per cent, implying a growth in labour productivity by 43 per cent. From 1970 to 2000, labour productivity in the EU increased by 40 per cent, that is, almost as rapidly as in the USA. Much of this productivity gain was allocated to increases of leisure time in Europe, while the opposite happened in the US.

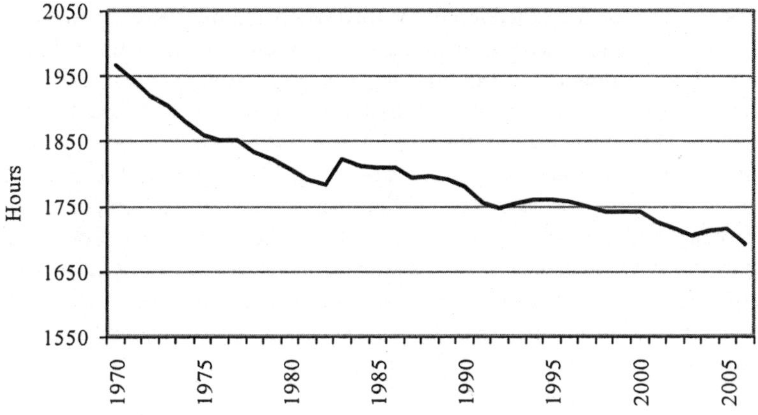

Note: Data for South Korea is missing.

Source: Data from OECD. Illustration, Maria Eriksson, JIBS, 2008.

Figure 8.1 Average yearly hours of working in OECD countries, 1970–2006

Table 8.3 PPP GDP per capita, per hour worked and hours worked per capita 1970 and 2000, USA and EU (15), USA Indices = 100

	GDP per capita		Hours worked per capita		GDP per hour worked	
	1970	2000	1970	2000	1970	2000
European Union	69	70	101	77	65	91

Source: Blanchard (2004).

GROWTH OF ECONOMIES – A GENERAL PATTERN

The rate of economic growth in the very long run has been estimated by Kuznets (1966), Maddison (1982, 1995) and others. The rate of economic growth of different industrializing economies has differed according to the timing of their start of their industrialization process. So far, three stages or waves of industrialization have been identified as is indicated by Table 8.4.

Currently South Korea and Taiwan, belonging to a fourth wave industrialization, have experienced five decades of a growth rate of approximately 6 per cent. The main explanation of the difference in growth rate favouring late-comers is the importance of learning by imitation. The late-comers have the advantage of drawing upon organizational and technological experiences accumulated by countries industrializing at earlier stages. When Japan and countries like Sweden, Norway and Denmark of the European periphery initiated their industrialization process at the end of the 19th century they could draw upon the massive knowledge accumulation of England, France, Germany and the United States as well as the increased possibilities of financing their investments with international loans supporting large import surpluses. During the 20th century, growth rates of real product and income per capita of different nations of waves 1 to 3 have stabilized at approximately 2 to 2.8 per cent per year.

Table 8.4 Long-term growth rates of real per capita GDP of industrialized market economies 1870–1979 and 1870–2002, per cent per annum

		1870–1979	1870–2002
Japan	wave 3	3.0	2.9
Sweden	wave 3	2.9	2.8
Finland	wave 3	2.7	2.7
France	wave 2	2.6	2.4
Germany	wave 2	2.6	2.6
Norway	wave 3	2.6	2.7
Austria	wave 2	2.4	2.4
Italy	wave 3	2.4	2.3
United States	wave 1–2	2.3	2.5
Canada	wave 2	2.3	2.4
Denmark	wave 2	2.3	2.3
Belgium	wave 1	2.1	2.2
Netherlands	wave 2	2.1	2.3
Switzerland	wave 2	2.1	2.1
Great Britain	wave 1	1.8	1.9
Median		2.3	2.3
Standard deviation		1.5	1.0

Sources: Maddison (1982, 1995); OECD: National Account Statistics, 2004.

As can be seen from Table 8.4 there is no general tendency towards divergence from the long-term steady rates of growth. There are of course fluctuations associated with business cycles but the long-term trends are indicating quite stable equilibrium processes.

Such a steady rate of growth is a remarkable property of the industrialized economies and is compatible with constant returns to scale of the expanding stocks of material, educational and other knowledge capital being accumulated by the industrialized countries.

HUMAN CAPITAL IN CLASSICAL ENDOGENOUS GROWTH THEORY

The macroeconomics of capital accumulation goes back to the early 20th century when the first models of economic growth were formulated. In these one-sector models of the economy, investment decisions were assumed to be based on insufficient capital to match the growing demand for products. The basic result of these early model exercises was the proposition that the growth rate of national income was determined as the ratio of the average propensity to save and the marginal capital–output ratio. Alternatively the rate of growth was determined as the product of the propensity to invest and the marginal productivity of material capital. The propensity to save (or to invest) was regarded as a behavioural constant, determined by cultural factors. The marginal capital–output ratio was assumed to represent the aggregate technology of the society.

Increasing knowledge, resulting in improved technology, would then be reflected in a decreasing marginal capital–output ratio, leading to an increasing rate of growth.

Gustav Cassel's theory of equilibrium growth, as formulated in *Theoretische Sozialökonomie* (1918), was used as a starting point in one of the generalizations of the growth theory by the mathematician and physicist John von Neumann in a paper published in the 1930s (von Neumann, 1937). Assuming a completely closed economy with a large number of producers, interconnected with each other by technological conditions of production, admitting possibilities of substitution of inputs and joint production, von Neumann proved that there would indeed exist a general equilibrium rate of growth and – as a saddle point property – a dual rate of interest equal to the rate of growth, that would ensure sustained economic growth with equilibrium relative proportions of all inputs and outputs of the expanding economy. For an exposition of this theory see for example Morishima (1964), Hicks (1965), Nikaido (1968), Andersson (1968).

The Cassel property of balanced growth in an economy subdivided into a large number of products can be proved with the aid of a simplified version of the von Neumann model. In this model of a growing economy we make the simplification that the economy can be subdivided into a finite number of sectors, each sector producing one product only. Thus, the index of a sector is also an index of a product. We also make the simplification that there is only one recipe for the production of a given product by a sector, that is constant input–output coefficients. This implies that there is no possibility of substituting different inputs in the production of an output. However, as has been remarked by Leontief and others, a sufficiently large number of sectors (products) can exhibit macroeconomic substitution as a consequence of reduction of the output of one sector in favour of an expansion of the output of another sector.

In similarity with the von Neumann model treatment of households, it is assumed that all households can be aggregated into a sector, producing labour by inputs of given amounts of products per unit of labour delivered.

In continuous time the model can be specified as follows:

$$Ax + B\dot{x} \leq x; \text{ with } \dot{x}_i = gx_i \qquad (i = j = 1,\ldots,n) \tag{8.6}$$

as the condition of balanced growth.

$$p^T A + rp^T B \geq p^T \tag{8.7}$$

with

$A = \{a_{ij}\}$ = current input of commodity i per unit output of j

$B = \{b_{ij}\}$ = capital stock input of i per unit of output of j

$x = \{x_i\}$ = vector of outputs

$\dot{x} = \{\dot{x}\}$ = vector of increases of output

$p = \{p_n\}$ = vector of relative prices.

Also, in this growth model there is a condition of equality between the rate of interest and the rate of growth at the sustainable equilibrium growth path of the economy. Furthermore, the growth path requires a given vector of relative prices as well as a given vector of output shares to be upheld as long as the technology of production is given by the square matrices (A, B).

We further assume that the economy can be closer to or further from full use of capacity as indicated by the parameter μ. A sustainable equilibrium is such that there is full use of capacity and a rate of growth of capacity compatible with full capacity use, that is, $\mu = 1$. In order to show the dual properties we can solve this problem by maximizing the rate of capacity use at some given, uniform rate of growth of capital and production. This corresponds to a Keynesian assumption of a possible 'unemployment equilibrium' (see Malinvaud (1977) or Benassy (1990)).

It is then reasonably easy to show a modified Cassel–Harrod–Domar condition of sustainable economic growth also to be ruling in the multi-goods growth model:

$$\max_{(x,\mu)} \mu \tag{8.8}$$

subject to:

$$\mu x_i = \sum_j a_{ij} x_j + \lambda_w \sum_j b_{ij} x_j \tag{8.9}$$

where

μ = rate of production capacity utilization
x_i = production of good i
a_{ij} = use of current input i per unit of output of j
λ_w = a given warranted rate of growth of capital
b_{ij} = capital input i per unit of output j.

This optimization problem corresponds to:

$$\max_{(x,\mu,p)} L = \mu - \sum_i p_i \left(\mu x_i - \sum_j a_{ij} x_j - \lambda_w \sum_j b_{ij} x_j \right) \tag{8.10}$$

with the necessary conditions of a maximum:

$$\frac{\partial L}{\partial \mu} = 1 - \sum_i p_i x_i = 0 \tag{8.11}$$

$$\frac{\partial L}{\partial x_i} = -p_i \left(\mu - \sum_k p_k a_{ki} - \lambda_w \sum_k p_k b_{ki} \right) = 0 \tag{8.12}$$

$$\frac{\partial L}{\partial p_i} = -\left(\mu x_i - \sum_j a_{ij} x_j - \lambda_w \sum_j b_{ij} x_j \right) = 0. \tag{8.13}$$

We now assume an iterative adaptation of the rate of growth of capital until $\lambda^* = \lambda_w$ which is sufficient to achieve full use of production capacity, i.e. such that $\mu = 1$. We can thus assume that there exists a warranted rate of growth equal to the maximal rate of growth at full employment. We then have the condition of maximal balanced growth:

$$\lambda^* = \frac{1 - \sum_k (p_k / p_i) a_{ki}}{\sum_k (p_k / p_i) b_{ki}} \tag{8.14}$$

$$= \frac{\text{profit ratio}}{\text{capital–output ratio}} = \frac{\text{real gross savings ratio}}{\text{capital–output ratio}}$$

in *value* terms.

All the technological knowledge of this model is represented by the elements of the A- and B-matrices.

By the Perron–Frobenius theorem on square semi-positive matrices (Frobenius, 1912; Klein, 1973; Debreu and Herstein, 1953) it can be shown that any exogenously determined decrease of an element in (A, B), ceteris paribus, must lead to an increasing rate of balanced growth. But not only the eigenvalue γ(max) of growth will change. There will also be a change in the eigenvector, representing the relative proportions of products (sectors) of the growing economy. An increase in the productivity of labour is represented by a drop in one or many of the vectors of labour input–output coefficients. An increasing efficiency of the education system is represented by a decrease in the values of the corresponding b-vector.

Increasing the profit or savings ratio, increasing productivity of human capital or decreasing capital–output ratios will thus imply an increasing balanced rate of growth.

NEW TECHNOLOGICAL OPPORTUNITIES IN THE CLASSICAL GROWTH THEORY

John von Neumann (1937) formulated an economic growth model, including possibilities of substitution as well as joint production. The assumption of joint production is an expedient way to handle depreciation as each sector of the economy can produce some goods and services and a reduced amount of capital as a generalized output. Production techniques are represented by two rectangular matrices Q and M. Each element of Q indicates the quantity of good or service i required per unit intensity of technique j. Each element of matrix M indicates the amount of good or service i per unit intensity of technique j. Labour is treated as any other service.

The model is as follows:

$$(M - gQ)x \geq 0$$

$$p(M - gQ)x = 0$$

$$p(M - rQ) \leq 0$$

$$p(M - rQ)x = 0$$

$$pMx > 0.$$

von Neumann growth theorem: A unique equilibrium solution with positive common rate of expansion $g^* = r^*$ exists. At the unique equilibrium solution there are associated non-negative vectors x^*, p^*.

For a proof see Klein (1973).

r can be interpreted as a rate of interest or rate of return on capital. M and Q are rectangular matrices with column vectors representing techniques of production.

Along Schumpeterian lines, new technological opportunities would be emerging more or less randomly from research in university departments and laboratories. These new techniques would then simply be additions to the M and Q rectangular matrices as new technological vectors and these would be chosen instead of earlier vectors, if they would lead to higher r^* and g^*.

A similar procedure can be introduced into the simpler Leontief growth model (Brody, 1970) in which a new technique a_{in}, b_{in} would be preferred to the old technique a_i, b_i, if $p(a_{in} + rb_{in}) < p(a_i + rb_i)$, i.e. if the unit cost of production is lower with the new technology.

GROWTH OF EDUCATION AND CAPITAL IN THE NEOCLASSICAL GROWTH MODEL

We can conveniently introduce knowledge as human capital leading to the definition of efficiency labour as:

$$\eta = hL_0 \tag{8.15}$$

where

η = total efficiency labour
h = human capital or education per unit of labour.

Total supply of labour (in working hours) is assumed to be constant.

We now define a production function with labour measured in efficiency units. The production function is assumed to be differentiable and concave.

$$q = f(k) \tag{8.16}$$

with $\eta q = Q$ and $\eta k = K$, where Q = total product and K = total material capital. Further define $a \equiv \dot{h}/h$ and $c \equiv$ consumption per capita. The capital accumulation equation is now:

$$\dot{k} = f(k) - c - (a+\delta)k. \tag{8.17}$$

We further assume a social welfare function to be maximized.

$$\text{Maximize} \int_{t=0}^{\infty} U(c)\, e^{-rt} dt = W$$

where $U(c)$ is assumed to be some differentiable, concave social utility function and W a measure of total social welfare,

$$\text{subject to } \dot{k} = f(k) - c - (a+\delta)k \tag{8.18}$$

$$c(0) = c_0$$

The current value Hamilton function to be maximized is thus:

$$H = U(c) + \mu\left[f(k) - c - (a+\delta)k\right] \tag{8.19}$$

with the optimality conditions:

$$\mu = \partial U / \partial c \tag{8.20}$$

$$\dot{k} = f(k) - c - (a+\delta)k \tag{8.21}$$

$$\dot{k} = -\mu\left[\partial f / \partial k - (a+\delta+r)\right]. \tag{8.22}$$

We can eliminate μ and $\dot{\mu}$ to arrive at two differential equations:

$$\dot{k} = f(k) - c - (a + \delta)k$$

$$\dot{c} = -\frac{\partial U}{\partial c} \Big/ \frac{\partial^2 U}{\partial c^2} \left[\frac{\partial f}{\partial k} - (a + \delta + r) \right]$$

On the equilibrium path:

$$f'(k) = a + \delta + r, \qquad \text{a modified 'golden rule'} \tag{8.23}$$

$$c = f(k) - (a + \delta)k. \tag{8.24}$$

At the steady state Q, C and η will be growing at the same rate, which implies that consumption per capita will be growing as long as knowledge in the form of educational capital is increasing over time.

ENDOGENOUS KNOWLEDGE ACCUMULATION IN NEOCLASSICAL GROWTH MODELS

We have shown that the growth of knowledge by human capital investments can be easily incorporated in the neoclassical growth theory, as originally modelled by Tinbergen (1942), Solow (1956, 1957) and Swan (1956).

The growth of knowledge in the form of technological progress can either be exogenous (i.e. determined as a time trend) or endogenous (i.e. determined *within* the economic growth model). The production function is mostly assumed to be linearly homogenous in K and L.

The classical analysis of knowledge growth as technological progress in the framework of neoclassical production functions was formulated in the 1950s and 1960s by Arrow (1962), Harrod (1939), Hicks (1965) and Solow (1957). Harrod was early in proposing neutrality of progress of knowledge (or technology) in the sense that it would leave the capital–output ratio unchanged. Thus Harrod-neutrality implies that the efficiency of labour increases according to:

$$Q = Q\,[K, A(t)\,L] \tag{8.25}$$

where

Q = output
K = capital services and
L = labour services.

Solow-neutrality of progress of knowledge implies, that $Q = Q\,[A(t)K, L]$; i.e. the knowledge progress increases the efficiency of capital.

Hicks- and Arrow-neutrality implies a general improvement of the efficiency of production:

$$Q = A\,(t)\,Q\,(K, L)\text{; Hicks-neutrality}$$
$$Q = A\,(K)\,Q\,(K, L)\text{; Arrow-neutrality.}$$

where Arrow assumes that K denotes the total accumulated capital stock of the economy as a whole. Arrow in this way obviously made the first attempt at modelling the publicness of knowledge or technology.

Technological progress $A(t)$ is Arrow- or Solow-neutral, if it leaves the labour productivity, (Y/L), unchanged at a *given marginal productivity of labour.*

$A(t)$ is Harrod-neutral if the productivity of capital (Y/L) is unchanged at a *given marginal productivity of capital.*

The currently most popular assumption about technological progress is Hicks-neutrality, which requires the marginal rate of substitution between labour and capital to be unchanging, as long as the capital–labour ratio, (K/L) is constant during the process of technological progress.

The Cobb–Douglas production function covers all these alternatives:

Neutrality type	Function
Arrow/Solow	$Y = A^{\alpha}\,K^{\alpha}\,L^{1-\alpha}$
Harrod	$Y = K^{\alpha}\,(A\,L)^{1-\alpha}$ or $Y = A^{1-\alpha}\,K^{\alpha}\,L^{1-\alpha}$
Hicks	$Y = A\,K^{\alpha}\,L^{1-\alpha}$

The Cobb–Douglas production function has consequently become a preferred function in most of neoclassical growth modelling.

Technological and organizational knowledge can be assumed to determine the rate of technological progress as:

$$A = \mu R$$

where the level of technology (A) is determined by the level of knowledge.

The first model of *endogenous technological progress* by accumulation of knowledge was proposed by Karl Shell (1966, 1967) and by H. Uzawa

(1965). The production function in Shell (1966) is neoclassical. Assuming a constant unit amount of labour the production function is now:

$$Y(t) = F\left[K(t), R(t)\right] \tag{8.26}$$

where

$Y(t)$ = national product at time period t
$K(t)$ = capital at time t
$R(t)$ = level of knowledge at time period t.

Suppose that the growth of capital ($\dot{K}$) is determined by the equation:

$$\dot{K} = s(1-\tau)F(K,R) - \delta_K K \tag{8.27}$$

where

s = the propensity to save (and invest)
τ = the relative share of savings allocated to accumulation of knowledge by R&D
δ_K = the rate of depreciation of capital.

The accumulation of knowledge is assumed to be determined by the equation:

$$\dot{R} = gs\tau F(K,R) - \delta_R R \tag{8.28}$$

where

g = the productivity of R&D activities
δ_R = rate of depreciation of knowledge.

With given parameters ($0 < s, \tau, \delta_K, \delta_R < 1$) a general equilibrium path would require that $\dot{K} = 0$ and $\dot{R} = 0$ or:

$$R/K = g\left[\tau/(1-\tau)\right](\delta_K/\delta_R). \tag{8.29}$$

The equilibrium knowledge-capital ratio would thus increase with:

1. An increase in the productivity of the R&D-activities
2. An increase in the relative share of savings (and investment) allocated to R&D-investments, and
3. A relative decrease of the depreciation of knowledge.

Hicks (1965) has criticized the idea of depreciation of knowledge. 'A change in technology must instead result in a *fall* in the capital stock, correctly measured'. 'Every technical improvement implies a loss of capital...'.

According to Hicks it would be more reasonable to assume that the rate of depreciation of capital *increases with an increasing growth of knowledge* while knowledge itself would not depreciate. Thus Equations (8.27) and (8.28) could be rewritten along Hicksian lines as:

$$\dot{K} = s(1-\tau)F(K,R) - \delta_K\left(\frac{\dot{R}}{R}\right)K\,; \quad \text{with } \partial\delta_K \Big/ \partial\left(\frac{\dot{R}}{R}\right) > 0 \qquad (8.30)$$

$$\dot{R} = gs\tau F(K,R). \qquad (8.31)$$

We would then arrive at a system of equations with a possible equilibrium solution property, i.e.

$$\left\{\begin{aligned} \lambda K &= s(1-\tau)F(K,R) - \delta_K(\lambda)K \\ \lambda R &= gs\tau F(K,R) \end{aligned}\right\} \qquad (8.32)$$

with $0 < s,\tau,g < 1$.

The non-linear system (8.32) will have an equilibrium growth rate $\lambda^* > 0$, if $\delta_K(\lambda^*) \le \varepsilon$, where ε is a small number, corresponding to positive net savings. Investment in capital is thus required to be larger than some maximum rate of depreciation of capital on an equilibrium growth trajectory. On the equilibrium growth trajectory:

$$\dot{Y}/Y = \dot{K}/K = \dot{R}/R = \lambda^*.$$

As the savings ratio s is assumed to be constant, consumption per unit of labour will also be growing at the rate λ^*. Endogenous growth of knowledge and capital is thus in this model consistent with a steady growth of consumption per capita.

RECENT MODELLING OF ENDOGENOUS KNOWLEDGE AND ECONOMIC GROWTH

After a period of more than one decade, analyses of macroeconomic endogenous knowledge and technological progress reappeared (for example

Andersson and Mantsinen (1980); Romer (1986, 1990); Grossman and Helpman (1991a, 1991b); Aghion and Howitt (1992, 1998); Zhang (1991)). There are two major characteristics of these models. First, knowledge is *not* assumed to be depreciating. Second, diffusion of knowledge is assumed to be important.

Assumptions on Technology

$$g_A = \frac{\dot{A}}{A} = k_i Q - \delta$$

Shell (1966).

$$g_A = \frac{\dot{A}}{A} = \beta (a_K K)^{\beta} (a_H H)^{\gamma} A^{\theta-1}$$

Andersson and Mantsinen (1980); Romer, P. (1986, 1990); Grossman and Helpman (1991a); Aghion and Howitt (1992, 1998); Romer, D. (2001).

where A = knowledge capital stock, Q = total product, K = material capital stock, H = stock of educational capital.

The parameter θ indicates the impact of the stock of knowledge on the growth of knowledge. If $\theta = 1$, there would be no impact from the stock of knowledge on the *rate of growth* of total factor productivity.

If θ is larger than 1, total factor productivity would be accelerating with an increasing stock of knowledge, or:

$$\frac{\partial \frac{\dot{A}}{A}}{\partial A} = (\theta - 1) \beta (a_K K)^{\beta} (a_H L)^{\gamma} A^{\theta-2} > 0.$$

The growth of capital is assumed to be determined by a Cobb–Douglas production function:

$$\dot{K} = \underbrace{s(1-a_K)^{\alpha}(1-a_H)^{1-\alpha}}_{c_1} K^{\beta} A^{1-\alpha} H^{1-\alpha}. \tag{8.33}$$

Further assume that human capital is growing at the exogenously determined rate g_H. In Equation (8.33) $(1 - a_K)$ and $(1 - a_H)$ give the share of capital and educational capital used in the goods-producing sector (which is also the sector producing capital). The parameters a_K and a_H are determined exogenously.

$$\dot{A} = \beta (a_K K)^{\beta} (a_H H)^{1-\beta} A^{\theta} \tag{8.34}$$

$$\text{or } \dot{A} = \underbrace{\beta a_K^{\beta} a_H^{1-\beta}}_{c_2} K^{\beta} H^{1-\beta} A^{\theta}.$$

We thus have a non-linear system of differential equations:

$$\dot{K} = c_1 K^{\alpha} H^{1-\alpha} A^{1-\alpha} \tag{8.35}$$

$$\dot{A} = c_2 K^{\beta} H^{1-\beta} A^{\theta} \tag{8.35a}$$

$$\dot{H} = \gamma H \tag{8.35b}$$

or $\dot{Z} = M(Z)$ with $M(Z) > 0$ for $Z > 0$, where no depreciation of capital or knowledge is a crucial assumption in this model $Z = (K, A, H)$. This implies the existence of a common equilibrium rate of growth:

$$\lambda^* = \dot{K}/K = \dot{A}/A = \dot{H}/H = \dot{Y}/Y$$

as long as $\theta \leq 1$. David Romer (2001) has provided a useful illustration of the model outside and on the equilibrium growth trajectory.

Crucial assumptions are the values of β and θ. If the sum of β and θ is less than 1, then the growth rates of capital g_K and the growth rate of knowledge g_A will be $\dot{g}_K = \dot{g}_A + \dot{g}_H$, where $\dot{g}_H$ is the rate of growth of human capital. Furthermore $\beta \dot{g}_K + \gamma \dot{g}_H + (\theta - 1)\dot{g}_A = 0$. By substitution we then have:

$$\dot{g}_A / \dot{g}_H = \frac{\beta + \gamma}{1 - (\theta + \beta)} > 0.$$

On an equilibrium trajectory the rate of growth of capital equals the rate of growth of knowledge.

If $\beta + \theta$ were to be larger than 1, we would have *divergence* of the rate of growth of income, capital and knowledge. If $\beta + \theta = 1$ the system converges to constant rates of growth of capital and knowledge.

INCREASING RETURNS IN A MACRO ECONOMY?

In our accounting for growth of the total net product we have proposed that the growth of material and knowledge capital are the factors explaining the rate of growth of the macro economy. Because of the public nature of research findings, Romer (1986) has argued in favour of increasing returns to knowledge capital within a national economy as a consequence of publicness of knowledge. Each sector of production i is assumed in Romer's model to have the product regulated by a production function $F(K_i)$ multiplied by an efficiency factor $A(K)$, where K is a measure of the general availability of knowledge as reflected by the total macroeconomic stock of knowledge, as embodied in material, human and research capital of the economy as a whole. Romer then assumes that the product of the A and F functions, i.e. the macro production function, would be an aggregate production function with increasing returns to scale.

There are two fundamental objections to the assumption that there would be increasing returns in a macroeconomic production function. The first argument is the long-term inconsistencies of a growth path, as brought out by Solow (1994). The second argument against increasing returns at the macro-economic level is associated with the role of transaction-, information- and transportation costs.

The long-term inconsistency of a growth path based on increasing macro-economic returns can be exposed as follows.

The total capital of the macro economy, K analysed, is assumed to consist of material and knowledge capital stocks in fixed proportions. Total labour supply is assumed to be constant. The growth of the economy is further assumed to be determined by the following differential equation:

$$\frac{dK}{dt} = gK^{1+\lambda} \tag{8.36}$$

$\lambda > 0$ indicates increasing returns to scale. How quickly would an economy with $\lambda > 0$ double its size? Equation (8.36) can be reformulated to answer this question:

$$dt = \frac{1}{g}\frac{dK}{K^{1+\lambda}}. \tag{8.37}$$

Considering a discrete time period t_0 to t_1 and the requirement that $K_1 = 2K_0$, we have:

$$\Delta t = t_1 - t_0 = \int_{t_0}^{t_1} dt = \int_{t_0}^{t_1} \frac{dK}{gK^{1+\lambda}} = \frac{1}{g\lambda K_0^{\lambda}}\left(1 - \frac{1}{2}\right). \tag{8.38}$$

Thus, the doubling time, $t_1 - t_0$, depends on the scale at t_0 if $\lambda > 0$. This implies that the time of doubling of the capital stock gets shorter the larger the size of the economy. As the economy grows, the time of doubling of the capital stock will become shorter and shorter. When t goes towards some *finite* T^* the capital stock will grow towards infinity (Mathews and Langenhop, 1966). Close to T^* the total capital stock will be congesting every conceivable spatial unit of the world.

Practically all available growth statistics also indicate that empirical evidence is incompatible with increasing returns to scale of (total) capital at the macro level of national (and) multinational economies (see p. 202).

The second argument against increasing returns to scale at the macro level has to do with the indecomposable role of information, transactions and transportation costs associated with transmission and use of material goods, services and knowledge.

The reasonable macroeconomic assumption is constant returns to scale where the macro economy is assumed to include resource uses by the transaction and transportation sectors of the economy.

Basing the analysis of competitive equilibrium on the analysis by Chamberlin (1933), Robinson (1933) and Triffin (1940) of monopolistic competition, Dixit and Stiglitz (1977) claim that a monopolistic competition general equilibrium would be compatible with increasing returns to scale in the production of firms. This is a consequence of the fact that in monopolistic competition each firm would face a downward sloping demand curve with respect to their own price.

However, there is a spatial reason for the downward sloping demand curve, implicit in most of microeconomic analysis of monopolistic competition. Information, transaction and transportation costs are preventing perfect competition. Enlarging a geographical market implies searching across a space that would be growing in proportion to the square of the increased distance from the production site. Such average costs are thus progressively increasing with an increasing scale of production. Limited accessibility of customers and their demand is thus the main explanation of the existence of increasing returns to production of goods, services and knowledge by firms. In Romer's models (1986, 1990), there is no limitation on accessibility, because of the non-existence of information, transactions and transportation activities and resource use within the model.

In the sequel we will show that macroeconomic modelling of knowledge and growth can include spatial frictions limiting the macroeconomic rate of growth.

EMPIRICAL STUDIES OF ECONOMIC GROWTH AND SPILLOVERS FROM RESEARCH AND DEVELOPMENT INVESTMENTS

In macroeconomic growth models there are two distinct strands of the relation between R&D investments and economic growth rates. In the models going back to Shell (1966) and Uzawa (1965), R&D investments are endogenously determined in the growth models assumed, without any assumptions about economies of scale in the use of knowledge. Important recent examples are given in Peretto (1995), Young (1998) and Braconier (1998).

The impact of R&D is in these models determined by the R&D intensity, that is, the *share* of R&D labour in total employment. Implicit is an assumption that there is no free lunch in the diffusion of knowledge but that labour (and other resources) are required in the absorption of new knowledge (Nelson and Rosenberg, 1993). Among the activities requiring resources in the absorption of new knowledge are:

- search and adaptation of machinery and labour
- organization of production and product designs.

The use by a firm of new knowledge created by scientists of universities or firms is thus a decision variable with associated expected revenues, costs and risks (Nelson and Winter, 1982; Mansfield et al., 1981). Although new knowledge is public in nature, the access is limited and costly.

In contrast to this reasoning P. Romer (1990) and Grossman and Helpman (1991a) have modelled the endogenous formation of new knowledge by R&D and the process of economic growth with an assumption of free use of new knowledge by all firms *within a country*.

The USA – being the largest economy of the world – would thus have a growth advantage as a consequence of economies of scale in the use of capital (including material, educational and research capital).

Specifying the production function to be $Q_i = A_i(R)K_i^{\alpha_{iK}} R_i^{\alpha_{iR}} H_i^{\alpha_{iH}}$ for a sector, the growth rate of total factor productivity would be determined as $\dot{A}_i / A_i = \alpha_{iR}\dot{R}$, which means that the rate of growth of total factor productivity of firm or industry is determined by the total amount of resources allocated to R&D in the national economy as a whole.

In the contrasting approach advocated by Young (1998) and Peretto (1995), and earlier by Nelson and Winter (1982), the growth of total factor productivity would be determined as:

$$\dot{A}_i / A_i = \alpha_{iy}\left(\dot{R}/n\right)$$

where

n = number of product lines of the economy as a whole
α_{iy} = the efficiency of the use of R&D-investments.

An alternative is R&D per capita = $\left(\dot{R}/L\right)$ as a proxy for $\left(\dot{R}/n\right)$.

Braconier (1998) has empirically estimated the impact on long-term rates of growth of per capita incomes 1960–95, contrasting the Romer-type economies of scale of R&D against the Young–Peretto R&D per capita. The database used is a sample of 62 countries. The results are the following for the best fit equation:

Table 8.5 Regression results. Dependent variable: percentage rate of per capita income growth

Variable	Coefficient	t-value
Intercept	+0.120	+5.40
R&D (investments per capita)	+0.290	+5.80
ln (income per capita in 1960)	–0.010	–4.20
ln (gross investment)	+0.013	+3.49
ln (human capital investment)	+0.010	+3.43
ln (population growth)	–0.006	–3.00

$R^2 = 0.63$

Formulations capturing Romer-type increasing returns are rejected in this hypothesis testing. On the basis of his hypothesis testing we can draw the conclusion that:

- The Romer, and Grossman and Helpman hypothesis of macroeconomic returns to scale in the use of knowledge created by R&D, is falsified.
- R&D intensity has a significant positive impact on macroeconomic growth rates.
- Accumulation of human and material capital has significant positive impacts on macroeconomic growth rates.
- There is a growth advantage of being initially backward (see also Kuznets, 1966).

SCIENTIFIC RESEARCH AND ECONOMIC GROWTH – A NEOCLASSICAL MODEL

Students of economic history have not failed to observe that the onset of the Industrial Revolution in England, which initiated the age of sustained economic growth in Europe and the West, was preceded by a few decades by the scientific revolution in the age of Newton, who gave the world both the calculus and the new principles of mechanics, which at that time made up not only the heart of physics but of all 'natural philosophy' or natural science.

This raises the question of how closely economic and scientific growth are tied together and perhaps also the chicken and egg question of which comes first – but that turns out to be resolvable and revealing on a closer examination in pages 225–30.

Pure basic research producing nothing of market value has always depended on outside financial support which may be forthcoming either from government income derived from taxation or otherwise from private sponsors. For purposes of this analysis both sources may be presumed to be in essence proportional to national income or, more simply, to GDP. Thus financial input into scientific research is presumably equal to or in any case limited by a fixed proportion of GDP.

What about manpower? At one time, observation of current trends revealed that the number of theoretical physicists was growing at 5 per cent per annum which far outstripped that of population growth in general, and thus encouraged some physicists to predict that by 2050 the physics establishment would be made up of the entire world population – an obvious fallacy. The growth of any subset of population P is at best restricted by a logistic law:

$$\dot{P} = aP(N - P) \tag{8.39}$$

where N is a limit of either absolute numbers or of a certain proportion in a growing total population.

This means in essence that in the long run, physicists or for that matter biologists or economists or witch doctors cannot expect to grow at a faster rate than that of the general population.

There are thus two restrictions posed on the growth of all science, one deriving from GNP and the other from population. With these limits scientific output may of course advance faster than either on account of technical progress in scientific research. That technical progress should operate not only because of industrial science but within science as well, is not only theoretically reasonable but empirically verifiable. Data on inputs and outputs of the engineering department at the University of Texas, Austin, when fitted to a Cobb–Douglas production function with technical progress, revealed a rate of technical change for the time span 1960 to 1990 of approximately 4 per cent.

Whatever the precise numerical value may be, there is thus no debating the possibility of technical progress in scientific research.

To the extent that financial support and manpower may, over intermediate periods, grow slightly faster than GDP and population, respectively, growth rates in science may temporarily exceed those in the economy, and to the extent that the rate of technical progress in science exceeds that in production. Generally, scientific output may grow even permanently at somewhat higher rates than output in the economy. This points to the importance of further study of technical progress in both science and industrial production, in order to obtain a more solid basis for forecasting sustained growth in either sector of the economy.

While budgets and manpower are hard facts, open to direct observation, the impact of scientific growth on technical progress is shrouded in considerable obscurity and even uncertainty. The relation between technical change and aggregate output in the economy, on the other hand, is again more firmly established.

Conventional wisdom has it that pure basic research, while never intended to bear any fruit in solid practical applications, invariably turns out to have an impact on applied science, if only with a time delay of often considerable and unpredictable length.

Illustrations are known for example from mathematics where the study of operators in Hilbert space turned out to be just what was needed for the foundations of quantum mechanics, or the perfectly 'pure' theory of numbers, especially of primes, which supplied essential tools to cryptography and cryptanalysis.

But how reliable is the presumed link between today's basic research and tomorrow's applied research and technology?

Suppose for a moment that the larger part of basic research never matures into useful applications but remains essentially what it is intended to be, an object of disinterested human curiosity. Suppose furthermore that in order to please, attract and motivate scholars and scientists, they must be allowed to spend a proportion of their research time on basic research while primarily in pursuit of applied research which they have been hired to do. In that case, basic research is just a sop or extra expense needed to motivate and employ fruitfully the army of scientists that carries out the business of the (applied) research establishment.

It is then only the proportion of total scientific effort actually devoted to applied research that is productive of technical innovations.

For purposes of calculating applicable scientific output this is still a function of manpower; in efficiency units and funds supplied as inputs into the scientific community. For simplicity of argument assume a Cobb–Douglas production function. Let:

R = scientific output resulting in technical progress
S = scientific manpower
M = funds to finance science.

$$R = bS^{\alpha}M^{\beta} \tag{8.40}$$

Whether basic research as a constant fraction of total research is ultimately useful to applied science resulting in technical progress will merely affect the productivity coefficient b, as long as basic research remains a fixed proportion of all scientific effort.

Allowing for technical progress in scientific research (8.40) should be modified as:

$$R = e^{\varepsilon t}S^{\alpha}M^{\beta} \tag{8.41}$$

where ε is the rate of exogenous technical progress in (applied) scientific research.

Turn now to the production Y of goods and services as recorded in GDP. Its inputs are labour (L) (efficiency units), capital (K) and research (R), which determines the state of technology and thus the effectiveness with which labour and capital can be employed.

In a national context, (R) represents research of this country. Even though science is international its results become effective only when reproduced in one's own country. In this sense, national output depends on national research. The productivity of national research is of course dependent on its integration with the international science community.

With Cobb–Douglas functions once more – but without exogenous technical progress, which is now represented by research output, (R) – we have:

$$Y = R^{\rho}L^{\lambda}K^{\mu} \tag{8.42}$$

where $\rho, \lambda, \mu > 0$ are constant output elasticities. Nothing is assumed about either constant, decreasing or increasing returns to scale.

Consider now the allocation of the nation's labour force (measured in efficiency units) (N), to research personnel (S) and manpower (L) in general production:

$$\begin{aligned} L &= xN \\ S &= (1-x)N \end{aligned} \tag{8.43}$$

with $0 < x < 1$.

Although there may be sections in the economy where no research is needed or undertaken, in the aggregate, some science input is essential to all under contemporary conditions.

Let savings be given as a constant fraction, s, of GDP. A fraction u of this saving will be invested in capital so that:

$$\dot{K} = usY \tag{8.44}$$

and an amount:

$$s(1-u)Y$$

is applied as funding input into research:

$$M = (1-u)sY. \tag{8.45}$$

Current output depends on these allocations as follows:

$$Y_t = \left\{b\left[(1-x)N\right]^{\alpha}\left[(1-u)sY\right]^{\beta}\right\}^{\rho}(xN)^{\lambda}\left(K_{t-1} + usY_{t-1}\right)^{\mu}. \tag{8.46}$$

In the short run, viz. this year, output is maximized by choosing x and u such that:

$$0 = \frac{\partial Y}{\partial x} = -\frac{\alpha\rho Y}{1-x} + \frac{\lambda Y}{x}$$

$$0 = \frac{\partial Y}{\partial u} = -\frac{\beta\rho Y}{1-u} + \frac{\mu S Y_t Y_{t-1}}{K_{t-1} + usY_{t-1}}$$

yielding:

$$x = \frac{\lambda}{\lambda + \alpha\rho} \tag{8.47}$$

$$u = \frac{1 - \dfrac{\rho\beta}{\mu}\dfrac{k}{s}}{1 + \rho\beta/\mu} \tag{8.48}$$

where

$$k = \frac{K_{t-1}}{Y_{t-1}}$$

is the capital–output ratio.

If last year's capital–output ratio k is too large, so that u in Equation (8.48) is negative, then all savings are put as funds into research until, as Y grows, the capital–output ratio k falls.

However, as neoclassical growth theory shows, the capital–output ratio will stabilize in the long run. At constant k, the proportions of manpower and of savings applied to research should then also be constant. Does this imply that the growth rates of science and of production in general will equalize?

Consider now the long-run growth rates that are generated by the production functions (8.40) and (8.41) when fixed proportions x and u (even non-optimal ones) are allocated to the research and production sectors of the economy.

Observe first that a constant capital–output ratio k implies $K = kY$:

$$\frac{\dot{K}}{K} = \frac{\dot{Y}}{Y} = g. \tag{8.49}$$

Now, from (8.41), (8.43) and (8.45) and (8.49) the growth h of science is:

$$h = \frac{\dot{R}}{R} = \varepsilon + \alpha\frac{\dot{N}}{N} + \beta\frac{\dot{Y}}{Y}$$

$$h = \varepsilon + \alpha n + \beta g \tag{8.50}$$

where n is the given rate of growth of efficiency units of labour and g denotes the growth rate of GNP.

$$g = \frac{\rho}{1-\mu}h + \frac{\lambda}{1-\mu}n \tag{8.51}$$

Substituting (8.51) in (8.50) the growth of science output is determined as:

$$h = \varepsilon + \alpha n + \frac{\beta\rho}{1-\mu}h + \frac{\beta\lambda}{1-\mu}n$$

$$h = \frac{1-\mu}{1-\mu-\beta\rho}\varepsilon + \frac{\alpha - \alpha\mu + \beta\lambda}{1-\mu-\beta\rho}n \tag{8.52}$$

so that:

$$g = \frac{\rho}{1-\mu-\beta\rho}\varepsilon + \frac{\lambda+\rho\alpha}{1-\mu-\rho\beta}n. \tag{8.53}$$

These growth rates are weighted sums of the external growth rates n of efficiency units of the labour force and ε of the effectiveness of scientific research. These weights are increasing functions of all the output elasticity α, β, λ, μ, ρ. Consider the difference in growth rates:

$$\begin{aligned} h-g &= \{(1-\rho-\mu)\varepsilon + [\alpha(1-\rho-\mu)+\lambda(\beta-1)]\}n \\ &\geq \alpha(1-\lambda-\mu)n + (1-\rho-\mu)\varepsilon \\ &\geq 0 \end{aligned}$$

on the assumption of non-decreasing returns in scientific research:

$$\alpha+\beta \geq 1$$

and:

$$\rho+\mu \leq 1;$$

non-increasing returns in production.

Even without technical progress in research, the science sector will then grow at least as fast as the production sector of the economy.

On the other hand, with non-decreasing returns in production $\lambda+\mu+\rho \geq 1$ and no technical progress plus non-increasing returns in research $\alpha+\beta \leq 1$ and $\varepsilon = 0$, the production sector will grow faster than the science sector.

With constant returns in both sectors, research will grow faster if and only if there is technical progress in scientific research $\varepsilon > 0$.

Without technical progress in research, both sectors will grow at the same rate $g = h$ if and only if both sectors have constant returns to scale:

$$\begin{aligned} \alpha+\beta &= 1 \\ \rho+\lambda+\mu &= 1\,. \end{aligned} \tag{8.54}$$

This constant growth rate turns out to be equal to that of growth of efficiency units of labour:

$$g = h = \frac{\lambda + \alpha + \rho}{\lambda + \rho + \alpha} n \tag{8.55}$$

so that, research notwithstanding, no increase in output per efficiency unit of labour is then possible.

This shows how restrictive the assumption of constant returns is, when technology or research inputs are included. The true effect of research must therefore be seen in its power to generate increasing returns, when capital and labour by themselves are capable only of constant returns to scale:

$$\rho + \lambda + \mu > \lambda + \mu = 1. \tag{8.56}$$

In fact with $\varepsilon = 0$, Equation (8.53) shows that:

$$g > n \Leftrightarrow \lambda + \mu + \rho(\alpha + \beta) > 1.$$

With constant returns in both research and production (and no exogenous increase in research productivity):

$$g - n = \rho.$$

The growth rate of output per efficiency unit of labour equals the output elasticity ρ of research.

DYNAMICS OF SCIENTIFIC AND APPLIED RESEARCH – A NEO-SCHUMPETER APPROACH

The field of 'dynamic synergetics' owes much of its development to the contributions of the German physicist Hermann Haken (1978). In a number of path-breaking studies, Haken has highlighted certain elements that are involved in synergetic processes. If we disregard certain less important components of this paradigm, we arrive at the following two conditions that must be fulfilled in a synergetic analysis:

1. The variables involved are dynamically and non-linearly interactive.
2. Timescales are separable, according to the relative speed of change in the dynamic sub-processes.

The first requirement, non-linear interactivity, excludes such standard economic methods as input–output models and most neoclassical growth models from synergetics. Instead, synergetics starts at the level of second-order interactions, which means that the interactions are irreducible to linear relations. Included among synergetic phenomena are catalysts, enzymes and similar physical, chemical and biological phenomena, all of which are interactive. An important economic analyst who has explored dynamic economic models from this standpoint is Tönu Puu (2003).

Fundamental to synergetic theory is the possibility of *adiabatic approximation*. This concept refers to the possibility of solving for approximate equilibria, using the actual difference of time scales of different processes as a vehicle of approximating the constancy of some process. This implies that synergetics is a theory and modelling procedure for real rather than idealized systems.

Synergetics is a theory containing possibilities of bifurcations (that is, phase transitions). Although growth and evolutionary equilibria may be typical outcomes, every synergetic system contains the potential for revolutionary changes to the structure. Stochastics can be essential to such phase transitions in synergetic models. Although of minor consequence during the stages of evolutionary equilibria of a specific system, there are situations – such as in the vicinity of a bifurcation – where and when even small stochastic swings can trigger a transfer from one evolutionary trajectory onto another, by way of a revolutionary disruption of the overall structure. In this sense, synergetics comes rather close to the thinking of Prigogine (for example given in Prigogine and Nicolis, 1989).

We can also use synergetic reasoning in the context of modelling the development of scientific ideas. Let us assume that such ideas are accumulated in nodes of an intellectual network. Let us further assume that some of these ideas are of a paradigmatic (that is, infrastructural) nature, which means that they are changing extremely slowly and only through continuous confirmations or falsifications of the fast processes – i.e. models consistent with the paradigmatic theory.

As an example, consider general equilibrium theory (GET) as such a slowly changing, paradigmatic process within a network of ideas. Assuming the components of such paradigmatic or infrastructural ideas to be interconnected with each other into a stable network of consistent ideas, this can coexist with very fast processes which generate more or less applicable models that are supported by the 'fundamental GET network'.

Parallel to the GET theory there exist other economic theories – for example, Neo-Keynesian Theory (NKT) or Evolutionary Economic Theory (EET). These theories could potentially be mutually compatible. We can illustrate these theoretical bodies with Figure 8.2.

Newly generated ideas can be either *critical* or *non-critical*. A critical idea is an idea that belongs to the slowly changing part of a theoretical paradigm. A critical idea therefore interconnects large subsets of the total network of ideas, generating an expanded infrastructure for further theoretical development. Such a synergetic, critical idea (e.g. a model or hypothesis) has two characteristics:

1. It provides a shortcut between formerly unconnected networks of ideas.
2. It triggers a large increase in the development potential of the field as a whole, in spite of being small in itself.

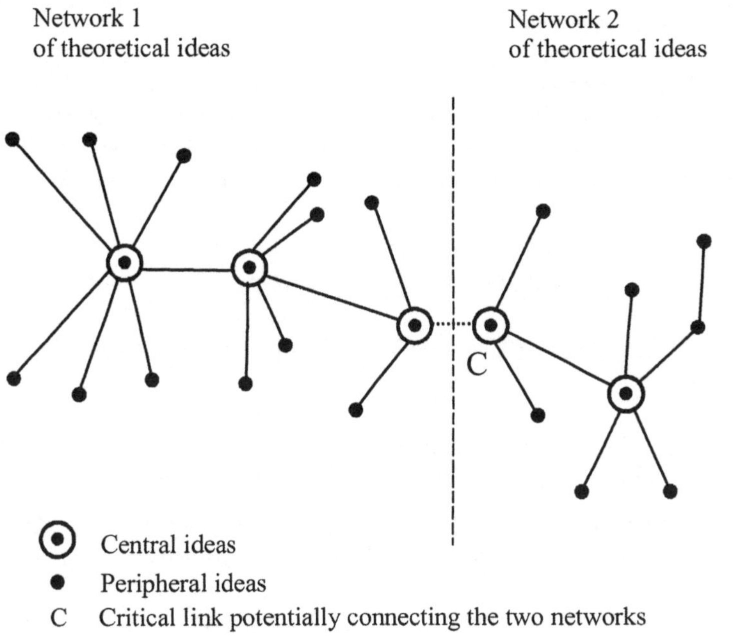

Figure 8.2 Networks of connected scientific ideas

Both these phenomena introduce fundamental non-linearities into theories of scientific development. The introduction of a small but sufficiently critical idea implies that a small change in one of the slowly changing variables causes a much greater shift in the structure of ideas as a whole. Thus we arrive at the typical case where an infinitesimal change in one variable causes substantial changes in other variables.

There are many examples of how critical (although innocuously small) contributions can trigger the development of totally new approaches to theoretical and applied research. One theoretical example is *Inequalities* by Hardy et al. ([1934] 1967). In that book, the three mathematicians reformulated many relations as inequalities rather than as equalities, which was the standard procedure before the publication of their book. This new approach was an example of a critical idea, which made it possible to use set theory in practical problem formulation and problem-solving. Most of the modern programming in economics (e.g. linear programming, non-linear programming, dynamic programming, optimal control theory) needed this critical link between applied mathematical modelling and its theoretical foundation. Similarly the CES-function of applied mathematical economics was completely analysed in *Inequalities* long before the introduction into economics in Arrow et al. (1961).

A similar relation exists between Newtonian physics in the 17th century and the development of mechanical engineering in the 18th and 19th century.

Synergetic theory can be used to model the dynamic interactions of scientific and applied knowledge. The growth of scientific knowledge is determined by the educational capital and other resources available for scientific research.

$$\Delta_1 R_S = F\left[H_S, Q(K, R_A) s\tau_S\right] \tag{8.57}$$

Applied industrial research is dependent on scientific knowledge and other resources.

$$\Delta_2 R_A = G\left[R_A, R_S, Q(K, R_A) s\tau_A\right] \tag{8.58}$$

Capital accumulation is dependent on applied industrial knowledge savings and allocation of savings to material and research investments.

$$\Delta_2 K = s(1 - \tau_A - \tau_S) Q(K, R_A) - \delta K \tag{8.59}$$

Δ_1 = change over a long time period
Δ_2 = change over a short time period.

$F\left[H_S, Q(K, R_A) s\tau_S\right]$ is a scientific production function, within which

H_S = the human (education) capital available for scientific research
$Q(K, R_A)$ = the macroeconomic production function with capital (K) and applied knowledge (R_A) as arguments
s = the rate of savings
τ_S = share of savings allocated to scientific research.

The applied industrial research is determined by the function:

$$G\left[R_A, R_S, Q(K, R_A)s\tau_A\right]$$

$$0 < \tau_A + \tau_S < 1.$$

The production function Q is assumed to be a Taylor-approximation of order three (Puu, 2003), allowing for increasing, constant and decreasing returns at different levels of production (see also Frisch, 1962).

The growth per year of scientific knowledge is slow compared to the growth of applied knowledge and other capital. Therefore a formulation of a differential equation system operating on the same timescale requires a reformulation of the system equations.

$$\dot{R}_S = \varepsilon F\left[H_S, Q(K, R_A)s\tau_S\right] \quad (8.57a)$$

$$\dot{R}_A = G\left[R_A, R_S, Q(K, R_A)s\tau_A\right] \quad (8.58a)$$

$$\dot{K} = s(1 - \tau_A - \tau_S)Q(K, R_A) - \delta K \quad (8.59a)$$

$0 < \varepsilon << 1$, is by orders of magnitude smaller than 1. A very small positive ε means that the level of scientific knowledge is (perceived to be) constant and thus provides a platform of science infrastructure facilitating and constraining the advances of applied knowledge by industrial research and development.

Using an adiabatic approximation we thus have the following system of differential equations.

$$\dot{R}_A = G\left[R_A, \bar{R}_S, Q(K, R_A)s\tau_A\right] \quad (8.58b)$$

$$\dot{K} = s(1 - \tau_A - \tau_S)Q(K, R_A) - \delta K \quad (8.59b)$$

$$\dot{R}_S \cong 0. \quad (8.57b)$$

This system can now be solved as:

$$\lambda R_A = G\left[R_A, \bar{R}_S, Q(K, R_A)s\tau_A\right] \quad (8.60)$$

$$\lambda K = s(1 - \tau_A - \tau_S)Q(K, R_A) - \delta K \quad (8.61)$$

giving a *temporary equilibrium rate of growth*, $\lambda^* > 0$. However, this is not a general equilibrium rate of growth. The slow and steady expansion of scientific knowledge will eventually lead to a bifurcation of the system (8.57a) to (8.59a). At such a critical point all three equations will interact and give rise to a new temporary equilibrium growth trajectory after a phase transition period. Such a phase transition period was termed a period of 'creative destruction' by Joseph Schumpeter (1912).

SPATIAL ACCESSIBILITY OF KNOWLEDGE AND GROWTH

Knowledge can be embodied in machinery and other material capital, as human capital embodied in the labour force and in units of research. For simplicity, we will assume that in each point of space there will be an aggregate of such knowledge capital, called K_i. We will further assume that the productivity of the K_i is declining monotonously with an increasing distance, d_{ji} from a user j to a holder of K_i. The maximal productivity is reached if $i = j$. Two reasonable and yet simple candidates of an accessibility function of i with respect to j are:

$$A_{ia} = \sum e^{-d_{ij}} K_j \qquad (8.62)$$

where A_i = accessibility and K_j = capital in node j.

$$A_{ib} = \sum d_{ij}^{-u} K_j ; \quad \text{with } d_{ij} \geq 1. \qquad (8.62a)$$

The production function of each node i of the network can be formulated as:

$$Q_i = F\left(A_i, \bar{M}_i\right); \quad i = 1, \ldots, n \qquad (8.63)$$

where

Q_i = production in node i
A_i = accessibility of material, educational and other knowledge capital in node i
$\bar{M}_i$ = economically useful area of node i.

Accumulation of knowledge capital of node i is determined by the equation:

$$\dot{K}_i = s_i F\left(A_i, \bar{M}_i\right); \quad i = 1,\ldots,n. \tag{8.64}$$

In order to illustrate some possible properties of such a differential equation assume that the production function can be decomposed into three factors: (1) local impact of knowledge, (2) spatial congestion, and (3) accessibility of knowledge, as indicated in Equation (8.65).

$$\dot{K}_i = \underbrace{s_i K_i^{\alpha}}_{(1)} \underbrace{\left(\frac{\bar{M}_i}{K_i}\right)^{\beta}}_{(2)} \underbrace{\left(\sum_{i \neq j} e^{-\gamma d_{ij}} K_j\right)^{\lambda}}_{(3)} \tag{8.65}$$

$$\dot{K}_i = s_i K_i^{\alpha-\beta} \bar{M}_i^{\beta} \left(\sum_{i \neq j} e^{-\gamma d_{ij}} K_j\right)^{\lambda} \tag{8.65a}$$

For simplicity we assume $\alpha = \beta$ and $\lambda = 1$.

$$\dot{K}_i = s_i \bar{M}_i^{\beta} \sum_{i \neq j} e^{-\gamma d_{ij}} K_j \qquad (i = 1,\ldots, n) \tag{8.65b}$$

$\dot{K}_i$ = investment in region i, $\bar{M}_i$ = available land in i, K_i = total capital stock in i, d_{ij} = distance from region i to region j and s_i = propensity to invest.

Assume a constant rate of growth i.e. $\dot{K}_i / K_i = g$ for all i, implying that $gk = Mk$, where

$$M = \left(s_i \bar{M}_i^{\beta} e^{-\gamma d_{ij}}\right),$$

and $k = [K_i]$. Every element

$$\bar{M}_i^{\beta} e^{-\gamma d_{ij}}$$

of the matrix M is larger than 0, because capital requires land and distances d_{ij} are always positive. For positive matrices, M, we have a theorem by Frobenius and Perron (see Klein, 1973). Accordingly, the balanced rate of growth, g, can be increased in four different ways:

1. By an increased propensity to save (composed of domestic rate of savings and import surplus)
2. By an increased efficiency of the transport and transactions infrastructure
3. By a decrease of any one of the transport and transaction links d_{ij} and
4. By an increased efficiency of land use.

An alternative model would be based on the idea that useful capital to region i from region j would be:

$$U_{ij} = \frac{K_j}{d_{ij}^{\mu}} \quad \text{with } d_{ij} \geq 1. \tag{8.66}$$

Production of region i would then be:

$$Q_i = \prod_j \left(\frac{K_j}{d_{ij}^{\mu}} \right)^{\alpha_{ij}} \tag{8.67}$$

$$\dot{K}_i = s \prod_j \left(\frac{K_j}{d_{ij}^{\mu}} \right)^{\alpha_{ij}} \tag{8.68}$$

$$\dot{K}_i = \lambda K_i \; ; \quad i = 1, \dots, n$$

$$\lambda K_i = s \prod_j \left(\frac{K_j}{d_{ji}^{\mu}} \right)^{\alpha_{ij}} \qquad i = 1, \dots, n \tag{8.69}$$

$$0 < \alpha_{ij} < 1$$

$$\sum_j \alpha_{ij} = 1$$

$$\lambda K_i = s \prod_j d_{ij}^{-\mu \alpha_{ij}} K_j^{\alpha_{ij}}. \tag{8.70}$$

This is a non-linear eigen-equation:

$$\lambda k = H(k). \tag{8.71}$$

A theorem applicable to Equation (8.71) is given on p. 235. As $H(k) > 0$ for all $k > 0$ we have a fixed point problem with $\lambda > 0$. The rate of growth at an equilibrium is thus the same in all nodes of the network and thus of the network economy, if seen as a macro economy.

MATERIAL CAPITAL, LABOUR AND KNOWLEDGE GROWTH ON NETWORKS

Accessibility to knowledge influences productivity in the nodes through the available stocks of knowledge on all nodes. The growth of productivity is thus dependent on the growth of the stocks of knowledge. Each node of the economic network is assumed to have a private sector of production producing the good, according to a production function.

Four factors of production are assumed to be available in the finite number of nodes.

Accessibility to knowledge in node i is defined as:

$$a_i = \sum_{j=1}^{n} e^{-\beta d_{ij}} R_j \qquad (8.72)$$

where

d_{ij} = distance (e.g. time of travel) from node i to node j
R_j = stock of knowledge in node j
β = distance friction parameter.

For simplicity we assume no trade between nodes of the economic network. All economic interaction is through accessibility to knowledge. Private capital accumulation is determined by the propensity to invest (s_i) and by the rate of investment in knowledge (τ_i):

$$\frac{dK_i}{dt} \equiv \dot{K}_i = s_i\left(1-\tau_i\right)Q_i\left(K_i, L_i, H_i, a_i\right) \qquad (i = 1, ..., n) \qquad (8.73)$$

where

K_i = capital
L_i = labour
H_i = human capital
a_i = accessibility to knowledge.

Expansion of labour supply in a node is assumed to be determined by consumption per capita = C_i = $\left[(1-s_i)(1-\tau_i)Q_i/L_i\right]$ and the total size of the labour force (L_i):

$$\dot{L}_i = F\left(C_i, L_i, H_i\right). \tag{8.74}$$

Assumptions:

$$\frac{\partial F}{\partial L_i} \geq 0; \quad \frac{\partial F}{\partial H_i} < 0$$

The sign of $\partial F/\partial C_i$ is uncertain. On the one hand, hours of work per capita tend to decline with increasing per capita consumption. On the other hand, an increasing average level of income would attract migration of labour. Investment in human capital depends upon income per capita as well as the level of education already achieved as shown empirically in Becker and Michael (1973) and Andersson and Lundqvist (1976).

Thus $\dot{H}_i = G\left[(1-s_i)(1-\tau_i)Q_i/L_2, H_i\right]$ (8.75)

Assumptions:

$$\partial G/\partial\left(Q_i/L_i\right) > 0 \text{ and } \partial G/\partial\left(H_i/L_i\right) > 0.$$

The growth of (disembodied) knowledge is assumed to be proportional to the share of total income allocated to the research sector of the economy. It is assumed that the research sector has a given labour force, which transforms the funds, $\tau_i Q_i$ into additions of knowledge with an efficiency of g_i. Thus the growth of knowledge is determined as:

$$\dot{R}_i = g_i \tau_i Q\left(K_i, L_i, H_i, a_i\right). \tag{8.76}$$

Compactly written we have a differential equation system:

$$\dot{x}_i = M(x) \tag{8.77}$$

where $x = \left(K_i, L_i, H_i, R_i\right)$ and $M(x)$ is a semi-positive mapping from x to $\dot{x}$. For such a system a theorem by Nikaido (1968) can be applied.

Assumptions:

(a) $M(x) = [M_i(x)]$ is defined for all $x \geq 0$.
(b) $M(x)$ is continuous as a mapping M: $R_+^n \to R_+^n$, except possibly at $x = 0$.
(c) $M(x)$ is positively homogenous of order m, $0 \leq m \leq 1$ in the sense that $M(x) \geq 0$ and $x \geq 0$.

Theorem:

Let $\Lambda = \{M(x) = \lambda x\}$ *for* $x \in p_n$

where

$$p_n = \left\{ x \middle| x \geq 0, \sum_{i=1}^{n} x_i = 1 \right\}$$

is the standard simplex. Then $M(x)$ contains a maximum characteristic value which is denoted $\lambda(M)$. Furthermore, if $M(x)$ is homogenous of degree 1, i.e. if $m = 1$ as a special case of assumption (c) then $\lambda(M)$ is the largest of all the eigenvalues of $M(x)$.

Proof: Nikaido (1968).

In the vicinity of an equilibrium $\lambda(M)$ can be locally linearized as $M[x(t)] = M(x^*)$, where x^* is x on the equilibrium trajectory. We then have the eigen-equation:

$$\gamma z = M\left(x^*\right) z \tag{8.78}$$

with the equilibrium growth rate $\lambda[M(x^*)]$. Applying the Frobenius–Perron theorem we can conclude that the growth rate γ will increase with:

(a) An increase of any research productivity g_i
(b) A decrease of any distance, d_{ij}
(c) A decrease of the general distance friction, β.

Changes of type (a), (b), (c) influence the rates of growth of all nodes to the same extent – in the long run.

The consequences of changes of the parameters s_i and τ_i cannot be determined qualitatively, because of the fact that these parameters enter the different model equations with different signs.

Instead of qualitative analysis of the non-linear model (8.77) a quantitative version of that model has been simulated:

$$Q_i = A\left(\alpha_1 K_i^{-\rho} + \alpha_2 L_i^{-\rho} + \alpha_3 H_i^{-\rho} + \alpha_4 a_i^{-\rho}\right)^{-1/\rho} \quad (8.79)$$

$$(i = 1, 2, 3)$$

where $a_i = \sum_{i=1}^{3} e^{-\beta d_{ij}} R_j$.

The evolution of the inputs is determined by:

$$\dot{K}_i = s_i\left(1-\tau_i\right)Q_2 \quad (8.80)$$

$$\dot{L}_i = C_{1i}\left[\left(1-s_i\right)\left(1-\tau_i\right)Q_i/L_i\right]^{\lambda} L_i^{\gamma_i} \quad (8.81)$$

$$\dot{H}_i = C_{2i}\left[\left(1-s_i\right)\left(1-\tau_i\right)Q_i/L_i\right]^{\delta}\left(H_i/L_i\right)^{\varepsilon}$$

$$\dot{R}_i = \tau_i g Q_i \quad (i = 1, 2, 3). \quad (8.82)$$

In the simulations the savings (or investments) ratio s_i is assumed to be the same in all nodes and equal to 30 per cent.

The distances between nodes of the network are $d_{12} = d_{21} = 500$; $d_{13} = d_{31} = d_{23} = d_{32} = 100$.

The distance friction $\beta = 0.1$. Node 2 is thus the most accessible, while node 3 is the least accessible, i.e. a periphery. Three kinds of simulations are analysed:

1. Changes of the elasticity of substitution in the production function, $1/(1 + \rho)$, are varied.
2. The distance matrix is changed to reduce the contrast between centre and periphery.
3. Economies of scale in the production function are assumed.

Initially the nodes are equipped with equal shares of total human capital and knowledge, while node 1 is assumed to have substantially larger stocks of capital and labour.

The research allocation parameter τ_i is assumed to be equal in the three nodes and then iteratively optimized. This parameter works in two opposite ways. On the one hand increases of τ decrease the growth of capital, on the other hand they increase the growth of and accessibility of knowledge of all regions. $0 < \tau < 1$ at an optimum.

Some further conclusions can be made:

(a) The optimal τ increases with the size of the elasticity of substitution in production.
(b) The optimal τ is lower, if consumption per capita is the object rather than production per capita.
(c) There are larger gains to the periphery than to the centre from increases of τ.

The average rate of growth depends on the elasticity of substitution. The larger the elasticity of substitution, the larger is the rate of growth and the level of τ, i.e. the relative advantage of knowledge accumulation. In all simulations this system is dynamically stable. When constant returns are assumed the system steadily converges towards constant relative proportions without fluctuations.

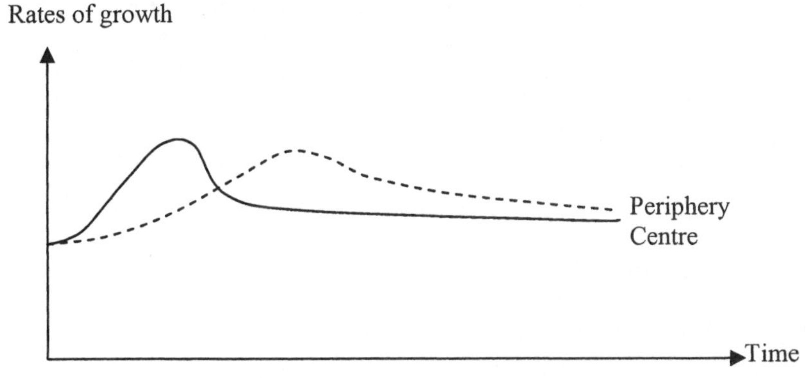

Figure 8.3 Patterns of growth in centre and periphery with a combination of economies of scale and frictions of distance

An assumption of increasing returns in production can be introduced in the CES production function by changing the exponent $-1/\rho$ to $-\eta/\rho$ with $\eta > 1$. Keeping all other assumptions of model (8.80) to (8.82) unchanged and setting $\eta = 1.5$ and $\tau = 0.5$ gives an interesting simulation result. The rates of growth are as expected much higher in this simulation than in comparable simulations with constant returns to scale. The time-pattern of growth is quite different from all simulated cases with constant returns to scale in production. Figure 8.3 shows the simulated rates of growth at different periods of time for the centre and periphery. The frictions of distance evidently give rise to delays in the production growth rates of the periphery in comparison with the centre.

These delays of the growth of the periphery are important for the development of inequality between nodes of an economic network. The well-known inverted U-curve in inequality, according to which per capita incomes of regions diverge in earlier stages of development towards a new economic structure, and only at quite late stages of development would there be convergence of regional income per capita.

ENDOGENOUS POLICIES AND GROWTH

So far the analysis of growth disregards the role of monetary institutions. The neutrality of monetary and interest policies has been an issue of intense debate since Keynes' macroeconomic theory was formulated in the 1930s (Keynes, 1936). Monetary policies can also be endogenized in the modelling of growth.

The quantitative rate of growth of the macro economy can be modelled along the theoretical lines of endogenous knowledge growth theory with material, human capital and R&D-capital as the growing inputs. The rate of growth of material plus human capital, g_K, can be assumed to depend on the real rate of interest r:

$$g_K = \alpha_0 - \alpha_1 r. \tag{8.83}$$

The quantitative rate of growth of the economy, g_y, can be assumed to depend on the rate of growth of capital (as defined) and a possibly positive rate of technological progress of production technology:

$$g_y = \beta_0 + \beta_1 g_K;$$

$$\text{by substitution of (8.83)} \quad \beta_0 + \beta_1 \left(\alpha_0 - \alpha_1 r\right) = g_y. \tag{8.84}$$

There is in this model approach nothing preventing non-linearities (e.g. increasing returns) in the dependency of g_y upon g_K, as long as there are institutions constraining the real rate of interest so as to avoid development of severe natural or labour resource bottlenecks. Such institutions are the Federal Reserve System and other central banks, regulating the floor level of interest rates. The financial regulatory institutions can be assumed to determine the rate of interest so as to avoid severe macroeconomic bottleneck problems, expected eventually to lead to inflation. An obvious variable determining the emergence of bottleneck problems is the quantitative rate of growth, g_y.

Taylor (1993) has analysed the interest rate policies of the USA and proposes the following interest rate determining equation:

$$r_t = a + (1+b)\hat{p}_t + c\left[\ln\left(y_t/\overline{y}_t\right)\right] \tag{8.85}$$

where

r_t = the central bank rate of interest in period t
$\hat{p}_t$ = expected rate of inflation
y_t = actual GDP
$\overline{y}_t$ = GDP at balanced rate of growth.

$\left(y_t/\overline{y}_t\right)$ and $\hat{p}_t$ can be seen as measures of expected bottleneck problems. Taylor has estimated the parameters to be $a = b = 0.5$.

If the expected rate of growth is assumed to be equal to realized rate of growth we have a reasonable real interest rate determination equation if the expected rate of growth equals the actual rate of growth.

$$r = B_0 + B_1 g_y \tag{8.85a}$$

Otherwise and more cumbersome:

$$g_y = g_{ye} + \varepsilon \tag{8.85b}$$

where ε is a random variable and g_{ye} = expected rate of growth.

An equilibrium quantitative growth path would then be determined by two equations:

$$g_y A_0 + A_1 r = 0; \quad \textit{Real part } (R) \tag{8.86}$$

$$g_y + B_0/B_1 - B_1^{-1} r = 0; \quad \textit{Financial part } (F) \tag{8.87}$$

This linear system has a growth and interest equilibrium that can be illustrated by Figure 8.4.

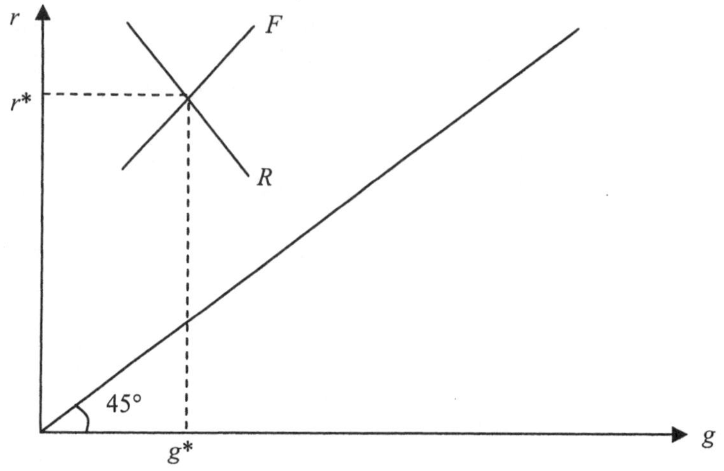

Figure 8.4 *Real (R), financial (F) and general macroeconomic equilibrium rates of interest and growth*

The real rate of interest is larger than the quantitative rate of growth, as long as the real rate of interest is institutionally determined by expected bottleneck problems (as for example, reflected by expected rates of inflation). Equality of the real rate of growth and the real rate of interest along the 45° line can only occur in an economy with no natural or labour resource bottlenecks occurring, for example in a von Neumann–Leontief–Cassel type of growing economy.

QUALITATIVE ECONOMIC GROWTH

Prices are assumed constant in most models of economic growth and technological progress. This implies that industrial R&D is wholly oriented to improvements of technology of production and not to generation of new or improved products. However, statistics on R&D investments show that most industrial research and development activities are oriented towards creation of new or improved products. This implies that the growth of the national product (GDP) should be decomposed into growth of quantity and growth of quality. Quality is primarily reflected in willingness to pay for the product. If the quality adjusted national product is defined as $y = \delta q$, where δ is the willingness to pay and q is the quantity produced (net of intermediate deliveries), then the rate of growth is:

$$\frac{\dot{\delta}}{\delta}+\frac{\dot{q}}{q}=\frac{\dot{y}}{y}.$$

$\dot{q}/q$ is the rate of quantitative growth, while $\dot{\delta}/\delta$ is the rate of growth of quality of the net national product. The willingness to pay δ_i for some good i must be relative to some substitute low quality reference good.

Qualitative growth by increasing value of goods is obviously more than improvement of production techniques related to the creative and innovative activities of society. Creation of new goods and their innovation is a highly uncertain economic process. In contrast to normal risk of investment, this type of risk is *epistemic* and can thus only be reduced by increasing knowledge, developing during the creation/innovation process.

In most societies financing of the creative processes is by financial means that are different from financing of projects with risks that can be compensated for by normal investment portfolio diversification procedures. For research of a scientific depth, the epistemic risk is large enough to warrant public funding. For product research venture capital or direct financing out of profits of firms are the normal sources of financing. This implies a required rate of return, exceeding required rates of return to most investments in material and human capital.

As is shown in Chapter 7 there are increasing returns to scale of investments in new products. This implies that countries like Switzerland, the Netherlands, Sweden and Finland with their large relative shares of large manufacturing corporations have larger than average relative proportions of their national products allocated to R&D investments, oriented to qualitative improvement of products.

EMPIRICAL STUDIES OF KNOWLEDGE ACCESSIBILITY AND GROWTH

A number of econometric studies of the impact of knowledge diffusion on economic growth have been performed by scholars of the Jönköping International Business School (see for example, Karlsson and Manduchi, 2001; Johansson et al., 2001; Andersson and Ejermo, 2004; Gråsjö, 2006).

One of the recent studies by Martin Andersson and Charlie Karlsson (2007), building on earlier work, provides a representative result from this type of econometric studies.

This econometric study is based on the following model:

$$Y_s = K_s^{\alpha}\left(A_s L_s\right)^{(1-\alpha)} \tag{8.88}$$

where

Y_s = product value of locality s
K_s = capital in locality s
A_s = accessible knowledge in locality s
L_s = labour in locality s.

Technological progress is assumed to be Harrod-neutral. The rate of change in output per unit of labour over time can be expressed as:

$$\frac{\Delta Y_s}{Y_s} = \alpha \frac{\Delta K_s}{K_s} + (1-\alpha)\frac{\Delta A_s}{A_s}. \tag{8.89}$$

In the estimation of changes over a short period of time the authors assume the rate of change of capital intensity to be approximately equal to zero and thus:

$$\frac{\Delta Y_s}{Y_s} = (1-\alpha)\frac{\Delta A_s}{A_s} \tag{8.90}$$

with:

$$\frac{\Delta A_s}{A_s} = \sigma_s(h_s)\frac{\Delta A_s}{Y_s} \tag{8.91}$$

where $\sigma(h)$ indicates the capacity to absorb knowledge as a function of human capital per unit of labour in each one of the localities s (Cohen and Levinthal, 1990). The econometric specification is:

$$\begin{aligned} \Delta Y_s = {} & \delta + \theta_1 \omega_s T_{sm} + \theta_2 \omega_s T_{sr} \\ & + \theta_3 \omega_s T_{se} + \theta_4 E_s \\ & + \theta_5 Popdens_s + \theta_6 Mig_s \\ & + \theta_7 Agr_s + \theta_8 Publ_s \\ & + \varepsilon_s \end{aligned} \tag{8.92}$$

where

ω_s = knowledge intensity of the labour force in location s
T_{sm} = accessibility to knowledge resources within the locality (i.e. municipality)
T_{sr} = accessibility to knowledge resources within the commuting region
T_{se} = accessibility to knowledge resources in all other localities of the country.

The accessibility measures are based on the exponential specification as given by Equation (8.62), with distances expressed as travel time by car.

ΔY_s = change in value added/employee, 1993–2001, in location s
E_s = number of one-employee firms in relation to total population
$Popdens_s$ = population per km^2 in locality s
Mig_s = 1, if net migration is positive, otherwise 0
Agr_s = 1, if more than 5 per cent of employment is in agriculture, otherwise 0
$Publ_s$ = 1, if more than 34 per cent of employment is in public sector, otherwise 0.

The knowledge resources are measured by the number of R&D man-years in universities of the localities. The econometric estimates are as follows:

$$\begin{aligned} \Delta Y_s = {} & 196082 + \underset{(2.4)}{314} \cdot \omega_s T_{sm} \\ & + \underset{(5.2)}{714} \cdot \omega_s T_{sr} \\ & - \underset{(-4.3)}{2239081} \cdot E_s \\ & - \underset{(-2.3)}{20069} \cdot Agr_s \end{aligned} \tag{8.93}$$

$R^2 = 0.41$; Obs: 286.

The parameters excluded from the estimated equation are not significantly different from zero.

In order to influence the growth of income, knowledge resources have to be located in the vicinity of the location of production. Local and regional accessibility is what counts.

These estimates strengthen the hypothesis that the macroeconomic growth impacts of knowledge spillovers are heavily spatially constrained.

IN NUCE

Industrial economies have in the very long run been growing at a moderate per capita growth rate. The long-term growth rates have on the whole had a tendency to converge towards a value close to 2.5 per cent per annum. Although business cycle fluctuations have been quite frequent, there is thus a general tendency towards a steady state rate of growth of economies beyond the initial stages of industrialization. However, newly industrialized countries seem to have productivity advantages of being late-comers in the industrialization process. The transformation from being an economy based on extraction and farming into an advanced industrial economy seems to require an increasingly shortened time. At the end of each transformation period into a fully industrialized economy, growth rates systematically decrease towards the long-term steady state rate of growth. Two growth factors have been notable during the 20th century. First, a steady expansion of the average level of education and more recently an increase in the relative GDP share of research and development investments.

In explaining the stable rate of growth there are basically three theoretical approaches. The first approach is associated with the theory of production interdependencies as modelled by von Neumann (1936) and Leontief (1951). These dynamic models have production functions representing constant returns to scale (with or without possibilities of substitution of different inputs).

A second class of models, the neoclassical growth models, is based upon a macro production function with capital and labour as inputs and with an assumption of an exogenously determined rate of technological progress (Solow, 1957). Technological progress can in these models be seen as a representation of expanding knowledge, increasing the productivity of labour, capital or both factors of production. In these models the rate of capital accumulation is determined endogenously and one of the results is that the propensity to save (and invest) cannot influence the rate of growth of the real income per capita.

A third class of models of macroeconomic growth has been called endogenous growth theory. In endogenous growth models, increasing technological efficiency is assumed to be determined by the growth of knowledge which is determined *within the model*. The first endogenous growth theories were proposed by Uzawa (1965) and Shell (1966), using an extended neoclassical production function and optimal control theory to arrive at closed form solutions. In these models of endogenous growth the propensity to save would be an important factor influencing the rate of growth per capita as well as the rate of growth of knowledge per unit of labour. The endogenous growth of knowledge as an equilibrium problem within an economy was explored by a number of economists in the 1980s and 1990s.

Early neoclassical endogenous theories of knowledge accumulation were based on an assumption of depreciation of knowledge on par with depreciation of material capital. This assumption had already been implicitly abandoned in the neoclassical theory of growth of the 1950s. In the new theories of endogenous growth of knowledge and production emerging in the 1980s the assumption of depreciation of knowledge was explicitly abandoned.

The idea of frictionless spillovers of knowledge (regarded as a public good) between different agents was proposed by some economists. According to some formulations the public character of knowledge would also imply economies of scale in knowledge accumulation at the macroeconomic scale of nations. Large economies like the USA, Russia and Japan would thus have a growth advantage over small economies like Finland, Sweden, the Netherlands, Taiwan and Korea, if they were to allocate similar relative shares of their GDP to investments in new knowledge. Accordingly, there would exist a size advantage of knowledge similar to the advantage of size of nations in warfare.

Empirical studies of long-term growth rates of industrialized national economies do not support the hypothesis that there is such a growth advantage of large size of nations. There are simply no studies showing positive correlations between size of national economies and their rates of economic growth. Constant returns to scale of total capital, including material, human and other knowledge capital, seems to be a more reasonable assumption.

There are general theoretical arguments supporting constant returns to scale in the long time perspective, relevant to theories of economic growth. A long-run equilibrium requires all firms to operate at minimal average (total) cost. Such an average cost includes costs of transactions and transport of inputs and outputs. In general, average transport and transaction costs increase with scale of operations. A long-run equilibrium scale would then permit a combination of increasing returns in production and decreasing returns in transactions and transportation. This combination of returns to scale would be compatible with constant returns to scale of the macro economy.

Different mechanisms constraining diffusion of new knowledge from inventors to innovators and between early and late adopters have been proposed. The simplest examples are the institutions of patents and copyrights. Another approach is to see all new applied knowledge as highly product-specific, limiting the net returns to imitators. The factor of importance would then be R&D investments in relation to the total number of products of the economy.

The number of products increases with the size of the economy. Two ratios indicating the knowledge intensity of the economy would thus be R&D investments in relation to the number of products or the GDP. The R&D intensity and total R&D have been empirically tested as predictors of the growth rate of GDP. These tests lead to the conclusion that the total R&D, implying increasing returns to knowledge investments, is *not* significantly related to the rate of economic growth, while the hypothesis of a positive relation between R&D intensity and economic growth is supported by data.

Another approach to analysis of knowledge diffusion and growth accepts the idea of diffusion of knowledge, but only subject to spatial frictions, constraining knowledge flows. This view of the matter has been a dominant idea among European and especially Scandinavian economists and economic geographers and more recently in the USA (Krugman, 1991).

The spatial frictions of knowledge production and use are most realistically modelled with accessibility measures, in which the value of knowledge as an input, which is generated in different localities is discounted by the distance between the knowledge generating and using localities at a spatial rate of discount. Empirical tests on Swedish data have shown that there is a significant positive relation between economic growth and accessibility to knowledge resources. These effects are primarily constrained to be substantial within a quite limited spatial area supporting the view that R&D and knowledge-dependent firms tend to be spatially clustered.

References

Aghion, P. and P. Howitt (1992), 'A model of growth through creative destruction', *Econometrica*, **60**, 323–51.
Aghion, P. and P. Howitt (1998), *Endogenous Growth Theory*, Cambridge, MA: MIT Press.
Alba-Ramirez, A. and M.-J. San Segundo (1995), 'The return to education in Spain', *Economics of Education Review*, **14** (2), 155–66.
Andersson, Å.E. (1968), 'From interest and prices to capital and growth', *Swedish Journal of Economics*, **70** (4), 221–41.
Andersson, Å.E. (1985), *Kreativitet, Storstadens Framtid*, Stockholm: Prisma (in Swedish).
Andersson, Å.E. (1988), *Universitetet – Regioners Framtid*, Stockholm: Prisma (in Swedish).
Andersson, Å.E. (2003), 'Quantitative and qualitative growth analysis', in S. Yousefi and J. Rosser Jr. (ed.), *Chaos, Solitons and Fractals*, Special Issue: Complex economic phenomena in time and space, in honour of Prof. Tönu Puu, **18** (3), Amsterdam: Elsevier, pp. 477–84.
Andersson Å.E. and D.E. Andersson (2006), *The Economics of Experiences, the Arts and Entertainment*, Cheltenham, UK and Northampton, MA, USA: Edward Elgar.
Andersson, Å.E. and B. Johansson (1984), 'Knowledge intensity and product cycles in metropolitan regions', WP–84–13, IIASA, Laxenburg, Austria.
Andersson, Å.E. and L. Lundqvist (1976), 'Regional analysis of consumption patterns', *Papers in Regional Science*, **36** (1), 117–31.
Andersson, Å.E. and J. Mantsinen (1980), 'Mobility of resources: accessibility of knowledge and economic growth', *Behavioural Science*, **25**, 353–66.
Andersson, Å.E. and O. Persson (1993), 'Networking scientists', *Annals of Regional Science*, **27**, 11–21.
Andersson, L. (1997), *Benefit Cost Analysis: A Practical Guide*, Lexington, MA: Lexington Books.
Andersson, M. and O. Ejermo (2004), 'Sectoral knowledge production in Swedish regions 1993–1999', in C. Karlsson, P. Flensburg and S.Å. Hörte (eds), *Knowledge Spillovers and Knowledge Management*, Cheltenham, UK and Northampton, MA, USA: Edward Elgar, pp. 143–70.
Andersson, M. and C. Karlsson (2007), 'Knowledge in regional economic growth – the role of knowledge accessibility', *Industry and Innovation*, **14** (2), 129–49.
Arai, M. and C. Kjellström (1999), 'Returns to human capital in Sweden', in R. Asplund and P.T. Pereira (eds), *Returns to Human Capital in Europe*, Helsinki: ETLA, The Research Institute of the Finnish Economy.
Arrow, K.J. (1962), 'The economic implications of learning by doing', *Review of Economic Studies*, **29**, 155–73. (Reprinted in J.E. Stiglitz and H. Uzawa (1969), *Readings in the Modern Theory of Economic Growth*, Cambridge, MA: MIT Press).

Arrow, K.J. (1971), *Essays in the Theory of Risk-Bearing*, Amsterdam: North Holland.

Arrow. K.J., H.B. Chenery, R.S. Minhas and R.M. Solow (1961), 'Capital–labor substitution and economic efficiency', *Review of Economics and Statistics*, **XLIII**, 225–50.

Asplund, R. (1999), 'Earnings and human capital: evidence for Finland', in R. Asplund and P.T. Pereira (eds), *Returns to Human Capital in Europe. A Literature Review*, Helsinki: ETLA, The Research Institute of the Finnish Economy, pp. 44–77.

Asplund, R. (ed.) (2001), *Education and Earnings. Further Evidence from Europe*, Helsinki: ETLA, Series B 183.

Barasinska, N., D. Schäfer and A. Stephan (2008), 'Do risk attitude and household portfolio diversification match?', mimeo, Berlin: DIW.

Barber, B. (1952), *Science and the Social Order*, New York: Free Press.

Barceinas-Paredes, F., J. Oliver-Alonso, J.L. Raymond-Bara, J.L. Roig-Sabaté and A. Skalli (2001), 'Does education improve productivity or earnings only? Evidence from France and Spain', in R. Asplund (ed.), *Education and Earnings. Further Evidence from Europe*, Helsinki: ETLA, Series B 183, pp. 65–96.

Barth, E. and M. Roed (1999), 'The return to human capital in Norway', in R. Asplund and P.T. Pereira (eds), *Returns to Human Capital in Europe*, Helsinki: ETLA, The Research Institute of the Finnish Economy, pp. 227–58.

Becker, G.S. and R.T. Michael (1973), 'On the new theory of consumer behavior', *Swedish Journal of Economics*, 378–96.

Beckmann, M.J. (1974), 'Der Diskontierte Bandit', *Methods of Operations Research (OR-Verfahren)*, **XVIII**, 9–18.

Beckmann, M.J. (1978), *Tinbergen Lectures in Organization Theory*, Heidelberg: Springer Verlag.

Beckmann, M.J. (1994), 'On knowledge networks in science: collaboration among equals', *Annals of Regional Science*, **28**, 233–42.

Beckmann, M. (1999), 'Bidding for research funds', in U. Leopold-Wildburger, G. Feichtinger and K.P. Kirchner (eds), *Modelling and Decisions in Economics: Essays in Honor of Franz Ferschl*, Heidelberg: Physica Verlag, pp. 229–38.

Beckmann, M.J. (2000). 'Diversification versus concentration: a note on the allocation of effort among risky research projects', *Pacific Economic Review*, **5** (3), 291–8.

Beckmann, M.J. (2008), 'A preview of the new economics of knowledge', *Asia-Pacific Journal of Accounting and Economics*, **15** (1), 1–9.

Beckmann, M.J. and H.-P. Künzi (1973–1984), *Mathematik für Ökonomen I–III*, Heidelberg: Springer Verlag.

Beckmann, M.J. and O. Persson (1995), 'Locating the network of interacting authors in scientific specialties', *Scientometrics*, **33** (3), 351–66.

Beckmann, M.J. and O. Persson (1998a), 'Scientific collaboration as spatial interaction', in M.J. Beckmann, B. Johansson, F. Snickars and R. Thord (eds), *Knowledge and Networks in a Dynamic Economy*, Heidelberg: Springer Verlag.

Beckmann, M.J. and O. Persson (1998b), 'The thirteen most cited journals in economics', *Scientometrics*, **42** (2), 267–71.

Beeching, H.C. (1880), 'The masque of B–ll—l', Balliol College, Oxford.

Bellman, R.E. (1957), *Dynamic Programming*, Princeton, NJ: Princeton University Press.

Benassy, J.P. (1990), 'Non-Walrasian equilibria, money and macroeconomics', in B.M Friedman and F.H. Hahn (eds), *Handbook of Monetary Economics*, Amsterdam: North-Holland, pp. 103–69.

Bernstein, J. and I. Nadiri [1991] (1997), 'Product demand, production cost, and interindustry R&D spillovers', CVS RR 90–53 (1990), NBER WP 3625 (1991), revised in 1997.

Blanchard, O. (2004), 'The economic future of Europe', *Journal of Economic Perspectives*, **8** (4), 3–26.

Bonitz, M. (1985), 'Journal ranking by selective impact – new method based on SDI results and journal impact factors', *Scientometrics*, **7** (3–6), 471–85.

Bonitz, M. (1990), 'Journal ranking by different parameters', *Scientometrics*, **18** (1–2), 57–73.

Borchardt, K. (1978), 'Wissenschaftliche Literatur als Medium Wissenschaftlichen Fortschritts', *Jahrbücher für Nationalökonomie und Statistik*, 481–89.

Borel, A. (1981), *Mathematik als Kunst und Wissenschaft*, Munich: Carl Friedrich von Siemens Stiftung.

Bowen, H.R. (1980), *The Cost of Higher Education*, San Francisco: Jossey-Bass.

Braconier, H. (1998), 'Essays on R&D and growth', *Lund Economic Studies*, 72, Department of Economics, Lund University.

Braithwaite, R.B. (1968), *Scientific Explanation*, Cambridge: Cambridge University Press.

Brenner, T. and S. Greif (2006), 'The dependence of innovativeness on the local firm population – an empirical study of German patents', *Industry and Innovation*, **13** (1), 21–39.

Brinkman, P.T. and L.L. Leslie (1986), 'Economies of scale in higher education: sixty years of research', *Review of Higher Education*, **10**, 1–28.

Brody, A. (1970), *Proportions, Prices and Planning – A Mathematical Restatement of the Labour Theory of Value*, Amsterdam: North-Holland.

Brown, G.E. (1992), 'Report of the task force on the health of research, US House of Representatives, 102nd Congress, Washington, DC.

Brunello, G., S. Comi and C. Lucifora (1999), 'Returns to education in Italy: a review of the applied literature', in R. Asplund, and P.T. Pereira (eds), *Returns to Human Capital in Europe*, Helsinki: ETLA, The Research Institute of the Finnish Economy, pp. 183–208.

Cassel, G. (1918), *Theoretische Sozialökonomie*, Leipzig: C.F. Winter.

Chaitin, G.J. (1966), 'On the length of programs for computing finite binary sequences', *Journal of the Association for Computing Machinery*, **13**, 547–69.

Chamberlin, E.H. (1933), *The Theory of Monopolistic Competition: A Re-Orientation of the Theory of Value*, Cambridge, MA: Harvard University Press.

Christensen, J.J. and N. Westergard-Nielsen (1999), 'Wages and human capital: the Danish evidence', in R. Asplund, and P.T. Pereira (eds), *Returns to Human Capital in Europe*, Helsinki: ETLA, The Research Institute of the Finnish Economy, pp. 30–42.

Chubin, D.E. (1976), 'State of the field. The conceptualization of scientific specialties', *Sociological Quarterly*, **17**, 448–76.

Chubin, D.E. (1985), 'Beyond invisible colleges: inspirations and aspirations of post-1972 social studies of science', *Scientometrics*, **7**, 221–54.

Cohen, W.M. and D.A. Levinthal (1990), 'Absorptive capacity: a new perspective on learning and innovation', *Administrative Science Quarterly*, **35**, 128–52.

Cohn, E. and J.T. Addison (1998), 'The economic returns to lifelong learning', *Education Economics*, **6** (3), 253–308.

Cohn, E., S.L.W. Rhine and M.C. Santos (1989), 'Institutions of higher education as multi-product firms: economies of scale and scope', *Review of Economics and Statistics*, **71**, 284–90.

Crane, D. (1972), *Invisible Colleges*, Chicago: University of Chicago Press.

De Groot, H., W.W. McMahon and J.F. Volkwein (1991), 'The cost structure of American research universities', *Review of Economics and Statistics*, **73**, 424–31.

Debreu, G. and I.N. Herstein (1953), 'Nonnegative square matrices', *Econometrica*, **21**, 597–607.

Denison, E.F. (1967), *Why Growth Rates Differ*, Washington: Brookings Institution.

DIW (Deutsches Institut für Wirtschaftsforschung) (2007), 'Innovationsindikator Deutschland', research report, Berlin. Downloadable at: http://www.diw.de/documents/publikationen/73/76418/diwkompakt_2007-033.pdf

Dixit, A. (1987), 'Strategic behavior in contests', *American Economic Review*, **77**, 891–8.

Dixit, A.K. and J.E. Stiglitz (1977), 'Monopolistic competition and optimum product diversity', *American Economic Review*, **67** (3), 297–308.

Engwall, L. (ed.) (1992), *Economics in Sweden: An Evaluation of Swedish Research in Economics*, London: Routledge.

Epple, D., R. Romano and H. Sieg (2006), 'Admission, tuition, and financial aid policies in the market for higher education', *Econometrica*, **74** (4), 85–92.

Ernst, H. (1996), *Patent Informationen für die Strategische Planung*, Wiesbaden: Deutscher Universitäts Verlag.

Fermi, L. [1954] (1994), *Atoms in the Family: My Life with Enrico Fermi*, Chicago: University of Chicago Press.

Fersterer, J. and R. Winter-Ebmer (1999), 'Human capital and earnings in Austria', in R. Asplund and P.T. Pereira (eds), *Returns to Human Capital in Europe*, Helsinki: ETLA, The Research Institute of the Finnish Economy, pp.13–29.

Flexner, A. (1930), *Universities: American, British, German*, New York: Oxford University Press.

Forman, P. (1974), 'Financial support and political alignment of physicists in Weimar Germany', *Minerva*, **12**, 39–66.

Frisch, R. (1962), *Innledning til Produksjonsteorien*, Oslo: Universitetsforlaget (in Norwegian).

Frobenius, G. (1912), 'Über Matrizen aus nicht-negativen Elementen', Berlin: Preussischen Akademie der Wissenschaften, pp. 456–77.

Funke, U.H. (1976), *Mathematical Models in Marketing: A Collection of Abstracts*, Berlin: Springer Verlag.

Gates, B. (1995), *The Road Ahead*, New York: Penguin.

Gottinger, H.W. (1996), 'Competitive bidding for research', *Kyklos*, **49** (3), 439–47.

Gråsjö, U. (2006), 'Spatial spillovers of knowledge production – an accessibility approach', JIBS Dissertation Series No. 034, Jönköping International Business School.

Greif, S. (2001), 'Patentgeographie', *Raumforchung und Raumordnung*, **59**, 142–53.

Griliches, Z. (1957), 'Hybrid corn: an exploration in the economics of technological change', *Econometrica*, **25** (4), 501–22.

Griliches, Z. and F. Lichtenberg (1984a), 'Interindustry technology flows and productivity growth: a re-examination', *Review of Economics and Statistics*, **66** (2), 324–9.

Griliches, Z. and F. Lichtenberg (1984b), 'R&D and productivity growth at the firm level: is there a relationship?', in Z. Griliches (ed.), *R&D, Patents and Productivity*, Chicago: University of Chicago Press, pp. 465–96.

Groote, P. de (1993), 'The conservation theorem revisited', *Proceedings of the International Conference on Typed Lambda Calculi and Applications*, TLCA'93, Springer LNCS, pp.163–78.

Grossman, G.M. and E. Helpman (1991a), *Innovation and Growth in the Global Economy*, Cambridge, MA: MIT Press.

Grossman, G.M. and E. Helpman (1991b), 'Endogenous product cycles', *Economic Journal*, **101**, 1214–29.

Haken, H. (1978), *Synergetics – An Introduction*, Heidelberg: Springer Verlag.

Haken, H. (1998), 'Can we apply synergetics to the human sciences?' in G. Altman and W.A. Koch (eds), *Systems – New Paradigms for the Human Sciences*, New York: de Gruyter, pp. 58–78.

Hall, B. H. (1995), 'The private and social returns to research and development: what have we learned?', Mimeo, NBER No. 3956.

Hardy, G.H. (1940), *A Mathematician's Apology*, Cambridge: Cambridge University Press.

Hardy, G.H., J.E. Littlewood and G. Pólya [1934] (1967), *Inequalities*, Cambridge: Cambridge University Press.

Harmon, C. and I. Walker (1995), 'Estimates of the economic return to schooling for the United Kingdom', *American Economic Review*, **85** (5), 1278–86.

Harmon, C. and I. Walker (1999), 'The marginal and average returns to schooling in the UK', *European Economic Review*, **43**, 879–87.

Harrod, R.F. (1939), 'An essay in dynamic theory', *Economic Journal*, **49**, 14–33.

Hicks, J.R. [1939] (1968), *Value and Capital: An Inquiry into Some Fundamental Principles of Economic Theory*, 2nd edn, Oxford: Oxford University Press.

Hicks, J.R. (1956), *A Revision of Demand Theory*, Oxford: Oxford University Press.

Hicks, J.R. (1965), *Capital and Growth*, Oxford: Oxford University Press.

Hilbert, D. (1900), 'Mathematical problems', Lecture delivered before the International Congress of Mathematicians at Paris in 1900. The original address 'Mathematische probleme' appeared in *Göttinger Nachrichten* (1900), pp. 253–97, and in *Archiv der Mathematik und Physik*, **3** (1) (1901), 44–63 and 213–37. The address was translated into English with the author's permission by Maby Winton Newson for *Bulletin of the American Mathematical Society*, **8** (1902), 437–79. A reprint appears in F. Brouder (ed.) (1976), *Mathematical Developments Arising from Hilbert Problems*, American Mathematical Society.

Hodges, A. (1983), *Alan Turing: the Enigma*, London: Burnett; New York: Simon & Schuster.

Holub, H.W., G. Tappeiner and V. Eberharter (1991), 'The iron law of important articles', *Southern Economic Journal*, **58** (2), 317–28.

Ichino, A. and R. Winter-Ebmer (1999), 'Lower and upper bounds of returns to schooling: an exercise in IV estimation with different instruments', *European Economic Review*, **43**, 889–901.

Isacsson, G. (1999), 'Estimates of the return to schooling in Sweden from a large sample of twins', *Labour Economics*, **6**, 471–89.

Johansson, B. and Å.E. Andersson (1998), 'A Schloss Laxenburg model of product cycle dynamics', in M.J. Beckmann, B. Johansson, F. Snickars and R. Thord (eds), *Knowledge and Networks in a Dynamic Economy*, Berlin: Springer Verlag, pp. 181–219.

Johansson, B., C. Karlsson and R.R. Stough (2001), *Theories of Endogenous Growth – Lessons for Regional Policies*, Heidelberg: Springer Verlag.

Jones, C.I. and J. Williams (1998), 'Measuring the social return to R&D', *Quarterly Journal of Economics*, **113**, 1119–35.

JPSIOD 96 (1997), Journal performance indicators on diskette, Institute for Scientific Information, Philadelphia.

Karlsson, C. and A. Manduchi (2001), 'Knowledge spillovers in a spatial context – a critical review and assessment', in M.M. Fischer and J. Frölich (eds), *Knowledge, Complexity and Innovation Systems*, New York: Springer Verlag, pp. 101–24.

Karlsson, C., U. Gråsjö and M. Andersson (2006), 'Regional knowledge accessibility and regional economic growth', Working Paper Series in Economics and Institutions of Innovation, 66, Royal Institute of Technology, CESIS – Centre of Excellence for Science and Innovation Studies, Stockholm.

Katz, J.S. (1994), 'Geographical proximity and scientific collaboration', *Scientometrics*, **31** (1), 31–43.

Kaufman, M. (1986), *The Capital Budgetary Handbook*, Homewood, IL: Dow-Jones/Irwin.

Kessler, M.M. (1963), 'Bibliographic coupling between scientific papers', *American Documentation*, **14**, 10–25.

Keynes, J.M. (1936), *The General Theory of Employment, Interest and Money*, London: Macmillan.

Klein, E. (1973), *Mathematical Methods in Theoretical Economics*, New York: Academic Press.

Knight, F.H. (1933), *Syllabus*, Chicago: University of Chicago Press.

Kochen, M. (1969), 'Stability in the growth of knowledge', *American Documentation*, **20**, 186–97.

Kolmogorov, A.N. (1965), 'Three approaches to the quantitative definition of information', *Problems of Information Transmission*, **1** (1), 1–7.

Koopmans, T.C. (1975), 'Concepts of optimality and their uses', Nobel Memorial Lecture, reprinted in *The Scandinavian Journal of Economics*, **78** (4), 542–60.

Koopmans, T.C. and M. Beckmann (1957), 'Assignment problems and the location of economic activities', *Econometrica*, **25**, 53–76.

Krugman, P. (1991), *Geography and Trade*, Cambridge, MA: MIT Press.

Kruse, P. and M. Stadler (1993), 'The significance of nonlinear phenomena for the investigation of cognitive systems', in H. Haken and A. Mikhailov (eds), *Interdisciplinary Approaches to Nonlinear Complex Systems*, Berlin: Springer Verlag, pp. 138–60.

Kuhn, T.S. (1970), *The Structure of Scientific Revolutions*, 2nd edn, Chicago: University of Chicago Press.

Kullback, S. and R.A. Leibler (1951), 'On information and sufficiency', *Annals of Mathematical Statistics*, **22**, 79–86.

Kuznets, S. (1966), *Modern Economic Growth: Rate, Structure and Spread*, New Haven, CT: Yale University Press.

Lancaster, K. (1966), 'A new approach to consumer theory', *Journal of Political Economy*, **74**, 132–57.

Leontief, W.W. (1951), *Studies in the Structure of the American Economy 1919–1939*, New York: Oxford University Press.

Lepenies, W. (1976), 'History and anthropology – historical appraisal of current contact between disciplines', *Social Science Information*, **15**, 287–306.

Liebowitz, S.J. and J.P. Palmer (1984), 'Assessing the relative impacts of economics journals', *Journal of Economic Literature*, **22**, 77–88.

Lintner, J. (1965), 'The valuation of risk assets and the selection of risky investments in stock portfolios and capital budgets', *Review of Economics and Statistics*, **47**, 13–37.

Luce, D. and H. Raiffa (1957), *Games and Decisions*, New York: Wiley.

Luukkonen, T., O. Persson and G. Sivertsen (1992), 'Understanding patterns of international scientific collaboration', *Science, Technology and Human Values*, **17** (1), 101–26.

Machlup, F. (1958a), *The Optimum Lag of Imitation Behind Innovation*, Festschrift to Frederik Zeuthen, Copenhagen: Nationalokonomisk Forening, pp. 239–56.

Machlup, F. (1958b), 'Can there be too much research?', *Science 28*, **128** (3335), 1320–25.

Machlup, F. (1962a), 'The supply of inventors and inventions', in R.R. Nelson (ed.), *The Rate and Direction of Inventive Activity*, Princeton, NJ: Princeton University Press, pp. 143–70.

Machlup, F. (1962b), *The Production and Distribution of Knowledge in the United States*, Princeton, NJ: Princeton University Press.

Maddison, A. (1982), *Phases of Capitalist Development*, Oxford: Oxford University Press.

Maddison, A. (1995), *Monitoring the World Economy: 1820–1992*, Paris: Organization for Economic Cooperation and Development.

Malinvaud, E. (1977), *The Theory of Unemployment Reconsidered*, Oxford: Basil Blackwell.

Mankiv, N.G., D. Romer and D.N Weil (1992), 'A contribution to the empirics of economic growth', *Quarterly Journal of Economics*, **107**, 407–37.

Mansfield, E. (1968), *The Economics of Technical Change*, New York: Norton.

Mansfield E., J. Rapoport, A. Romeo, E. Villani, S. Wagner and F. Husic (1977), *The Production and Application of New Industrial Technology*, New York: Norton.

Mansfield, E., M. Schwarz and S. Wagner (1981), 'Imitation costs and patents: an empirical study', *Economic Journal*, **91** (364), 907–18.

Marshakova-Shaikevich, I. (1996), 'The standard impact factor as an evaluation tool of science fields and scientific journals', *Scientometrics*, **35** (2), 283–90.

Mathews, J.C. and C.E. Langenhop (1966), *Discrete and Continuous Methods in Applied Mathematics*, New York: Wiley.

Merton, R.K. (1968), 'The Matthew effect', *Science*, **159**, 56–63.

Merton, R.K. (1969), 'Behavior pattern of scientists', *American Scientist*, **57**, 1–23.

Merton, R.K. (1970), *Sociology of Science*, New York: Columbia University Press.

Mill, J.S. (1975) [1859], *On Liberty*, edited by David Spitz. Toronto: W. W. Norton.

Miller, P., C. Mulvey and N. Martin (1995), 'What do twins studies reveal about the economic returns to education? A comparison of Australian and US findings', *American Economic Review*, **85** (3), 586–99.

Mincer, J. (1974), *Schooling, Experience, and Earnings*, New York: National Bureau of Economic Research.

Moore, W.J. (1972), 'The relative quality of economics journals: a suggested rating system', *Western Economic Journal*, **10** (2), 156–69.

Morishima, M. (1959), 'The problem of intrinsic complementarity and separability of goods', *Metroeconomica*, **11**, 188–202.

Morishima, M. (1964), *Equilibrium, Stability and Growth*, London: Oxford University Press.

Morse, S.P. (1968), 'A mathematical model for the analysis of contour-line data', *Journal of the ACM* (Association for Computing Machinery), **15** (2), 205–20.

Mossin, J. (1966), 'Equilibrium in a capital asset market', *Econometrica*, **34** (4), 768–83.

Mullins, N.C. (1968), 'The distribution of social and cultural properties in informal communication networks among biological scientists', *American Sociological Review*, **33**, 786–97.

Nelson, R.R. and N. Rosenberg (1993), 'Technical innovation and national systems', in R.R. Nelson (ed.), *National Innovation Systems: A Comparative Analysis*, Oxford: Oxford University Press, pp. 3–21.

Nelson, R.R. and S.G. Winter (1982), *An Evolutionary Theory of Economic Change*, Cambridge, MA: Belknap Press of Harvard University Press.

Neumann, J. von (1936), 'On a certain topology for rings of operators', *Annals of Mathematics 2nd Ser*, **37** (1), 111–15.

Neumann, J. von (1937), 'Über ein ökonomisches Gleichungssystem und eine Verallgemeinerung des Brouwerschen Fixpunktsatzes', in *Ergebnisse eines Mathematischen Kolloquiums*, **8**, 1935–1936, Franz–Deuticke, pp. 73–83. [Translated: 'A model of general economic equilibrium', *Review of Economic Studies*, **13**, 1–9.]

Nickell, S. (1979), 'Education and lifetime patterns of unemployment', *Journal of Political Economy*, **87** (5), S117–31.

Nikaido, H. (1968), *Convex Structures and Economic Theory*, New York: Academic Press.

NSF (National Science Foundation) (1998), 'Grant proposal guide', NSF 99–2, Washington, DC.

OECD (1986), *Science and Technology Indicators: R&D, Invention and Competitiveness*, Vol. 2, OECD, Paris.

OECD (1990), *Main Science and Technology Indicators*, Vol. 2, OECD, Paris.

OECD (1995), *Education and Employment*, Centre for Educational Research and Innovations, OECD, Paris.

OECD (1997), *Human Capital Investment: An International Comparison*, OECD, Paris.

OECD (2001a), *Education at a Glance: OECD Indicators 2001*, OECD, Paris.

OECD (2001b), *Education Policy Analysis 2001*, OECD, Paris.

OECD (2004), National Account Statistics, OECD, Paris.

OECD (2007a), National Account Statistics, OECD, Paris.

OECD (2007b), *Science and Technology Indicators*, OECD, Paris.

Palacios-Huerta, I. and O. Volij (2004), 'The measurement of intellectual influence', *Econometrica*, **72** (3), 963–77.

Palme, M. and R. Wright (1992), 'Gender discrimination and compensating differentials in Sweden', *Applied Economics*, **24**, 751–9.

Patrinos, H.A. (1995), 'Education and earnings differentials', mimeo, World Bank.

Peretto, P.F. (1995), 'On rivalry, variety and spillovers in endogenous growth', Duke University. Available at SSRN: http://ssrn.com/abstract=35181 or DOI: 10.2139/ssrn.35181 (2008-02-06)

Perron, O. (1907), 'Zur Theorie der Matrizen', *Mathematische Annalen*, **64**, 248–63.

Persson, O. (1991), 'Regional collaboration in science. Data on Nordic co-authorships 1988–1990', CERUM Working Paper CWP–1991:16, Umeå University, Umeå.

Polya, G. (1945), *How to Solve It: A New Aspect of Mathematical Method*, Princeton, NJ: Princeton University Press.

Price, D.J. de Solla (1961), *Science since Babylon*, Clinton, MA: Colonial Press.

Price, D.J. de Solla (1963), *Little Science, Big Science*, New York: Columbia University Press.

Price, D.J. de Solla (1965), 'Networks of scientific papers', *Science*, **149**, 510–15.

Price, D.J. de Solla (1967), 'Nations can publish or perish', *Science and Technology*, **70**, 84–90.

Prigogine, I. and G. Nicolis (1989), *Exploring Complexity*, New York: W.H. Freeman.

Psacharopoulos, G. (1994), 'Returns to investment in education: a global update', *World Development*, **22** (9), 1325–43.

Psacharopoulos, G. (2000), 'The economic costs of child labor, by the sweat and toil of children', Department of Labor, Washington, DC.

Psacharopoulos, G. (2005), 'Why some university systems are collapsing: realities from Europe', paper presented at the ACA conference 'The Future of the University', 30 November – 2 December, Vienna.

Psacharopoulos, G. and H.A. Patrinos (2002), 'Returns to investment in education: a further update', World Bank Policy Research Working Paper No. 2881, Washington, DC.

Psacharopoulos, G. and H.A. Patrinos (2004), 'Returns to investment in education: a further update', *Education Economics*, **12** (2), 111–34.

Puu, T. (1997a), *Economics of Space and Time, Scientific Papers of Tönu Puu*, edited by Å.E. Andersson, M.J. Beckmann, K.-G. Löfgren and A. Stenberg, Heidelberg: Springer Verlag.

Puu, T. (1997b), *Nonlinear Economic Dynamics*, 4th edn, Berlin: Springer Verlag.

Puu, T. (2003), *Attractors, Bifurcations and Chaos: Nonlinear Phenomena in Economics*, Berlin and Heidelberg: Springer Verlag.

Puu, T. (2006), *Arts, Sciences and Economics. A Historical Safari*, Berlin, Heidelberg, New York: Springer Verlag.

Ramsey, F.P. ([n.a.] 1990), 'Weight or the value of knowledge', *British Journal for the Philosophy of Science*, **41**, 1–4, reprint of documents 005–20–01 and 005–20–03, the Frank Ramsey Collection, Archives of Scientific Philosophy in the Twentieth Century, Hillman Library, University of Pittsburgh.

Reif, F. (1961), 'The competitive world of the pure scientist', *Science*, **134**, 1957–62.

Reskin, B.F. (1976), 'Sex-differences in status attainment in science – the case of the postdoctoral fellowship', *American Sociological Review*, **41** (4), 597–612.

Riksrevisionsverket (1996), *Samhällsvetenskaplig forskarutbildning – four years – not for years*, RRV 1996:52 (in Swedish).

Robinson, J. (1933), *The Economics of Imperfect Competition*, London: Macmillan.

Romer, D. (2001), *Advanced Macroeconomics*, 2nd edn, New York: McGraw Hill.

Romer, P.M. (1986), 'Increasing returns and long run growth', *Journal of Political Economy*, **94**, 1002–37.

Romer, P.M. (1990), 'Endogenous technological change', *Journal of Political Economy*, **98** (5), 71–102.

Ross, S. (1976), 'The arbitrage theory of capital asset pricing', *Journal of Economic Theory*, **13** (3), 341–60.

Rouse, C.E. (1999), 'Further estimates of the economic return to schooling from a new sample of twins', *Economics of Education Review*, **18** (2), 149–57.

Russell, B.A.W. (1912), *The Problems of Philosophy*, London: Williams and Norgate.

Sahlin, N.E. (1990), *The Philosophy of F.P. Ramsey*, Cambridge: Cambridge University Press.

Sandelin, B. and N. Sarafoglou (1997), 'Artikelpublicering – vad säger amerikanska databaser?', *Ekonomisk Debatt*, **25** (3), 155–60 (in Swedish).

Sarafoglou, N. and K.E. Haynes (1996), 'University production in Sweden: a demonstration and explanatory analysis for economics and business programs', *Annals of Regional Science*, **30** (3), 285–304.

Savigny, K.F. von (1832), *Wesen und Wert der Deutschen Universitäten*, Berlin: Ranke's Historisch Politische Zeitschrift.

Scherer, F.M. (1982), 'Interindustry technology flows and productivity growth', *Review of Economics and Statistics*, **64**, 627–34.

Scherer, F.M. (1984), 'Using linked patent and R&D data to measure interindustry technology flows', in Z. Griliches (ed.), *R&D, Patents and Productivity*, Chicago: University of Chicago Press, pp. 417–64.

Schmookler, J. (1996), *Invention and Economic Growth*, Cambridge, MA: Harvard University Press.

Schumpeter, J.A. (1912), *Theorie der Wirtschaftlichen Entwicklung*, Leipzig: Duncker & Humblot.

Schumpeter, J.A. (1934), *The Theory of Economic Development*, Cambridge, MA: Harvard University Press.

Science Citation Index (1988–90), Institute for Scientific Information, Philadelphia.

Shanghai Institute of Technology (2005), 'Academic ranking of world universities', Institute of Higher Education, Shanghai Jiao Tong University. Available at: http://ed.sjtu.edu.cn/ranking2005.htm (2008-12-02).

Shannon, C.E. and W. Weaver (1949), *The Mathematical Theory of Communication*, Chicago: University of Illinois Press.

Sharpe, W.F. (1963) 'A simplified model of portfolio analysis', *Management Science*, **9**, 277–93.

Sharpe, W.F. (1964), 'Capital asset prices: a theory of market equilibrium under conditions of risk', *Journal of Finance*, **19** (3), 425–42.

Shell, K. (1966), 'Toward a theory of inventive activity and capital accumulation', *American Economic Review*, **56** (2), 62–8.

Shell, K. (1967), 'A model of inventive activity and capital accumulation', in K. Shell (ed.), *Essays on the Theory of Optimal Economic Growth*, Cambridge, MA: MIT Press, pp. 67–85.

Shils, E.A. (1972), *The Intellectuals and the Powers and Other Essays*, Chicago: University of Chicago Press.

Simonton, D.K. (1984), *Genius, Creativity, and Leadership – Historiometric Inquiries*, Cambridge, MA: Harvard University Press.

Small, H.G. and B.C Griffith (1974), 'The structure of scientific literatures I: identifying and graphing specialties', *Science Studies*, **4**, 17–40.

Smith, A. (1904 [1776]), *The Wealth of Nations*, 5th edn, London: Methuen & Co. Ltd.

Smith, G.J.W. and I.M. Carlsson (1990), 'The creative process: a functional model based on empirical studies from early childhood up to middle age', *Psychological Issues, Monograph 57*, New York: International Universities Press.

Smyth, D.J. (1991), 'A model of quality changes in higher education', *Journal of Economic Behavior and Organizations*, **15**, 151–9.

Snickars, F. and J.W. Weibull (1977), 'A minimum information principle: theory and practice', *Regional Science and Urban Economics*, **7** (1–2), 137–68.

Social Science Citation Index, Institute for Scientific Information, Philadelphia.

Solow, R.M (1956), 'A contribution to the theory of economic growth', *Quarterly Journal of Economics*, **70**, 65–94.

Solow, R.M (1957), 'Technical change and the aggregate production function', *Review of Economics and Statistics*, **39**, 312–20.

Solow, R.M. (1994), 'Perspectives on growth theory', *Journal of Economic Perspectives*, **8** (1), 45–54.

Stackelberg, H. von (1932), *Grundlagen Einer Reinen Kostentheorie*, Vienna: Verlag von Julius Springer.
Statistics Sweden (1992), 'Census of population and housing 1990', Stockholm.
Stephan, P. (1996), 'The economics of science', *Journal of Economic Literature*, **34**, 1199–235.
Stewart, I.N. and P.L. Peregoy (1983), 'Catastrophe theory modeling in psychology', *Psychological Bulletin*, **94** (2), 336–62.
Stigler, G.J. (1947), *The Theory of Price*, New York: Macmillan.
Stigler, G.J., S.M. Stigler and C. Friedland (1995), 'The journals of economics', *Journal of Political Economy*, **103** (2), 331–59.
Stiglitz, J.E. and H. Uzawa (eds) (1969), *Readings in the Modern Theory of Economic Growth*, Cambridge, MA: MIT Press.
Stone, L.D. (1975), *Theory of Optimal Search*, New York: Academic Press.
Suzumura, K. (1995), *Competition, Commitment and Welfare*, Oxford: Clarendon Press.
Sveikauskas, L. (1981), 'Technological inputs and multifactor productivity growth', *Review of Economics and Statistics*, **63**, 275–82.
Swan, W. (1956), 'Economic growth and capital accumulation', *Economic Record*, **32**, 334–61.
Taylor, J. and J. Johnes (1992), 'The citation record of regional studies and related journals 1980–89', *Regional Studies*, **26** (1), 93–7.
Taylor, J.B. (1993), 'Discretion versus policy rules in practice', *Carnegie-Rochester Conference Series on Public Policy*, **39**, 195–214.
Taylor, J.B. (ed.) (1999), *Monetary Policy Rules*, Chicago: University of Chicago Press.
Terleckyj, N. (1980), 'Direct and indirect effects of industrial research and development on the productivity growth of industries', in J. Kendrick and B. Vaccara (eds), *New Developments in Productivity Measurement and Analysis*, Chicago: University of Chicago Press, pp. 359–77.
Thünen, J.H. von (1826), *Der Isolierte Staat in Beziehung auf Landwirtschaft und Nationalökonomie*, Perthes: Hamburg (Translated by C.M. Wartenberg (1966), *Von Thünen's Isolated State*, Oxford: Pergamon Press).
Tinbergen, J. (1942), 'Zür Theorie der langfristigen Wirtschaftsenttwicklung', *Weltwirtschaftliches Archiv*, **55**, 511–49.
Triffin, R. (1940), *Monopolistic Competition and General Equilibrium Theory*, Cambridge, MA: Harvard University Press.
Uzawa, H. (1965), 'Optimum technical change in an aggregative model of economic growth', *International Economic Review*, **6**, 18–31.
Veblen, T. (1918), *The Higher Learning in America: A Memorandum on the Conduct of Universities by Business Men*, New York: Huebsch.
Verry, D. and B. Davies (1975), *University Costs and Outputs*, Studies on Education, vol. 6, Amsterdam: Elsevier.
Weber, B. and S. Wolter (1999), 'Wages and human capital: evidence from Switzerland', in R. Asplund and P.T. Pereira (eds), *Returns to Human Capital in Europe*, Helsinki: ETLA, The Research Institute of the Finnish Economy, pp. 325–50.
Weinberg, S. (1993), *The First Three Minutes: A Modern View of the Origin of the Universe*, New York: Basic Books.
White, H.D. and B.C. Griffith (1981), 'Author co-citation: a literature measure of intellectual structure', *Journal of the American Society for Information Science*, **32**, 163–72.

Wibe, S. (1988), 'Storlek, kostnader och produktivitet inom högskolesektorn', in Å.E. Andersson (ed.), *Universitetet – Regioners Framtid*, Stockholm: Prisma (in Swedish).

Wicksell, K. (1898), *Geldzins und Güterpreise*, Jena: G. Fischer.

Wilson, A. (1970), *Entropy in Urban and Regional Modelling*, London: Pion.

Young, A. (1998), 'Growth without scale effects', *Journal of Political Economy*, **106** (1), 41–63.

Zhang, W.-B. (1991), *Synergetic Economics: Time and Change in Non-linear Economics*, New York & Berlin: Springer Verlag.

Index